AF344732

LSSI
LEAN SIX SIGMA INSTITUTE

Certification Manual

LEAN SIX SIGMA BLACK BELT

MARGE BOOKS

Collection: Lean Six Sigma
Director: David Soler

LEAN SIX SIGMA BLACK BELT. CERTIFICATION MANUAL
1st edition, February 2024

© Luis Vicente Socconini Pérez Gómez
© of this edition, ICG Marge, SL

Publisher: Marge Books
Brutau, 160 – 08203 Sabadell (Barcelona)
Tel. 931 429 486 – marge@margebooks.com
www.margebooks.com

Publisher Manager: Héctor Soler
Edition: Núria Gibert, Adrià Gibernau
Edition coordination: Karina Serrano
Make-up editor: Mercedes Lara
Printed by: Safekat, SL (Madrid)

ISBN printed edition: 978-84-19109-68-2
ISBN digital edition: 978-84-19109-69-9
Legal Deposit: B 3609-2024

This work is for informational purposes only and its content may not be relied upon in support of any claim or appeal. Neither the author nor the publisher assumes responsibility for the information, opinion or action based on said content, regardless of whether every effort has been made to ensure the accuracy of the information contained on its pages.

All rights reserved. No part of this edition, including the cover design, may be reproduced, stored, transmitted, distributed, used, communicated publicly or transformed through any means or system, whether electrical, chemical, mechanical, optical, recording or electrographic, without the prior written permission of the publisher, except as provided by law. Contact Cedro (Centro Español de Derechos Reprográficos, www.conlicencia.com) if you need to photocopy, scan or make digital copies of any fragment of this work.

 The paper used in this book has not been bleached with elemental chlorine (CI_2).

About the author

LUIS SOCCONINI

He holds a bachelor's degree in Industrial Engineering and a master's degree in Quality and Productivity from Monterrey Tec. He is also a Master Black Belt in Lean Six Sigma and a distinguished professor at several prestigious universities in Mexico.

Luis is certified in Strategic Management by Stanford University, in Leading Product Innovation by Harvard University, and in Industry 4.0 by MIT. He has worked as a business consultant for the Wharton Business School in Pennsylvania, as a process engineer for Grolsch Brewery in the Netherlands, and as a manufacturing engineer at IBM.

As director of Lean Six Sigma Institute, Luis develops high-impact projects for companies such as Abbott Laboratories, Kraft Heinz, Coca-Cola, BMW, Bimbo, and Fender – to name a few. He has a broad base of experience and is continually developing productivity applications in diverse industries such as construction, mining, agriculture, government, energy, service, and more.

Luis is the author of *Lean Six Sigma Yellow, Green and Black Belt certifications manuals, Lean Company, Lean Manufacturing, 5S practical guide to improve quality and productivity,* as well as co-author of *Lean Six Sigma Management System and Lean Energy 4.0.*

SOCCONINI

www.socconini.com

Content

Foreword

Dear reader, I warmly welcome you on this journey to obtain the Lean Six Sigma Black Belt Certification and I want to congratulate you because having this certification manual in your hands means that you seek to contribute to social Development through the improvement of people, processes, and organizations – which ultimately leads to the well-being of our communities.

This certification manual is born from the need to share what we at Lean Six Sigma Institute (LSSI) teach people who participate in organizational processes – including managers, business owners, government officials, engineers, operators, and students. All of them receive training to transform today's key processes and design the organizations of the future.

At first, this manual was part of the material delivered to LSSI course participants across the world. Until one day, our regional Director in Spain suggested that our manuals could also be distributed in bookstores – allowing anyone to access the knowledge that is revolutionizing business thinking and the way organizations work today. We know that as long as people are trained and – above all – committed to a new spectrum of design and improvement possibilities, organizations will grow stronger as they face the new challenges posed by the ever-changing world we live in.

In this manual you will find a particularly useful toolbox that will help you successfully develop and continuously improve organizational activities. This toolbox is the result of decades of best practices proven to help organizations maximize value and achieve their goals.

You will find management tools that leaders must understand and implement in order to plan and execute strategies, analyze results, design organizational structures, nourish new talent, and develop a new financial thinking that accurately reflects real costs.

Throughout the Black Belt certification course you will obtain the expert knowledge and skills needed to identify new opportunities, coach and mentor staff, and lead high-impact Lean Six Sigma projects in all areas of an organization.

You will be presented with several tools through a methodology which presents a step by step process for implementing and developing high impact projects.

It's highly critical that you continuously develop improvement projects utilizing your new understanding. The improvement process is a path that has a beginning but it knows no end. It requires that we develop good habits created by constantly repeating and performing Lean Six Sigma exercises.

The objectives for these tools are that you can understand, apply, and teach your collaborators new work methods, so that the subsequent generation can be well equipped in an effective manner to confront the complex and ever changing environments businesses are faced with everyday.

I want to thank you for trusting me by giving me the opportunity to present to you a widely contrasting method to address current business complications and for granting me the responsibility to help you in your improvement path. Specially in a world where the decision to continuously improve is in one's hands.

Luis Socconini
CEO and founder of Lean Six Sigma Institute

LSSI
LEAN SIX SIGMA INSTITUTE

Certification Manual

LEAN SIX SIGMA
BLACK BELT

Introduction to Black Belt

Leaders designing the future

Learning objectives

Upon completion of the Black Belt training, project leaders will be able to understand:

1. How Black Belts help organizations identify and implement improvement projects and transform organizational culture.
2. How to use advanced Lean Six Sigma tools and expert project management methodologies.
3. Training and coaching skills to help people achieve their maximum potential.

Content

> Background
> What is a Black Belt?
> Responsibilities

Background

Many organizations today have trained and certified Lean Six Sigma personnel. However, very few have certified Black Belts dedicated mainly to continuous process improvement.

Why are Black Belts so important?

Black Belt professionals:

- Develop projects that have a high impact on financial results and organizational culture.
- Work as full-time trainers and coaches that help employees achieve their full potential.
- Act as leaders who guide projects across all areas in an organization.
- Help organizations achieve high returns on investments and performance.

Training & Certification

Professional Development

LSS Company
6 **Work Systems**
- Innovation
- Value Streams
- Sustainability

Lean Six Sigma
5 **Robust Design**
- Agile Design
- Project Management
- Products & services

Six Sigma
4 **Optimization**
- Control Key Variables
- Statistical Tools
- Reduce Variability

Lean
3 **Effectiveness**
- Value Stream Mapping
- Continuous Flow
- Eliminate waste

Kaizen
2 **Stability**
- Visual Management
- 5S Housekeeping
- Standardization
- Reduce Overburden

Philosophy
1 **Leadership**
- Strategy & KPIs
- Value Stream Teams
- Training & Coaching

What is a Black Belt?

A certified Lean Six Sigma Black Belt is a professional who is trained in advanced Lean Six Sigma tools and methodologies to solve complex problems, and who serves as:

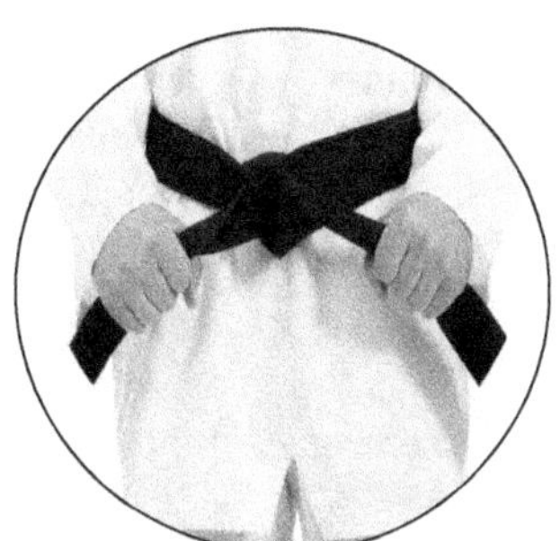

- A guide in the development of continuous improvement processes and organizational culture.

- A leader who promotes and ensures changes in work culture that result in improved work environments.

- A coach and trainer of Lean Six Sigma tools, methodology, implementation, and philosophy.

Black Belts are expert problem-solvers, business coaches, and leaders who help drive change and achieve improvements.

Responsibilities

Lean Six Sigma Black Belts are coaches and guides who work full-time to help organizations reach their maximum potential and achieve world-class processes.

The term Black Belt is related to martial arts, where a Black Belt is the expert who masters a specific field of knowledge and trains, coaches and mentors teams and individuals.

Among the skills that each Black Belt should develop are:

- Evaluating areas of opportunity and identifying the path to improvement.
- Quantifying the financial impact and the multiple benefits obtained from the improvements.
- Training and coaching teams responsible for project implementation.

> **Black Belts serve as internal coaches for personnel at all levels of the organization.**

Category	Description
Identifier	Discover areas of opportunity that will help the organization to reduce costs, increase capacity, improve margins, reduce inventory, etc.
Trainer	Train people within the different levels of Lean and Six Sigma 4.0 and ensure that everyone understands their role as well as the appropriate and correct implementation of tools.
Coach	Provide support to both teams and individuals in their respective areas and guide them in discovering improvement opportunities and executing projects.
Mentor	Develop a network of Lean Six Sigma individuals from all areas and functions of the organization that work as cross-functional teams and develop impactful projects.
Influencer	Motivate people from all areas and functions in order to maintain the continuous improvement philosophy as a main priority to achieve the goals of the organization and establish a learning system that improves the quality of life for everyone.

Knowledge Required

Certification	Who	Knowledge	Duration	Accum.
Lean Champion	Leaders	Philosophy – Tools – Transformation Process – Results	8 h	8 h
White Belt	Everyone	Introduction – Essential Tools	8 h	16 h
Yellow Belt	20 – 50%	Lean Tools & Methodologies	24 h	40 h
Green Belt	10 – 20%	Six Sigma Tools & Methodologies	40 h	80 h
Black Belt	1 – 3%	Leadership – Project Management – Advanced Tools	40 h	120 h
Master BB	1 %	Strategy Management – Innovation	40 h	160 h

LSSI
LEAN SIX SIGMA INSTITUTE

Lean Six Sigma is for the entire organization

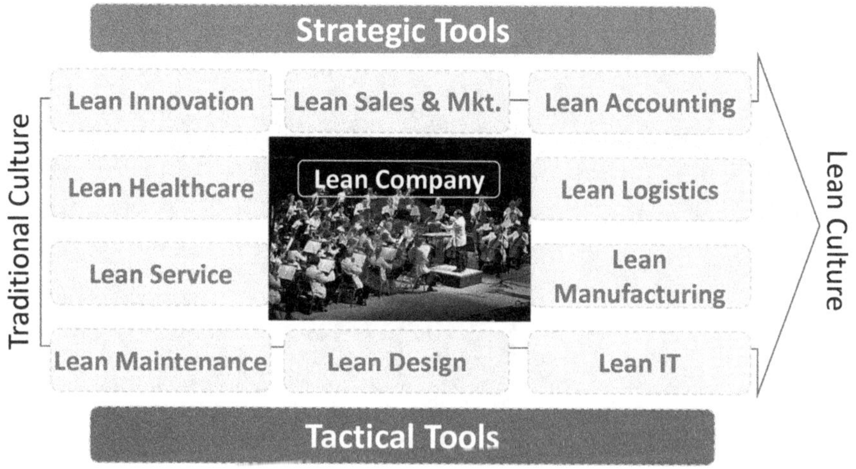

Scrum

"The art of doing twice the work in half the time."

Jeff Sutherland, Software Developer

Learning objectives

1. Understand how Scrum works to develop projects in an agile way with collaborative teamwork.
2. Understand the roles and responsibilities of each member of the Scrum team.
3. Understand how to use Scrum artifacts and develop Scrum ceremonies.
4. Understand the importance of developing successful projects that align with business strategy.

Contenidos

> Background
> What is Scrum?
> What is it used for?
> Key elements
> Who participates?
> When is it used?
> How long does it take?
> Procedure

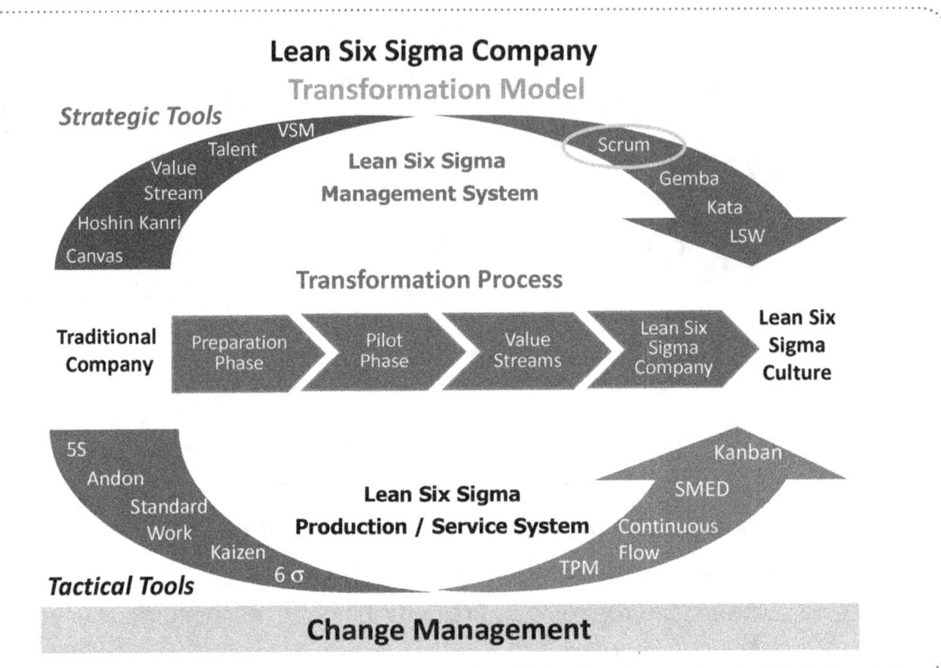

- Less than 20% of all companies develop a strategic plan.
- Of those that do, only 8% succeed in the implementation of their strategy.
- The main cause of failure is inadequate project management.
- Very few companies dedicate enough resources to tracking and managing strategic projects.

Traditional project management models are obsolete.

Source: *Harvard Business Review*

1986 – Article: "The New Product Development Game."
Hirotaka Takeuchi and Ikujiro Nonaka *(Harvard Business Review)*

- The authors studied teams from the most productive and innovative organizations in the world: Honda, Fuji-Xerox, 3M, etc.
- They asserted that the old, sequential approach to developing new products ("Waterfall planning") was no longer viable.
- Instead, they identified that the top-performing organizations were using a faster, more flexible method.
- These organizations' teams were adaptable, flexible, multidisciplinary, and self-organizing.
- Their managers did not give orders; they instead were leaders and facilitators dedicated to eliminating project obstacles.
- Their collaborative work was analogous to the performance of a rugby team moving up the field as a single unit using the **Scrum** method.

Project Management Methodologies

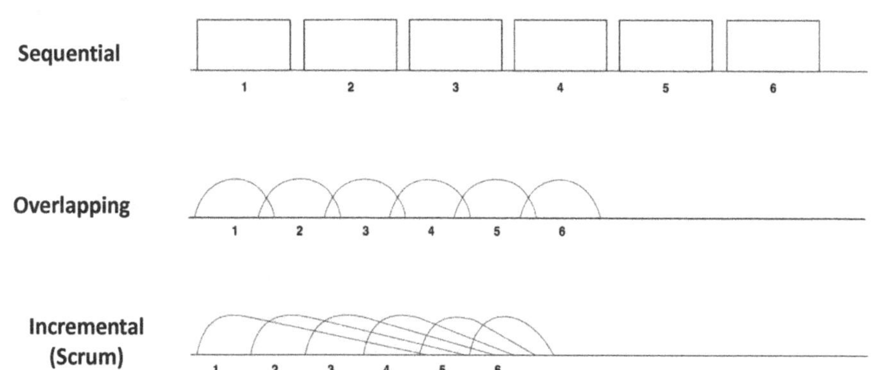

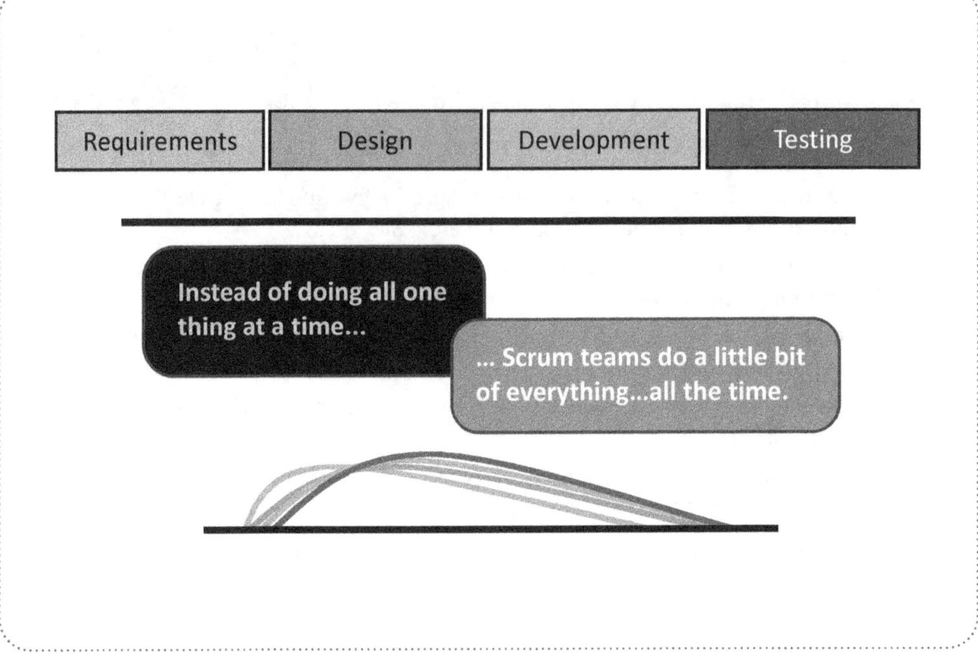

Lean Startup

Making the best decisions in high-risk, complex environments.

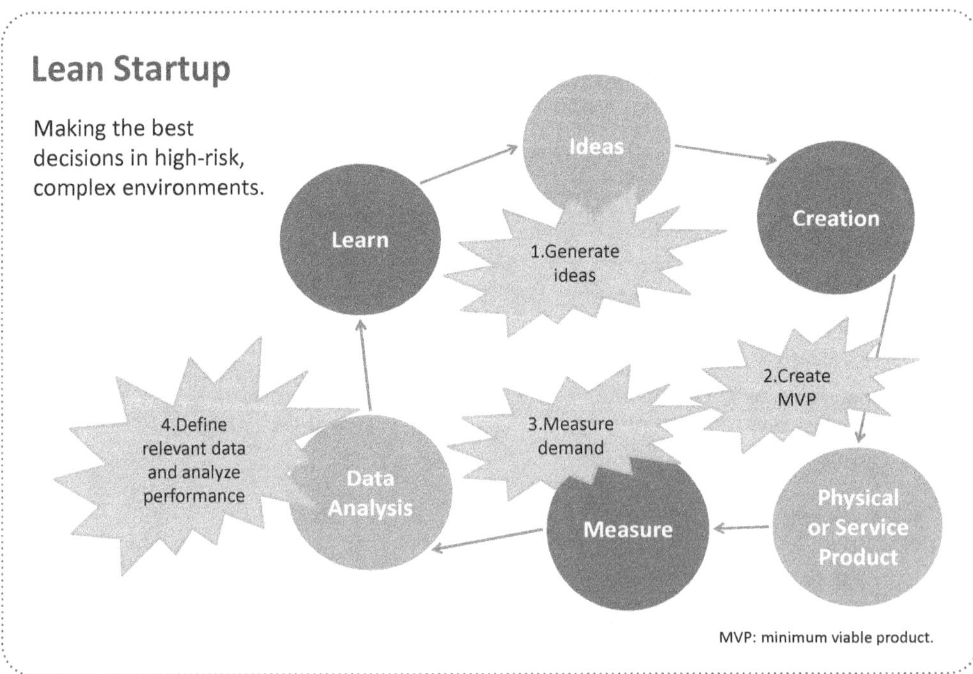

LSSI LEAN SIX SIGMA INSTITUTE

Origin of the word Scrum

- Takeuchi and Nonaka found that the development teams from Canon, Xerox, and Honda were highly productive and followed certain behavior patterns.

- They developed a framework that is very similar to the way rugby teams work.

  - **Scrum** is a method where players are packed closely together and **work *as a unit* to gain possession of the ball.**

    In the project management setting, team members share tasks and responsibilities and work as a unit to deliver final work products.

The origin of Scrum

Software developers Ken Schwaber and Jeff Sutherland developed the Scrum concept and framework around the Lean philosophy – which they call *Agile*.

They developed the following elements of Scrum:

- Participant roles.

- Ceremonies.

- Artifacts.

What is Scrum?

A Project Management System

> " A *framework* within which people can address complex adaptive problems, while productively and creatively delivering **products of the highest possible value.**

Ken Schwaber / Jeff Sutherland

Agile Manifesto

Individuals & Interactions	over	**Processes & Tools**
Functional Products	over	**Project Documentation**
Customer Collaboration	over	**Contract Fulfillment**
Response to Change	over	**Following a Plan**

LSSI
LEAN SIX SIGMA INSTITUTE

12 Principles behind the Agile Manifesto

1. Our highest priority is to satisfy the customer through early and continuous delivery of valuable software.

2. Welcome changing requirements, even late in development. Agile processes harness change for the customer's competitive advantage.

3. Deliver working software frequently, from a couple of weeks to a couple of months, with a preference for the shorter timescale.

4. Business people and developers must work together daily throughout the project.

5. Build projects around motivated individuals. Give them the environment and support they need, and trust them to get the job done.

6. The most efficient and effective method of conveying information to and within a development team is face-to-face conversation.

7. Working software is the primary measure of progress.

8. Agile processes promote sustainable development. The sponsors, developers, and users should be able to maintain a constant pace indefinitely.

9. Continuous attention to technical excellence and good design enhances agility.

10. Simplicity – the art of maximizing the amount of work done – is essential.

11. The best architectures, requirements, and designs emerge from self-organizing teams.

12. At regular intervals, the team reflects on how to become more effective, then tunes and adjusts its behavior accordingly.

Source: Agile Alliance

What is it used for?

Finance

Ensures projects achieve financial goals.

Monitors costs of projects.

Performs cost-benefit analysis.

Results

Ensures projects achieve expected results.

Identifies and quantifies the value that projects contribute to final results.

Evaluates and mitigates risks to achieve results.

Resources

Identifies the required resources.

Gathers the right team.

Provides follow-up for team members.

Development

Ensures projects are properly implemented.

Uses the right tools relevant to the objectives of the project.

Implements methods that ensure a successful project development execution.

Benefits of Scrum

Proper implementation will help:

- Increase speed of development.

- Align individual and corporate objectives.

- Create a culture driven by performance.

- Support shareholder value creation.

- Achieve stable and consistent communication of performance at all levels.

Source: Jeff Sutherland's *Scrum Handbook*

The 5 Values of Scrum

Employing the Scrum framework the right way requires compliance with its five values:

Team members pay close attention to results. — **Focus**

Team members hold each other accountable. — **Openness**

Team members ensure that everyone is engaged. — **Commitment**

Team members have the courage to engage each other and work through challenging problems. — **Courage**

Team members build trust by respecting each other. — **Respect**

LSSI
LEAN SIX SIGMA INSTITUTE

Scrum Characteristics

Agile Project Managements

Transparency	Inspection	Adaptation
▪ The main aspects of the process should be defined by common standards. ▪ All participants must share a common language for the process. ▪ A common definition of "Done" should be established for the team members who accept the deliverables and product.	▪ **Scrum** users must frequently inspect the models used to ensure that objectives are being met. ▪ Inspections should not interrupt or stop progress; they must be agile. ▪ Inspections are effective since they are carried out in the presence of the project owners or their representatives – who keep the established objectives in sight.	▪ The process should be adjusted when an inspection reveals that the deliverables are unacceptable. ▪ Sprint Planning. ▪ Daily Scrum. ▪ Sprint Review. ▪ Sprint Retrospective.

Who uses Scrum?

Illumina		FBI
Microsoft		Yahoo
Nielsen Media		Google
First American Real Estate		Electronic
BMC Software		High Moon Studios
John Deere		Lockheed Martin
Lexis Nexis		Philips
Sabre		Siemens
Salesforce		Nokia
Time Warner		Capital One
Turner Broadcasting		BBC
British Telecom		Fidelity Investments
General Electric		Bank of America
Apple		

What type of projects are most suitable for Scrum?

- New product development.
- Software development.
- Construction.
- Pricing.
- Financial applications.
- ISO 9001 Certificate.
- Design of space missions.
- Design of defense equipment.
- Provider development.
- Mobile telephony.
- Mobile apps.
- Medical products.
- Food and beverage.
- Technology transfer.
- Video game development.
- Development of new facilities.

Key Elements

Roles
- Product Owner
- Scrum Master
- Development Team

Ceremonies
- Sprint Planning
- Daily Scrum
- Sprint Review
- Sprint Retrospective

Artifacts
- Product Backlog
- Sprint Backlog
- Burndown Charts

LSSI
LEAN SIX SIGMA INSTITUTE

Who Participates?

Scrum teams are self-organizing and cross-functional

Product Owner

Responsible for maximizing the value of the product and the work of the development team.

Manages the product backlog and defines priorities.

Development Team

Self-organizing groups of 5 – 10 cross-functional members: QA, Designers, Engineers, etc.

Teams may vary between Sprints.

Scrum Master

Ensures that Scrum is understood and implemented correctly.

Organizes meetings and monitors project development.

Product Owner

Roles

- Vision and roadmap
- Empowerment
- Budget

- Business model
- Revenue sources
- Cost structure
- Channels

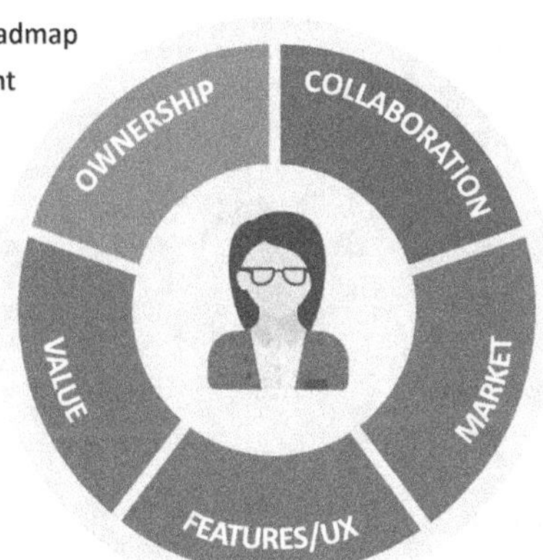

- Incubator/Colocation
- Joint backlog grooming
- Analyze delay
- Joint meetings

- Customers
- Feedback
- Data obtained from exposing product increments to customers

- User stories
- Product canvas
- Product backlog

Scrum Master

Roles

- Face-to-face communication
- Self-organization & transparency
- Adaptability to change

- Meetings & Scrum ceremonies
- Team's release planning
- Maintain sustainable pace

- Monitoring & tracking
- Burndown Charts, Status Boards
- Performance feedback
- Maintaining Scrum tool

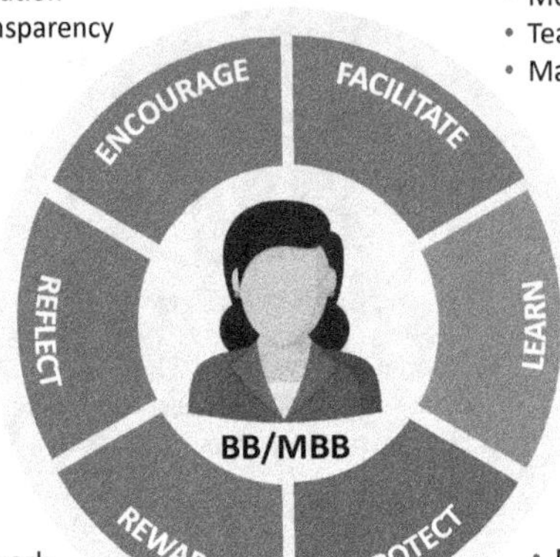

- Continuous self-learning
- Provide ongoing feedback to the team
- Interact & exchange experiences

- Take pride in good work performance
- Celebrate success

- Mediate and resolve conflict
- Protect the team from external obstacles

Scrum Master Interactions

Roles

- Provides coaching on self-organization and teamwork
- Removes obstacles in the Development Team's way
- Helps the Development Team to create high-value products
- Facilitates the implementation of Scrum

Product Owner   **Development Team**   **Scrum Master**   **Organization**

- Identifies effective Product Backlog management techniques
- Helps the Scrum team understand the need for clarity and conciseness of the Product Backlog items
- Facilitates the implementation of **Scrum**

- Leads and coaches the organization in its Scrum adoption
- Plans Scrum implementation and training throughout the organization
- Helps employees and stakeholders understand Scrum at the theoretical and empirical levels

LSSI
LEAN SIX SIGMA INSTITUTE

Scrum Ceremonies: 5 Levels of Planning

5 Levels of Planning			
Level	Freq	Main Actors	Output
1 Product Vision	1–2 times/yr	Product Owner	Vision
2 Roadmap	2–3 times/yr	Product Owner	Roadmap + Initial producto B/L
3 Release Planning	3–4 times/yr	Product Owner + Team + SH	Release Plan
4 Sprint Planning	Every Sprint	Product Owner + Team	Sprint Backlog
5 Daily Planning	Every Day	Team	Updated B/L Impediments

The five levels of planning help address these important aspects: priorities, estimates, and commitments.

They help create consistency and minimize the need for unnecessary meetings.

Their frequency depends on the organization, project, team size, requirements, etc.

When is it used?

- When developing complex projects.

- When requirements are not clearly defined.

- When the probability of making changes is high.

- When time is a constraint.

- When the project priority is to achieve the greatest benefits with the highest quality.

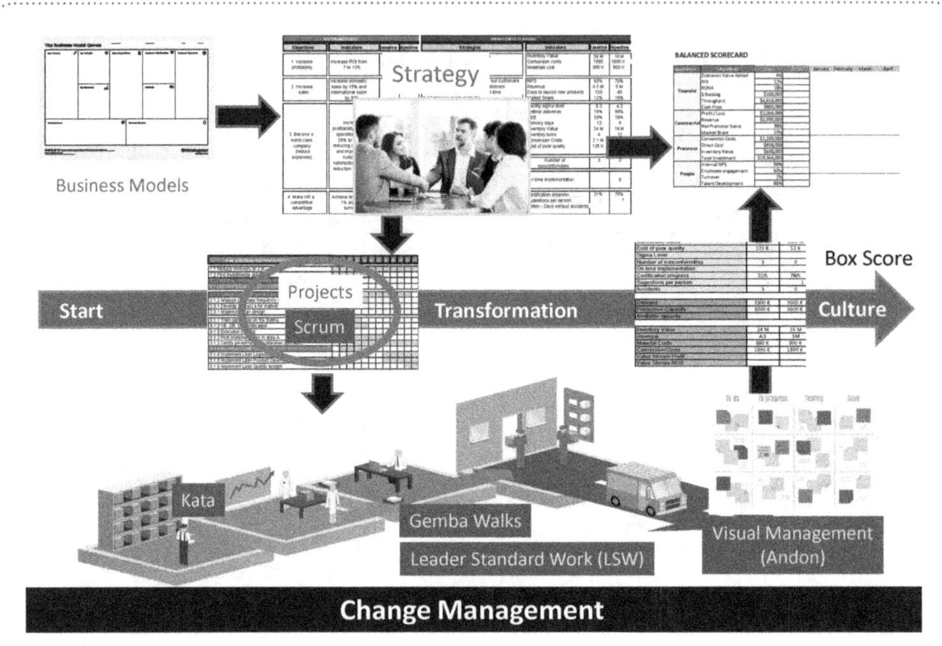

How long does it take?

- Project timelines will vary depending on their complexity.

- Each project is divided into sprints that represent viable and shippable product.

  - Each sprint has a fixed time period ranging from 1 to 4 weeks.

- Projects developed with Scrum tend to have far shorter cycle times than waterfall projects– reducing the total project time by up to 50%.*

*Source: *The Scrum Papers* by Jeff Sutherland and Ken Schwaber.

Stages and key aspects for agile project management:

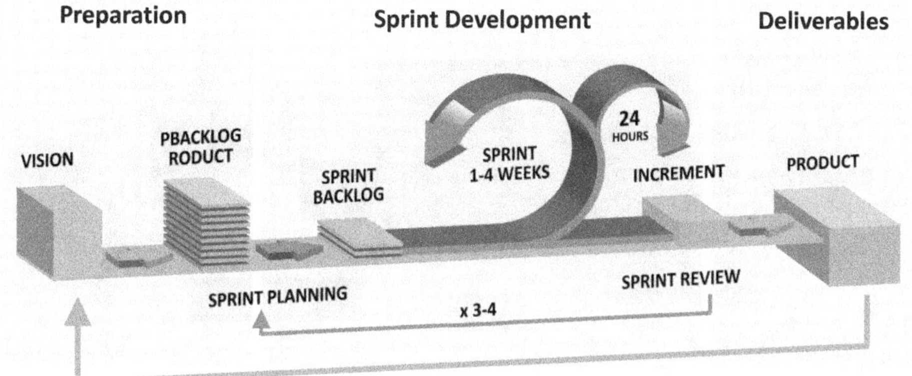

Scrum procedure to generate value

Stage 1: Vision

Description: The goals for the project/product and its alignment with the company's strategy
Person responsible: Product Owner
Frequency: 1 – 2 times during the project

Stage 2: Product Roadmap

Description: Holistic view of project/product features that create the vision
Person Responsible: Product owner
Frequency: 2 – 3 times during the project

Stage 3: Release Planning

Description: Release timing for specific product functionality
Person responsible: Product Owner
Frequency: When necessary

Stage 4: Sprint Planning

Description: Establish specific iteration goals and tasks
Person Responsible: Product Owner and Development Team
Frequency: At the start of each sprint

Stage 7: Sprint Retrospective

Description: Team refinement of environment and processes to optimize efficiency
Person Responsible: Product Owner
Frequency: At the end of each sprint

Stage 6: Sprint Review

Description: Demonstration of working product
Person Responsible: Product Owner
Frequency: At the end of each sprint

Stage 5: Daily Scrum

Description: The team gets together to establish and coordinate priorities of the day
Person Responsible: Development team
Frequency: Daily

Preparation | Execution

Stage 1: Vision

Preparation Phase

What: The vision of the project/product is developed according to the business strategy and the value proposition.

When: Project initiation phase.

Who: Management Team, Product Owner, Development Team and Scrum Master.

Responsible: Product Owner.

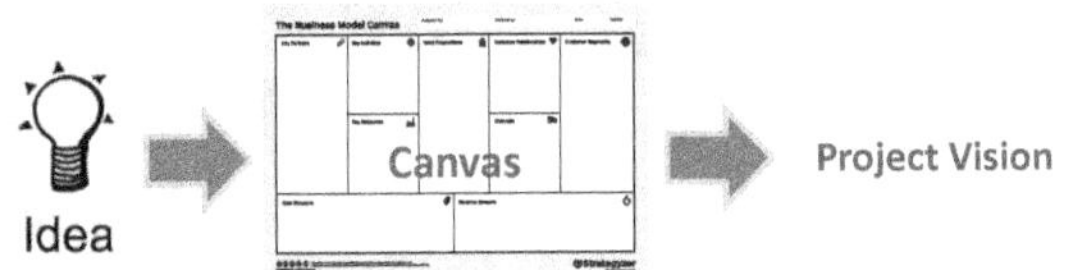

Idea → Canvas → Project Vision

- Define the Vision of the project (objectives) in terms of the value it creates.
- The Vision is a statement that can be communicated as an elevator pitch.
  - It must be written in two or three sentences.

Template:

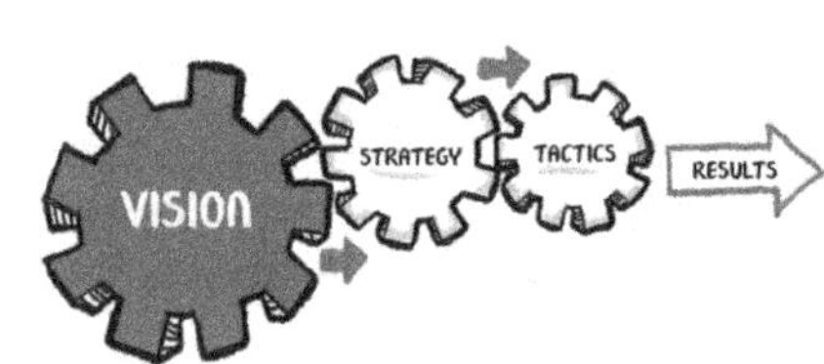

- For *<target customer>*
- Who *<statement of need>*
- The *<product name>*
- Is a *<product category>*
- That *<key benefit, irresistible reason to buy it>*
- Different from *<main alternative>*
- Our product *<final declaration of main differentiation>*
- Which supports our strategy to *<company strategy>*

Example

- Smartphone application: **Mobile bank**

For *ACME Bank customers*	< target customer
who *need to access their bank wherever they are*	< declaration of need
the *Pocket Bank*	< product name
is a *mobile application*	< product category
that provides *secure access when customers need it*	< key benefit
different from *online banking from a PC*	< main alternative
our product *allows users immediate access*	< main differentiation
which supports our strategy *to attract more customers*	< key strategy that supports

Vision – Product Roadmap – Release Planning – Sprint Planning – Daily Scrum – Sprint Review – Sprint Retrospective

Stage 2: Product Roadmap

Preparation Phase

What: A high-level view of the project/product requirements.

A list of characteristics that make the Vision attainable.

- Prioritized and organized by affinity.
- Delivery stages are defined.

When: Created at the beginning of the project and revisited 2 to 3 more times to redefine the characteristics.

Who: Management Team, Product Owner, Development, Team and Scrum Master.

Responsible: Product Owner.

Time: As much as is needed (usually 4 - 16 hours).

Vision – Product Roadmap – Release Planning – Sprint Planning – Daily Scrum – Sprint Review – Sprint Retrospective

Categories →	1. Account Organization	2. Money Transfers	3. Automatic Payments	4. Investments	5. Help
Requirements	1.1. User Access	2.1. Transfers between internal accounts	3.1. Creditor Registration	4.1. Information about investments	5.1. FAQs
	1.2. Visualize Accounts	2.2. Transfers to other banks	3.2. Payments Scheduling	4.2. News & Recommendations	5.2. Phone Contact
	1.3. View Statements		3.3. 'Lack of Funds' Alert	4.3. Stock Market	5.3. Chat With Customer Service
	1.4. View Account Balance			4.4. Investment Portfolio	
	1.5. Download transactions to Excel				
	1.6. Message Center				

The product roadmap is a high-level plan that shows how the project will evolve. It typically includes several deliverables.

Benefits:

- Follow-up on project's Vision (objectives).
- Alignment among team members.
- Helps in the management of the project portfolio.
- Prioritization of features and deliverables.

Product Vision →

Product Roadmap

Stage 3: Release Planning

Preparation Phase

What: A high-level timetable for the release of project deliverables. On average, a release will include 3 to 5 Sprints.

When: 3 to 4 times during the project. Sprints are planned at the beginning of each release.

Who: Product Owner, Development Team and Scrum Master.

Responsible: Product Owner.

Time: 2-4 hours.

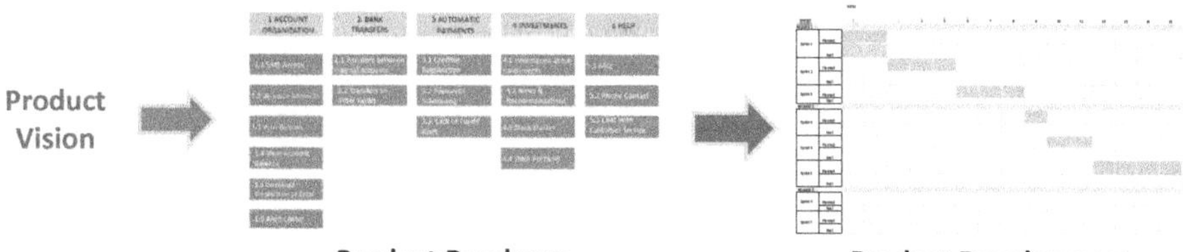

Product Vision → **Product Roadmap** → **Product Development**

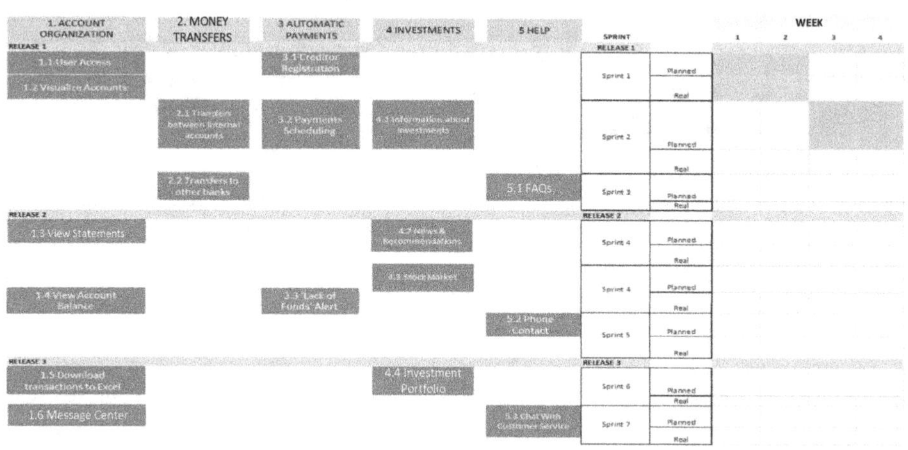

WEEK

SPRINT		1	2	3	4	5	6	7	8	9	10	11	12	13	14	15	16	17	18	19	20	21	22	23	24	25	26	26
Release 1																												
Sprint 1	Plan																											
	Real																											
Sprint 2	Plan																											
	Real																											
Sprint 3	Plan																											
	Real																											
Release 2																												
Sprint 4	Plan																											
	Real																											
Sprint 5	Plan																											
	Real																											
Sprint 6	Plan																											
	Real																											
Release 3																												
Sprint 7	Plan																											
	Real																											
Sprint 8	Plan																											
	Real																											

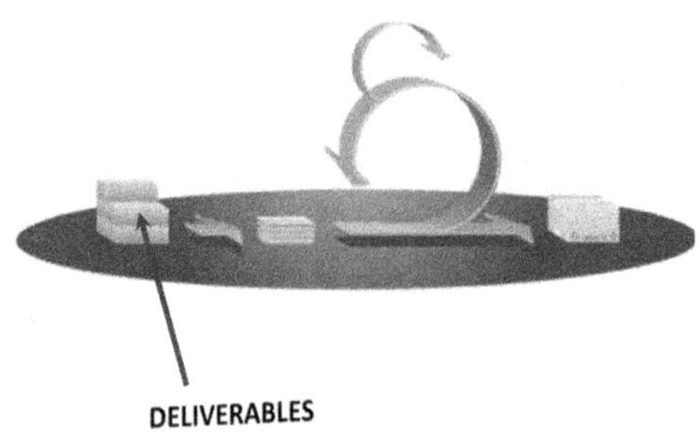

DELIVERABLES

- Project requirements are defined and listed as project/product deliverables.

- These deliverables are expressed as a list of **User Stories**, which are evaluated according to their complexity.

- Deliverables are prioritized by the Product Owner.

- They are reprioritized at the beginning of each Sprint.

Stage 4: Sprint Planning

Execution

What: Establishes the goals and plan for what can be delivered in the upcoming Sprint. In other words, it establishes the rhythm of the project. Each Sprint, or iteration, lasts between 1-4 weeks.

It allows for the development of speed and knowledge.

When: At the beginning of each Sprint.

Who: Product Owner, Development Team, and Scrum Master.

Responsible: Product Owner.

Time: 2 hours per week of Sprint.

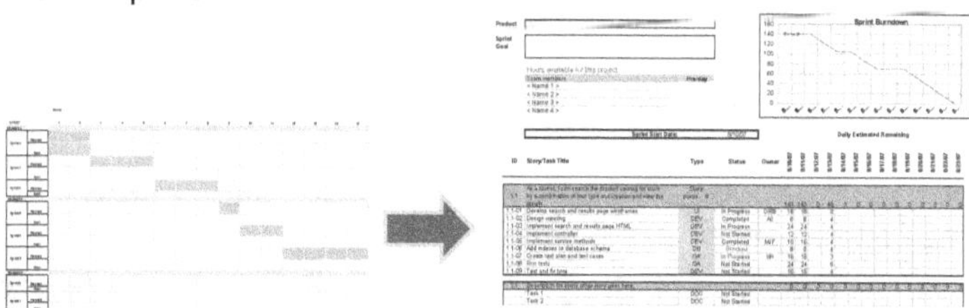

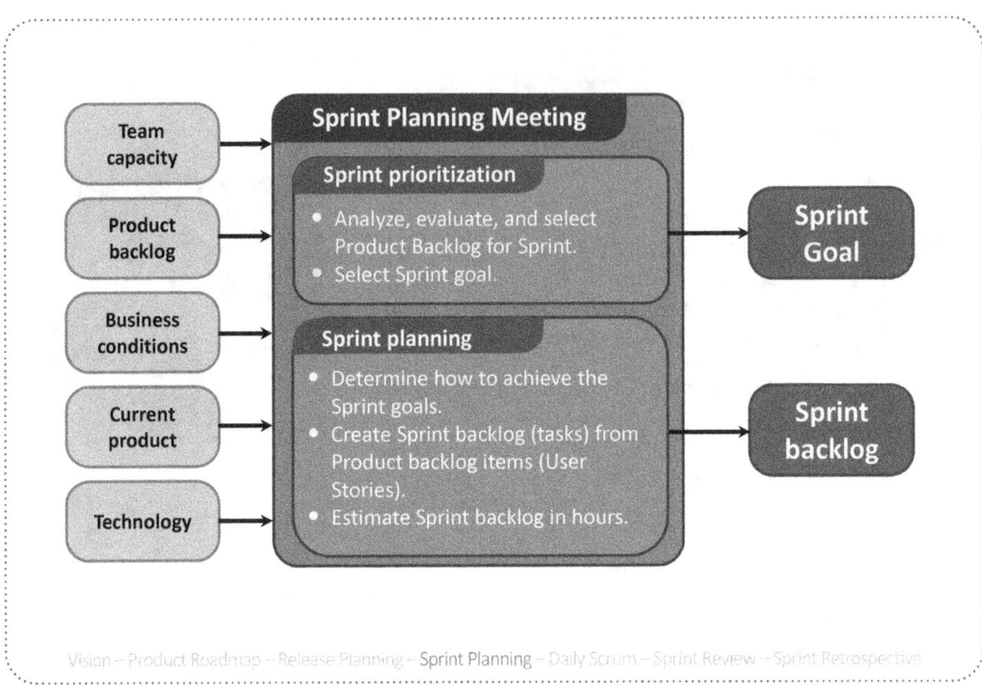

User Story

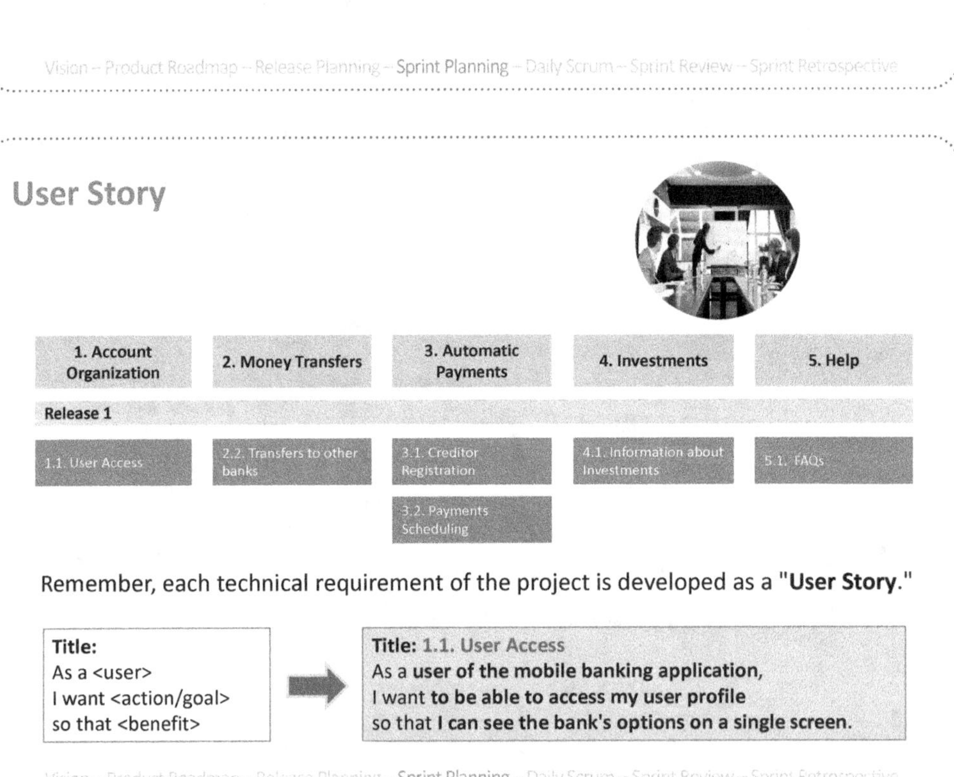

Remember, each technical requirement of the project is developed as a "**User Story**."

Complexity score

- **User Stories** have different levels of complexity.

- The **Team** must assign a score for each User Story according to its complexity.

- The **most common** score is selected.

Size	Points
XtraSmall (XS)	1
Small (S)	2
Medium (M)	3
Large (L)	5
XtraLarge (XL)	8

Preparation - Execution

- Each Sprint is planned by the Team.

- The Team's capacity (available time) for work is estimated.

- Tasks are estimated in hours.

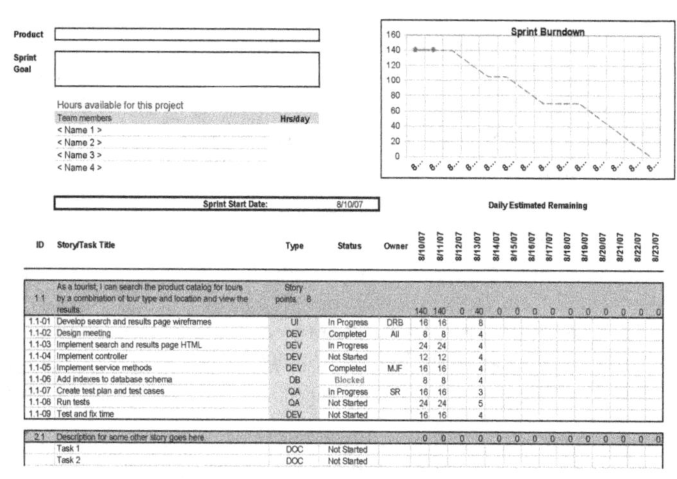

ID	Story/Task Title	Type	Status	Owner	8/10/07	8/11/07	8/12/07	8/13/07	8/14/07	8/15/07	8/16/07	8/17/07	8/18/07	8/19/07	8/20/07	8/21/07	8/22/07	8/23/07
1.1	As a tourist, I can search the product catalog for tours by a combination of tour type and location and view the results.	Story points 8			140	140	0	40	0	0	0	0	0	0	0	0	0	0
1.1-01	Develop search and results page wireframes	UI	In Progress	DRB	16	16	8											
1.1-02	Design meeting	DEV	Completed	All	8	8	4											
1.1-03	Implement search and results page HTML	DEV	In Progress		24	24	4											
1.1-04	Implement controller	DEV	Not Started		12	12	4											
1.1-05	Implement service methods	DEV	Completed	MJF	16	16	4											
1.1-06	Add indexes to database schema	DB	Blocked		8	8	4											
1.1-07	Create test plan and test cases	QA	In Progress	SR	16	16	3											
1.1-08	Run tests	QA	Not Started		24	24	5											
1.1-09	Test and fix time	DEV	Not Started		16	16	4											
2.1	Description for some other story goes here				0	0	0	0	0	0	0	0	0	0	0	0	0	0
	Task 1	DOC	Not Started															
	Task 2	DOC	Not Started															

Burndown Chart

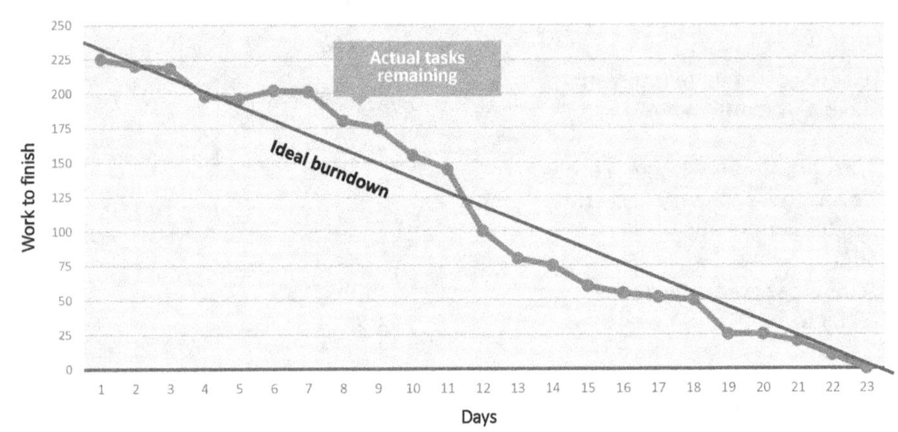

Stage 5: Daily Scrum

Execution

What: Also known as the Daily Stand-Up; each Team member presents:

- What he/she accomplished yesterday.
- What he/she plans to accomplish today.
- What his/her obstacles are.

When: At the beginning of the day - every day - everyone stands up.

Who: The entire Team presents, the Product Owner receives the information, the guests observe, and the Scrum Master moderates. You can invite other people. Only Scrum members can speak.

Responsible: Sprint Development Team.

Time: No more than 15 minutes. This is not a meeting to solve problems. It helps avoid having unnecessary meetings.

Daily Sprint Meeting: Scrum Board - Kanban

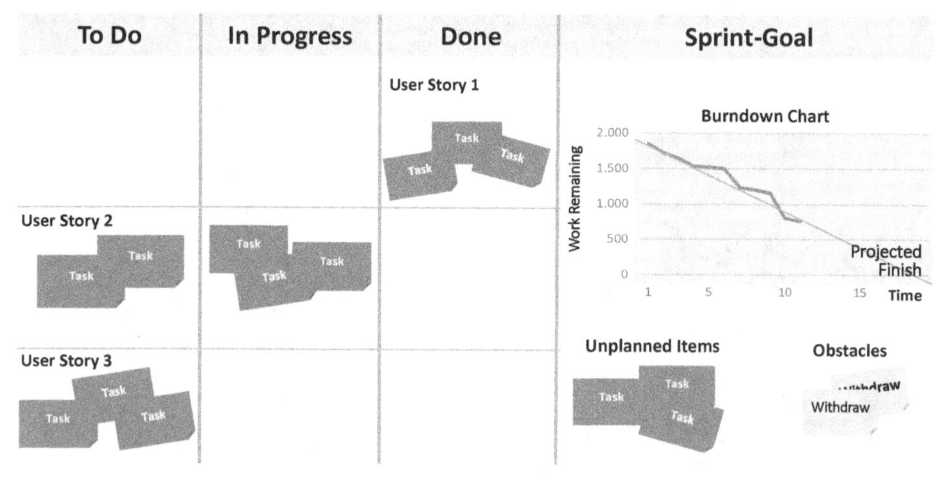

Use the Pomodoro technique

- The **Pomodoro technique** is a time management method developed by Francesco Cirillo in the late 1980s.

- The technique uses a clock to divide the time spent on a job in 25-minute intervals - called **"Pomodoros"** - and separates them with short breaks.

> A key objective of the technique is to eliminate [internal and external] interruptions on focus and flow.

1. Decide the task to be performed.
2. Set the **Pomodoro** (clock or stopwatch) at 25 minutes.
3. Work on the task until the clock rings and record it with an X.
4. Take a short break (5 minutes).
5. Take a longer break (15-20 minutes) after every 4 **Pomodoros**.

[it.] *pomodoro* = tomato [Eng]

Command and Control teams vs. self-organized teams

Command and Control

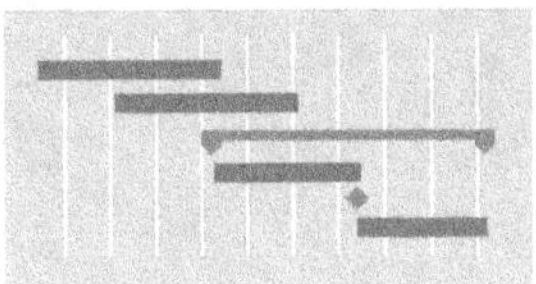

Orders:
Work is assigned to
the Team.

Control:
The project manager
continuously monitors
progress and updates
the status of the
project.

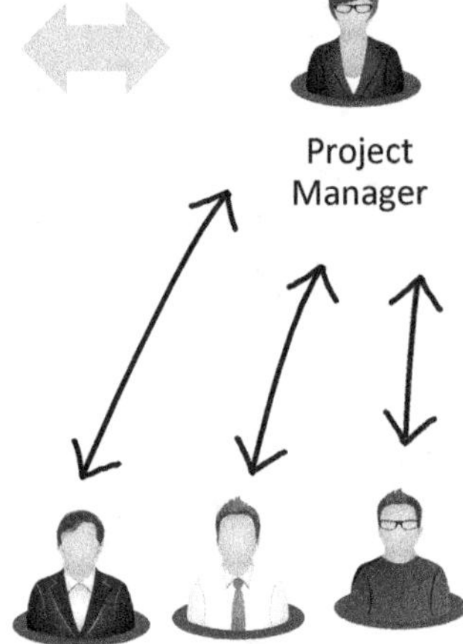

Self-organized Team

Scrum Board

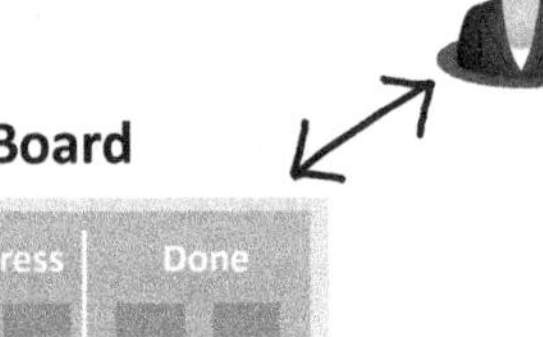

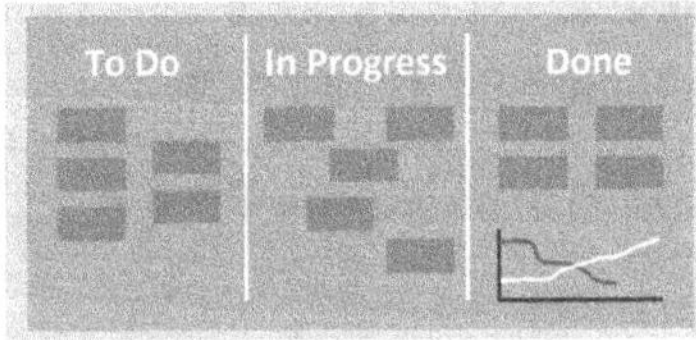

The team plans
and takes on the
work that needs to
be done during the
Sprint.

LSSI
LEAN SIX SIGMA INSTITUTE

Stage 6: Sprint Review

Execution

What: The Team presents the work completed during the Sprint. **Minimum Viable Products (MVP) are generated.**

When: At the end of each Sprint (1 - 4 weeks).

Who: The Product Owner presents the results achieved during the Sprint. The Development Team demonstrates the operation of the product.

Responsible: Sprint Development Team.

Time: 1 hour for each Sprint week.

- Informal.
- Preferably without PowerPoint presentations.
- No rigid demonstrations (demos).

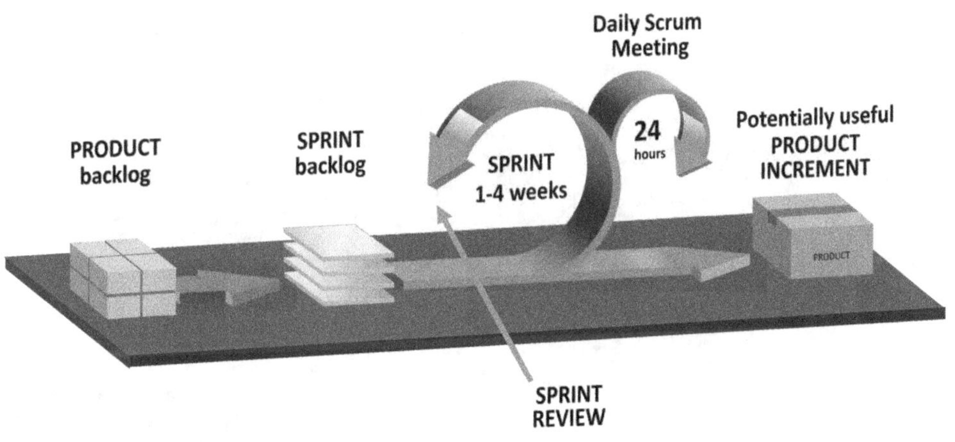

Stage 7: Sprint Retrospective

Execution

What: The Team discusses how the Sprint went and plans for future improvements. Three questions are asked:

- What do you think went well?
- What would you like to change?
- How should we implement those changes?

When: At the end of each Sprint (1-4 weeks).

Who: Development Team, Product Owner, and Scrum Master. Customers of product and personnel involved.

Responsible: Sprint Development Team.

Time: 45 minutes for each Sprint week.

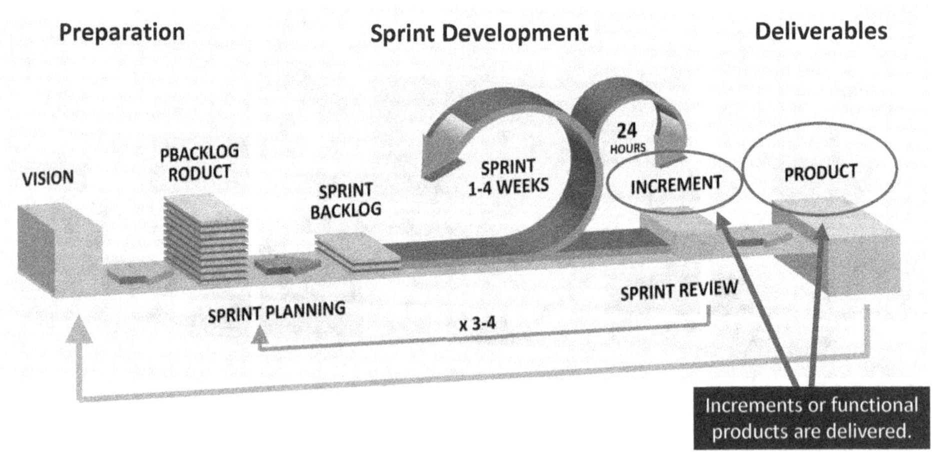

Coaching Leaders

Leaders designing the future

Learning objectives

1. Acquire the ability to plan, coordinate, and execute training sessions.
2. Build the necessary skills to deliver training sessions in the most effective manner.
3. Develop the skills to train teams and individuals to unlock their potential and maximize results.

Content

> Background
> Course Preparation
> Course Delivery
> Coaching

Background

I. Background	1. Introduction
II. Course Preparation	2. Training and Coaching
III. Course Delivery	3. Communication
IV. Coaching	

1. Introduction

Lean Company

Design	Manufacturing
Logistics	Maintenance
Accounting	Safety
Human Development	Quality
Products & Services	IT

Improve **Prevent** **Solve**

Define: QFD, A3, Kano, Canvas, etc.
Measure: VSM, Sampling, Gauge R&R, etc.
Analyze: Statistics, Balance Chart, FMEA, etc.
Improve: Kanban, Continuous Flow, SMED, TPM, etc.
Control: SPC, Control Plan, Poka Yoke, Std. Work

5 S
Visual Administrator   **Basic Tools**
Standardized Work

Strategic Planning, Canvas, Box Score
LSW, Gemba, Kata, Scrum   **Management**
Value Stream Structures   **Tools**
Talent Development

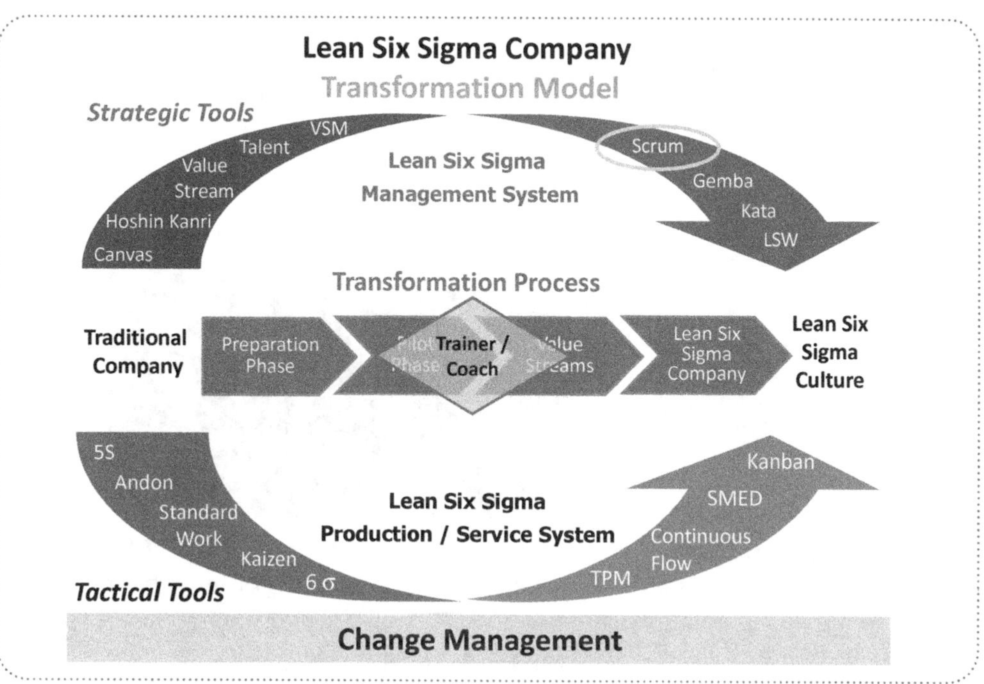

Important Leadership Knowledge & Skills
Training Within Industry

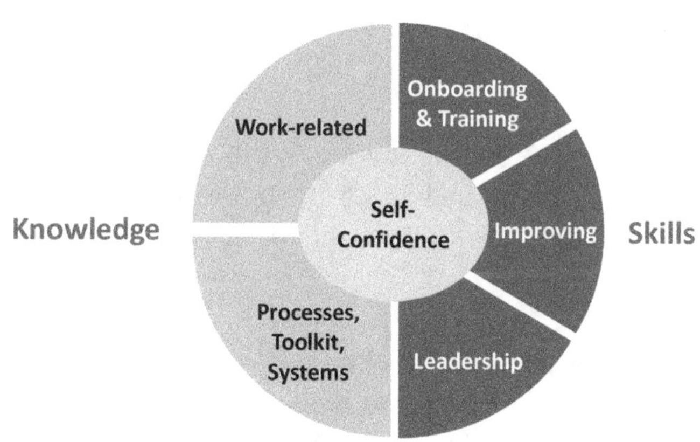

Motivation for learning
Coaching Leader

- **Motivated by the content:** The course content itself is engaging.

- **Motivated by usefulness:** The student understands the importance of learning as a useful instrument to pursue and accomplish his/her goals.

- **Motivated by the didactic method(s):** The student is engaged by the teaching methods, not only because the content is interesting, but also due to the encouragement to participate, the intellectual challenge presented, the higher-order mental processes required, etc.

- **Motivated by the teacher:** The trainer sets the environment in terms of rapport and helps build a strong motivational purpose though his/her interaction with the student during the teaching-learning process.

- **Motivated by the taste of success:** It is well known that experiencing success reinforces and strengthens one's motivation to pursue the fulfillment of tasks and objectives.

2. Training and Coaching

Training ensures people learn about the tools and helps them create a common language.

Coaching guides the correct implementation of tools to achieve practical solutions (i.e., turning knowledge into solutions).

The **Black Belts** play an important role as trainers and coaches. They help:

- Promote personal growth and business success.
- Produce a positive and productive workplace environment.
- Increase the skillsets of team members.

Leader Standard Work

LSSI   NAME: JEFF SALES

Time	Daily Task	Notes / Comments / Obstacles	Day	Time	Periodic Task
8:00 AM	Meeting (on-the floor)		Mon	9:00am	Production plan and shipping schedule
8:15 AM	Gemba Walk				
8:30 AM	Review Alicia's and George's LSW				
8:45 AM	Emails/ Voice Mail		Tue	11:00am	
9:00 AM	Meeting prep				
9:15 AM	Meeting				
9:30 AM	Meeting		Wed	9:00am	Training Session
9:45 AM	Production board / Open items				
10:00 AM	Review first production run performance				
10:15 AM					
10:30 AM	Task follow-up				
10:45 AM					
11:00 AM	Project time				
11:15 AM	Project time				
11:30 AM	Project time				
11:45 AM	Project time				
12:30 PM	Review 2nd production run performance				
12:45 PM					
1:00 PM	Results presentation meeting and task follow-up				
1:15 PM	Time for pending tasks				
1:30 PM	Time for pending tasks				
1:45 PM			3rd Tue	9:00 AM	Cross-training review
2:00 PM	Training session				
2:15 PM					
2:30 PM					
2:45 PM					
3:00 PM	Review 3rd production run performance				
3:15 PM	Costing simulations				
3:30 PM					
3:45 PM					
4:00 PM					
4:15 PM	Review on-time delivery performance				

3. Communication

- **The message:** Composed of the educational content, the subject matter, and the knowledge set that is intended to be transmitted.

- **The sender:** The teacher acts as the source of information and communication.

- **The receiver:** The student receives and decodes the message.

- **The channel:** Knowledge is obtained visually and/or audibly. The employment of different visual aids should be tailored to the audience being addressed and it should complement the verbal presentation.

How our Brain Works
The 4 Cardinal Points

LSSI
LEAN SIX SIGMA INSTITUTE

How our Brain Learns

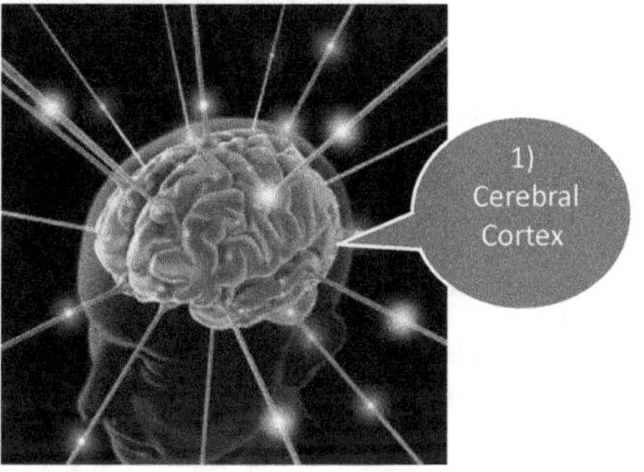

A. Information intake

- The external layer of our cerebral cortex receives sensory inputs from the outside world.

- Our cerebral cortex registers these inputs, which serve as raw material for learning.

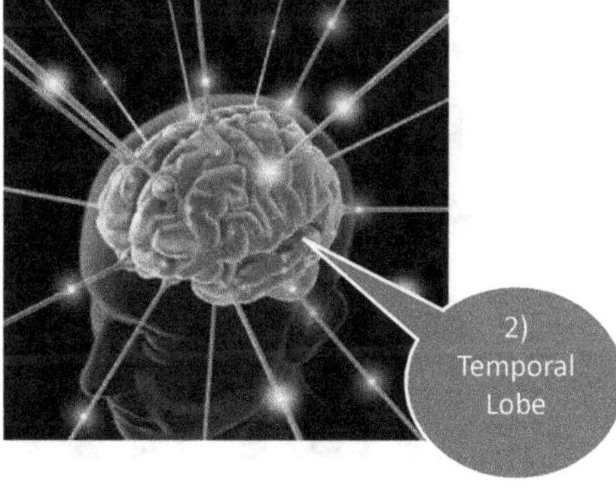

B. Creation of meaning

- The temporal lobe is involved in processing sensory input into derived meaning.

- Basically, if we can make sense of the content being taught, the information gets transferred to the working memory.

C. Abstraction

- This process is kicked off once the executive brain from the prefrontal cortex is fully **engaged**.

- The student receives and processes information, which is then used to create new knowledge, establish relationships, and form new abstractions.

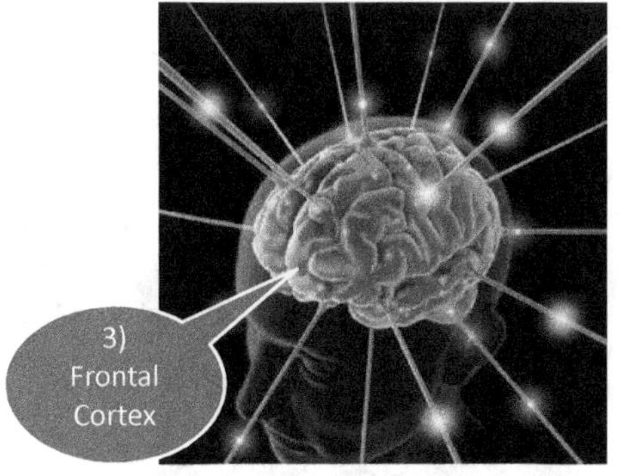

D. Learning experiments

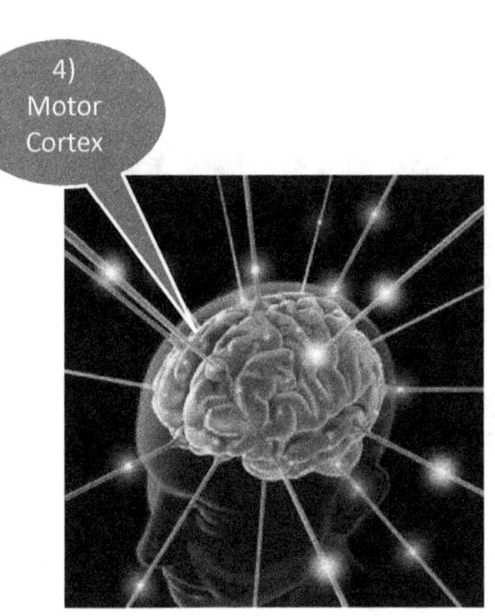

- Led by the motor cortex, the brain conducts experiments to test what has been learned.

- At this point, the brain uses the concepts it has learned as guidelines for active experimentation and the development of new learning.

LSSI
LEAN SIX SIGMA INSTITUTE

Course Preparation

I. Background

II. Course Preparation

III. Course Delivery

IV. Coaching

1. Situation analysis
2. Defining learning objectives
3. Course content
4. Choosing didactic methods
5. Material development
6. Didactic guidelines
7. Evaluation
8. Attendance list
9. Checklist
10. Lessons learned

1. Situation Analysis

1. Situation analysis
2. Objectives
3. Course content
4. Didactic methods
5. Material dev.
6. Guidelines
7. Evaluation
8. Attendance list
9. Checklist
10. Lessons learned

- Before designing a course, it is important to identify and analyze the knowledge needs of the people in your organization.

- Courses are created as a direct response to identified, specific knowledge needs.

- The opportunity to design a course presents itself when a discrepancy between the current and the desired working performance is identified.

Example

- After the introduction of new services, team members have regularly been making errors in the formulation, preparation, and processing of orders. It has been identified that the root cause of the problem is team member lack of knowledge regarding the characteristics of the new services. For this reason, it is important to deliver courses to advance knowledge development and reduce errors.

- The following are examples of common situations in the workplace:
  - Lack of awareness or clarity for specific activities or functions
  - Errors and inefficiencies
  - Incomplete understanding of the requirements of the customer or the company
  - Poor results in any given activity or function

2. Defining Learning Objectives

1. Situation analysis
2. Define objectives
3. Course content
4. Didactic methods
5. Material dev.
6. Guidelines
7. Evaluation
8. Attendance list
9. Checklist
10. Lessons learned

- An objective is the expected behavior a learner engages in as a result of specific training activities. It is important for this behavior to be observable and prone to evaluation.

- Defining objectives is a fundamental part of the teaching-learning process, and they can be broken down into general and specific ones. These objectives should be clearly communicated and easily understood.

LSSI
LEAN SIX SIGMA INSTITUTE

For objectives to be applicable and useful for the educational process, they must be:

- Explicit.
- Precise.
- Time-bound.
- Achievable.
- Observable.
- Measurable.
- Communicable.

Breakdown

- **General objective example:**

  "By the end of this course, participants will be able to successfully prepare and deliver a course independently".

- **Specific objectives examples:**
  - Master communication techniques.
  - Apply didactic techniques.
  - Develop course content.

3. Course Content

1. Situation analysis
2. Define objectives
3. Course content
4. Didactic methods
5. Material dev.
6. Guidelines
7. Evaluation
8. Attendance list
9. Checklist
10. Lessons learned

- Make sure that the general and specific points of the course content cover all of the learning objectives.

- External sources of information can be used when creating content.

- The content should not be ambiguous, but rather clear and transparent.

- The content should be ordered in a logical and sequential manner.

- The content should be relevant and engaging.

Example

1. Introduction
2. Background
3. Training & coaching
4. Communication
5. Didactic methods
6. Methods of learning
7. Course preparation
8. Course delivery
9. Conclusions

4. Choosing of Didactic Methods

1. Situation analysis
2. Define objectives
3. Course content
4. Didactic methods
5. Material dev.
6. Guidelines
7. Evaluation
8. Attendance list
9. Checklist
10. Lessons learned

- The didactic and research methods selected – as well as the rationale behind them – must follow flexible rules.

- If there is no clear choice of which didactic methods will be employed, then it will be difficult for the course participants to achieve the learning objectives.

Didactic Methods

1. Presentation
2. Presentation with supporting material
3. Discussion
4. Q&A Session
5. Demonstration
6. Work Session
7. Case Method
8. Learning exercises, experiments, excursions, and field trips

5. Material Development

1. Situation analysis
2. Define objectives
3. Course content
4. Didactic methods
5. Material dev.
6. Guidelines
7. Evaluation
8. Attendance list
9. Checklist
10. Lessons learned

- Training material is a key element for effective knowledge transfer.

- Examples of material:
  - PowerPoint presentations.
  - Videos.
  - Games.

PowerPoint is a powerful tool for delivering presentations.

Benefits include:

- It is an inexpensive, ubiquitous and relatively easy-to-use tool.
- It is capable of providing robust high-quality delivery through a coordination of texts, images, and movies.
- It can be used to present information in a dynamic and organized manner.
- It can be used to emphasize specific information.
- It facilitates the sequential delivery of content with the use of transitions.
- It can help engage the audience with captivating animations.
- It can stimulate learning energy and be more impactful by adding supplemental audio relevant to the content being presented.

Games and Simulations

- Games and simulations are also a very effective method for transferring knowledge – especially when they are interactive in nature and guide students through an analogical path to the learning objective.

- Benefits includes:
  - Authentic, engaging learning.
  - Learning based on emotions and logic.
  - Assessment of team effectiveness.
  - Stimulates ingenuity and spontaneity.
  - Sense of accomplishment.
  - Clarity about the learning.
  - Stimulates sudden insight and discovery (Aha Moments).

Videos

- Using videos is a simple, clear, and easy method to transfer knowledge and information.

- Some pedagogical benefits include:
  - Increases learner engagement.
  - Short, limited time.
  - Clear and direct; transparent.
  - Communicates message effectively.
  - Assists with mastery learning.
  - Increases retention for visual learners.

6. Didactic Guidelines

1. Situation analysis
2. Define objectives
3. Course content
4. Didactic methods
5. Material dev.
6. Guidelines
7. Evaluation
8. Attendance list
9. Checklist
10. Lessons learned

Didactic guidelines help define:

- Specific content topics to cover.
- Duration per topic.
- Duration per course.
- Material used per topic.
- Assessments and learning exercises.
- Necessary equipment.

Didactic Guidelines

Course	White Belt		Duration		2 Hours	
No.	Activity	Duration	Total Accum. Dur.	Material	Notes	
1	Introduction	0:20	0:20	Slides 1-6	Lean y Six Sigma complement each other	
2	Productivity and its Limitations	0:25	0:45	Slides 7-13	Detailed explanation of Waste and Variability	
3	Toyota Production System	0:10	0:55	Slide 14	Provide brief background info.	
4	Lean Tools	0:25	1:20	Slides 15-22	Briefly explain each and write them on the board	
5	5S Housekeeping	0:40	2:00	Slides 23-46	Provide examples for each	
6	5S Game (Numbers)	0:20	2:20	5S Game	Only if there is time at the end of No. 5	

7. Evaluation

1. Situation analysis
2. Define objectives
3. Course content
4. Didactic methods
5. Material dev.
6. Guidelines
7. Evaluation
8. Attendance list
9. Checklist
10. Lessons learned

- It is important to develop and implement a course evaluation for the purpose of providing insight into the level of knowledge, understanding, and skills possessed by the participants.

- The evaluation can be implemented at the beginning (as a diagnostic assessment), during the teaching process (to adjust teaching and boost learning), and/or after the course has been completed to evaluate learning outcomes.

- Course evaluations can be done in oral, written or practice form.

- Some question types include:
  - Open-ended.
  - Multiple choice.
  - True or False.
  - Ordered list.
  - Fill-in-the-blank.
  - Matching.
  - Essay.
  - Computational.

Knowledge Evaluation

ASSESSMENT	
Full Name	
Company Name	
Title	
Date	

What are two benefits of continuous flow?
Employees' performance is optimized and response times are significantly reduced.

List the three main problems companies usually face.
Lack of standardized work
Lack of strategic planning
Misinformation and lack of communication

What is quality?
Fulfilling customer's requirements and exceeding their expectations.

What does a Future Value Stream Map (VSM) represent?
The short-term improved solution that we want to incorporate into the service system.

What is Talent Development?
A methodology used to develop a learning culture by attracting, training, and retaining employees.

GRADED BY	
DATE	
COMMENTS	

Course Evaluation

- Likewise, the student's perception and satisfaction with the course received must be evaluated, with the aim of detecting opportunities for improvement.

COURSE EVALUATION	
Full Name	
Company Name	
Title	
Date	

On a scale of 1 - 10 (10 = "Excellent" and 1 = "Poor"), please rate the following and provide an explanation.

A. Quality of the course.
    1   2   3   4   5   6   7   8   (9)   10
The mix of presentations and interactive games really helped me understand the material thoroughly.
The course is very relevant to my job and I already know of areas where I can implement this new knowledge.

B. Quality of the instructor's teaching.
    1   2   3   4   5   6   7   (8)   9   10
The instructor is very knowledgeable and well-prepared, but it was hard to communicate with him after course hours.

C. How willing would you be to recommend this course?
    1   2   3   4   5   6   7   8   (9)   10
The course is very relevant to my business and the issues we face regarding rising costs due to inefficiencies.
It felt a bit rushed, but it really covered all learning objectives. I only wish we had more time!

D. What would you recommend we do differently to improve your experience (score of 10)?
I would encourage the use of more interactive games. They really helped me understand the lessons!

REVIEWED BY	
DATE	
COMMENTS	

LSSI — LEAN SIX SIGMA INSTITUTE

8. Attendance List

1. Situation analysis
2. Define objectives
3. Course content
4. Didactic methods
5. Material dev.
6. Guidelines
7. Evaluation
8. Attendance list
9. Checklist
10. Lessons learned

- It is important for the trainer to establish a record's log.

- That keeps track of participants' attendance and any compliance requirements.

Attendance List

Event			Start date	
Objective			End date	
			Duration	
Place			Project	
			Instructor	

No.	Full Name	Area	Company

Notes / Comments

9. Checklist

1. Situation analysis
2. Define objectives
3. Course content
4. Didactic methods
5. Material dev.
6. Guidelines
7. Evaluation
8. Attendance list
9. Checklist
10. Lessons learned

A **checklist** is a useful instrument for coordinating course logistics, defining items such as:

- Location/Date.
- Attendee list.
- Teaching material/supplies.
- Furniture layout.
- Equipment.
- Classroom capacity.
- Clock.
- Preparation activities.
- Course and post-course activities, etc.

CHECKLIST

Course provider	
Course name	
Date	
No. of participants	

Quantity	COMPONENTS Description	APPLICABLE Yes	No	MET Yes	No
Installation					
1	Classroom (capacity: 30 people)	X			
3	Power outlet	X			
-	Lighting	X			
Safety and Hygiene					
1	Fire extinguisher	X			
2	Trashcan	X			
1	Restroom	X			
Furniture layout					
1	Writing board	X			
20	Desks	X			
20	Chairs	X			
Equipment					
1	Video projector	X			
1	Screen	X			
1	Computer	X			

10. Lessons Learned Form

1. Situation analysis
2. Define objectives
3. Course content
4. Didactic methods
5. Material dev.
6. Guidelines
7. Evaluation
8. Attendance list
9. Checklist
10. Lessons learned

- The "Lessons-Learned" form is useful for recording all positive and negative experiences that occur during the course.

- In future courses it serves to improve or anticipate possible unwanted situations.

LESSONS LEARNED

Course provider	
Course name	
Date	
No. of participants	

OVERVIEW

What went well

Participants feedback emphasized clear course content and good examples used in presentations.

Good time allocation. All material was covered, and lessons always ended a few minutes ahead of time, which allowed for Q&A.

What could have been done better

Instructor could have been more involved in class exercises. Lack of guidance created confusion.

Audio system and speakers should have been checked before course kickoff. There were some audio difficulties

IMPROVEMENTS

Next Steps / Action Items	Responsible Person / Team	Action Taken
Re-design exercises to allow for more instructor participation.	Instructor	Yes
Ensure audio system and speakers work properly.	IT	No

I. Background

II. Course Preparation

III. Course Delivery

IV. Coaching

1. Preparation
2. Kickoff
3. Development
4. Assessment

LSSI
LEAN SIX SIGMA INSTITUTE

1. **Preparation**
2. **Kickoff**
3. **Development**
4. **Assessment**

- The teaching-learning process is developed through several phases.

- It is essentially a communication process between the teacher and the student, enhanced by student practice, participation and interaction.

1. Preparation

1. **Preparation**
2. **Kickoff**
3. **Development**
4. **Assessment**

- The trainer prepares himself/herself prior to the course in order to ensure optimal delivery.

- The learning objectives and teaching plans are developed

- During this phase, the trainer **reviews the course material,** formats, templates, and presentations. He/She also **"visualizes" the teaching process** and confirms the course is ready for kickoff.

- It is important to avoid overconfidence and always prepare as if you're teaching the course for the very first time... every time.

2. Kickoff

1. **Preparation**
2. **Kickoff**
3. **Development**
4. **Assessment**

- In this stage, **educational objectives and work plans are formulated,** tailored to the intended goals.

- The trainer starts the course by setting a welcoming and encouraging learning environment for the participants.

- Participants develop their first emotional reactions towards the course during this stage.

The following points should be considered during the course kickoff:

- Engaging welcome.

- Instructor and participant introductions.

- Expectation-setting.

- Learning objectives presentation.

- Rules and Agreements.

- Ice-breakers (optional).

LSSI
LEAN SIX SIGMA INSTITUTE

3. Development

1. Preparation
2. Kickoff
3. Development
4. Assessment

Following the course kickoff, **the trainer applies the didactic methods and explanations** – setting the teaching process in motion.

Session Structure

E. Transformation
The student has become the master.

D. Practice
Students are motivated to apply what they have learned in practical manners.

C. Demonstration
Development of easily-employed examples and exercises to test concepts and methods.

A. Awareness
During the Introduction and Background portions of the course, the students' attention must be captured by using information, facts, and examples they can relate to.

B. Information
Information is communicated once students are ready (Who, What, When, Where, How, Didactic Methods, etc.)

- Trainers should use a variety of methods and techniques to facilitate the learning process.

- It is important to ask yourself what is it that you want to teach, and what are the best ways to help participants understand and related to the course content.

- Once you are teaching, try to make the best use of all five of your senses. One cannot really understand how a flower smells by just reading about it. One can not determine the ground texture just by staring at it.

  - All five senses (sight, hearing, smell, taste, and touch) are the entrance doors to the mind.

Development: Do's

- Using an appropriate tone of voice when speaking with the participants.
- Use body language appropriately to face participants at all times.
- Make eye contact and scan the group constantly.
- Walk towards participants.
- Use friendly gestures and facial expressions.

- Observe and read your audience.
- Smile.
- Nod affirmatively.
- Use appropriate tone of voice as it helps set the environment for the class in terms of engagement.
- Always attempt to face your audience, even when writing on a board.

LSSI
LEAN SIX SIGMA INSTITUTE

Development: Don'ts

- Speak while facing visual aids (instead of your audience) or reading off notes.
- Stare at specific individuals or avoid eye contact altogether.
- Ignore some students.
- Place too much distance between the group and yourself.
- Constantly shuffle or move papers or notes during the training session.
- Stay in the same place for extended periods of time or move too quickly across the room.
- Check your watch frequently or get distracted with objects around you.
- Turn your back to your audience at any time.

Useful tools

Video Projector/Display Monitor

Using a video projector/display monitor allows for:

- A faster delivery of a presentation.
- The ability to pick up on previously discussed topics.
- The convenience of pointing out specific areas on the screen.

The Writing Board

- The writing board is an instructor's most commonly used visual aid and the least likely to be omitted from the classroom space anytime soon.

- Given the appropriate content and delivery, a writing board is an easy-to-use device that allows for a clean visualization for the participants.

  - Use chalk sticks or dry-erase markers with the boldest colors.
  - Write clearly and legibly.

- Position your body to allow maximum visibility while writing on the board.

Its appropriate use requires certain considerations:

- **Comprehensive and organized presentation:** It is recommended to comment on the way the writing board will be used prior to the training session. A disorganized mix of written and oral presentations will make it harder for students to assimilate knowledge.

- **Clear and legible handwriting:** Clear, legible descriptions and explanations are fundamental to help students understand the content being taught.

- **Coordination between oral presentation and visual aids:** Trainers should be able to provide verbal explanations as they write on the board.

4. Assessment

1. Preparation
2. Kickoff
3. Development
4. Assessment

During this phase, a knowledge assessment is administered **to verify the achievement of the learning objectives** and the added-value for the participants.

- Final knowledge assessment.
- Course evaluation and feedback.
- Certificates of completion or certification are awarded.

LSSI
LEAN SIX SIGMA INSTITUTE

I. Background

II. Course Preparation

III. Course Delivery

IV. Coaching

1. What is coaching?
2. Objectives of coaching
3. Benefits of coaching
4. Qualities of a good coach
5. Your role as a successful coach
6. The coaching session

1. What is Coaching?

- Informal one-to-one or group interaction.
- Opportunity to encourage, advise, motivate, and develop.
- Essential supervisory tool.
- Talent management philosophy.

Coaching for superior employee performance.

2. Objectives of Coaching

3. Benefits of Coaching

- Improves quality, performance, and productivity.

- Boosts enthusiasm and morale.

- Strengthens relationships and communication.

- Increases job satisfaction.

- Improves teamwork.

- Builds trust and reinforces loyalty.

LSSI
LEAN SIX SIGMA INSTITUTE

Coaching is an important part of your job.

- It helps you to keep in touch with employees.

- It lets you stay close to your teams.

- It allows you to work and interact with employees.

- It uses everyday situations to improve performance.

4. Qualities of a good Coach

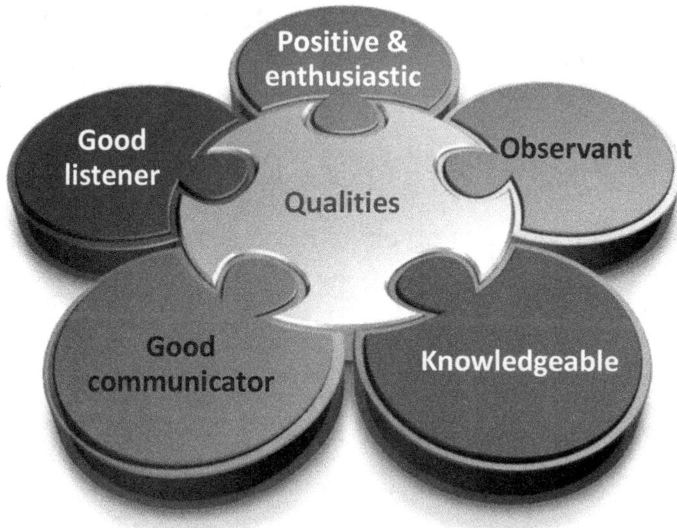

Effective coaching is immediate

- Coaching is oftentimes spontaneous.

- Coaching is most effective when it follows events and behavior closely.

Effective coaching is specific

Emphasizes:

- What is done well and what needs improvement.

- Required skills and knowledge.

- Standards of good performance.

- Significance of the job.

- Corrective action.

Effective coaching is interactive

- Discuss rather than give orders.

- Ask questions.

- Listen to what employees have to say.

- Pay attention to body language.

LSSI
LEAN SIX SIGMA INSTITUTE

5. Your role as a successful coach

- Observe employees at work.

- Show concern for them as individuals.

- Find out what motivates them.

- Focus on cooperation and collaboration, not competition.

- Emphasize growth and development.

- Provide new challenges.

- Give support and assistance.

- Create a positive work environment.

6. The coaching session

- Define the agenda.
- Focus on one or two issues at a time.
- Begin by checking progress.
- Show appreciation.
- Look ahead.
- Aim high, but keep goals within reach.
- Thank employees for their input and participation.
- Set a date for the next coaching session.

- Ask for feedback.
- Discuss problems and potential solutions.
- Allow time for questions.
- Agree on an action plan.

Coaching top performers

- Provide feedback.
- Be specific.
- Ask for opinions and input.
- Keep them consistently challenged.
- Provide adequate and relevant recognition and rewards.

LSSI
LEAN SIX SIGMA INSTITUTE

Coaching average performers

- Determine employees' potential.

- Identify factors preventing them from achieving their full potential.

- Reinforce strengths.

- Clarify standards.

- Develop a plan.

Coaching poor performers

- Consider root-causes.

- Encourage employee input and opinion.

- Work to develop solutions.

- Renegotiate goals and objectives.

- Agree on an action plan.

- Schedule follow-up sessions.

Coaching employees through periods of change

- Explain the situation.
- Offer reassurance.
- Involve employees in the change process.
- Teach them new skills.
- Define clear goals.
- Monitor development and performance.

Effective coaching

It is important to understand:

- Your role as a successful coach.
- How to conduct coaching sessions.
- Coaching techniques for top, average, and poor performers.
- How to coach employees through periods of change.

LSSI LEAN SIX SIGMA INSTITUTE

Key points to remember

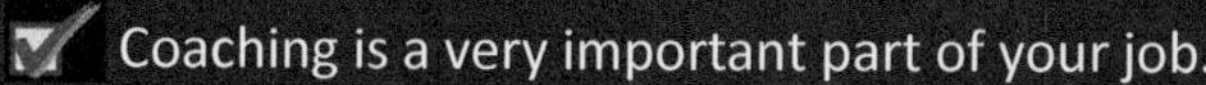

Lean Management

- ✔ Coaching is a very important part of your job.

- ✔ Coaching helps employees improve performance and grow professionally.

- ✔ Coaching helps you develop and strengthen meaningful and effective working relationships with employees.

- ✔ You already possess the inherent qualities that will make you a good coach.

Project Financial Evaluation

Learning objectives

1. Demonstrate how LSS projects can financially impact organizations.
2. Understand the profit model.
3. Analyze the 5 ways Lean Six Sigma creates financial impact.

Content

> Background
> Profit Model
> The 5 project financial keys
  - Cost Reduction
  - Increase in Capacity
  - Increase in Demand
  - Increase in Contribution Margin
  - Improvement in Capital Structure

Project Financial Evaluation

Background

- In many cases, finance and accounting provide important yet indecipherable reports.

- Finance rarely addresses leaders' needs in **understanding the financial impact** of the decisions being made.

> It is very important to demonstrate how Lean Six Sigma improvement projects financially impact an organization.

Profit Model

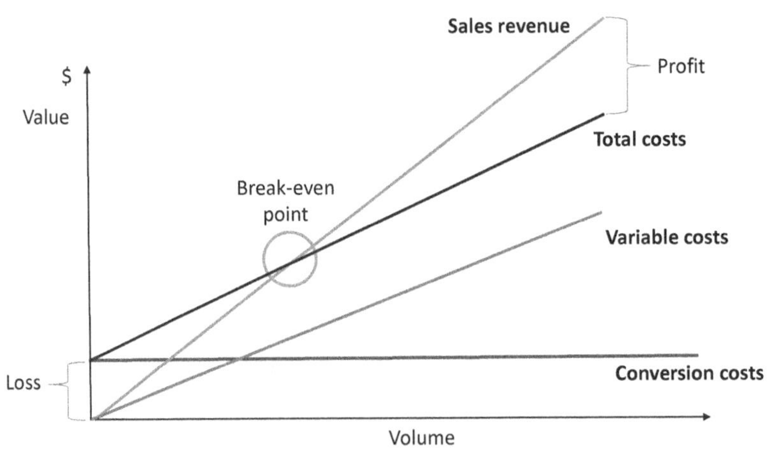

LSSI
LEAN SIX SIGMA INSTITUTE

Dimensions

- **Horizontal line:** Resources (i.e., Conversion costs). These are costs that remain unchanged regardless of sales volume.

    Examples: Resources such as rent, employee salaries, benefits, utilities (water, electricity, phone, etc.).

- **Sloped line:** Variable costs that change in proportion to the sales volume. The slope of the line is proportionate to the contribution margin % of products at different volume levels.

    Examples: Materials, transportation, tariffs, etc.

How to Calculate Contribution Margin

When you deliver a service or make a product and deduct the variable costs of delivering that service or product, the leftover revenue is the contribution margin.

- Sales Revenue: $100,000
- Variable costs: $25,000
- Contribution margin ($): $75,000
- Contribution margin (%): 75%

Break-Even Point

Exercise 1

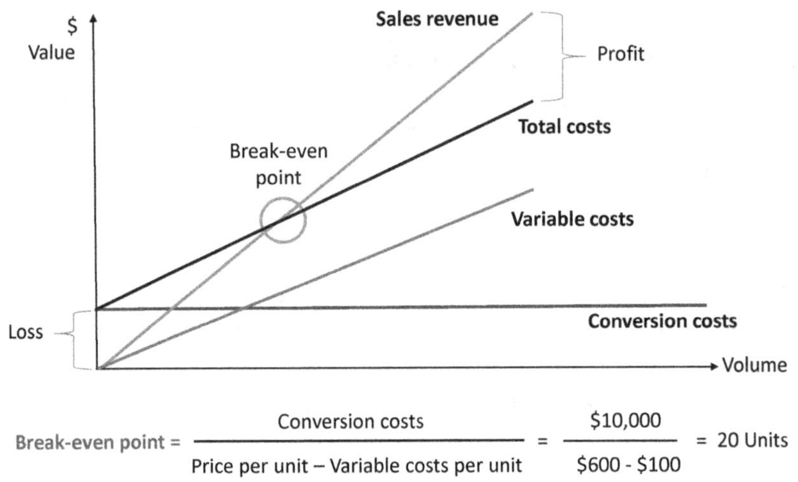

$$\text{Break-even point} = \frac{\text{Conversion costs}}{\text{Price per unit} - \text{Variable costs per unit}} = \frac{\$10,000}{\$600 - \$100} = 20 \text{ Units}$$

The 5 project financial keys

Lean Six Sigma creates financial impact in:

1. Reduction in costs.

2. Increase in capacity.

3. Increase in demand.

4. Increase in contribution margin.

5. Improvement in capital structure.

Source: *The Value Add Accountant* by Jean Cunninngham.

LSSI
LEAN SIX SIGMA INSTITUTE

1. Cost Reduction

Cost reduction occurs **when a company eliminates an existing cost** – meaning, when a company does not incur the expense any longer.

Examples:

- Eliminating or reducing late payment fees.
- Eliminating materials used to repair defective products.
- Eliminating shipping costs caused by returns or replacements.

Profit Model: Reduce conversion costs
Exercise 2

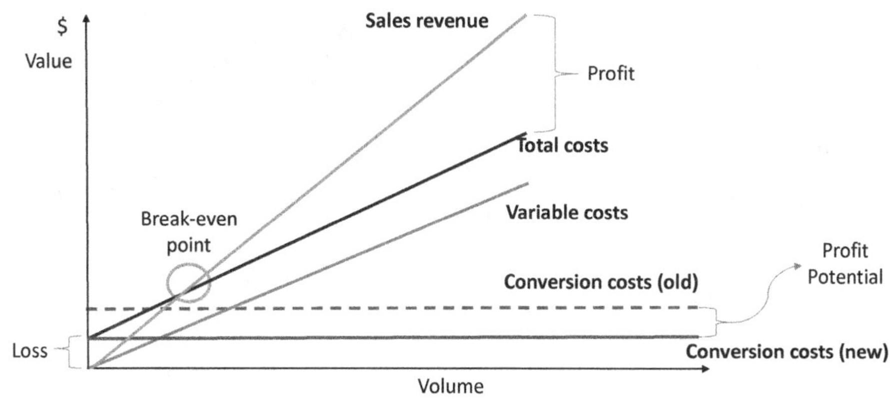

Cost savings are translated to potential profits and fewer unit sales are required to cover expenses.

Examples: Cost Reduction

- Eliminate or reduce overtime costs by reducing lead times.

- Eliminate or reduce direct costs by not hiring new personnel after an employee has quit his/her job, since capacity has increased.

- Reduce rent expense by reducing the amount of space needed to operate.

Cost Reduction: Energy

- Lighting.
- Office equipment.
- Heating, air conditioning and refrigeration.
- Thermal insulations.
- Transformers.
- Water heaters.
- Compressed air.

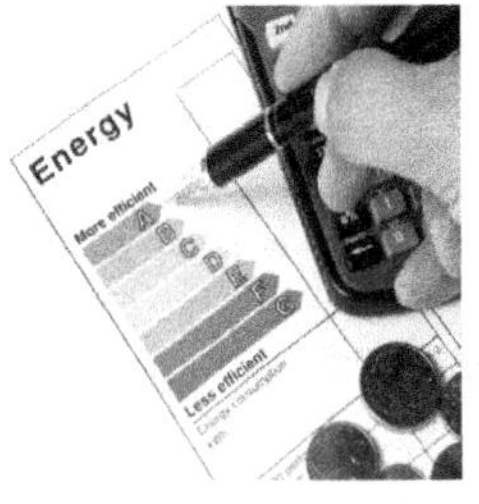

- Perform correlation analysis on energy consumption.
- Favorable contracts.
- Energy consumption during specific timeframes.
- Good habits and best practices.
- Improve power factor.

10 - 20% of total cost is energy-related.

LSSI
LEAN SIX SIGMA INSTITUTE

Mistakes in calculating cost reductions

- Although reducing setup time can lead to increases in available capacity, a key factor that creates value, this by itself does not necessarily reduce costs.

- Similarly, improving layout to reduce the space needed to conduct operations, also helps increase capacity, but this by itself also does not necessarily impact costs.

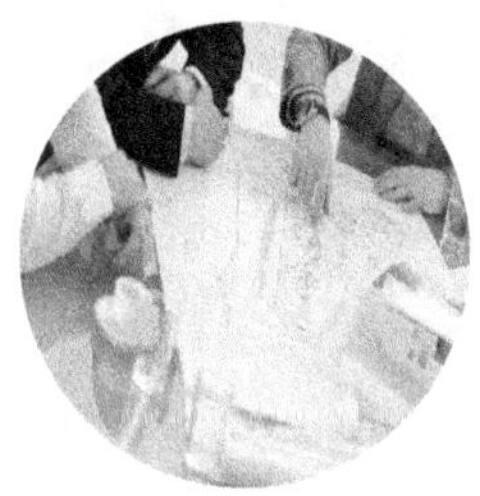

Target Cost

The following table shows the relationship between product, procurement and process improvements and achieving the target cost and improving profitability.

		ZX12 Product		
	Current	Product Kaikaku	Procurement Kaizen	Process Kaizen
Price	$400.00	$400.00	$400.00	$400.00
Required Profit Margin	57.00%	57.00%	57.00%	57.00%
Target Cost	$172.00	$172.00	$172.00	$172.00
Conversion Cost	$50.84	$49.12	$49.12	$43.75
Material Cost	$155.00	$135.00	$128.25	$128.25
Total Cost	$205.84	$184.12	$177.37	$172.00
Difference	$33.84	$12.12	$5.37	$0.00
Demand	500	500	500	500
Sales	$200,000	$200,000	$200,000	$200,000
Total Actual	$102,920	$92,060	$88,685	$86,000
Total Target Cost	$86,000	$86,000	$86,000	$86,000
Gap	$16,920	$6,060	$2,685	$0
Profit Margin	48.54%	53.97%	55.66%	57.00%

Product or Service profit evaluation

Exercise:
Which product would you choose to sell?

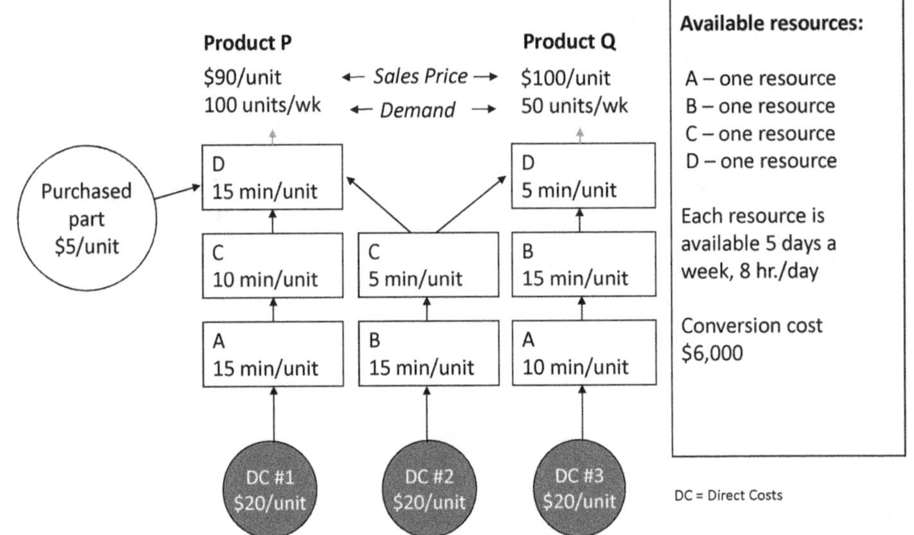

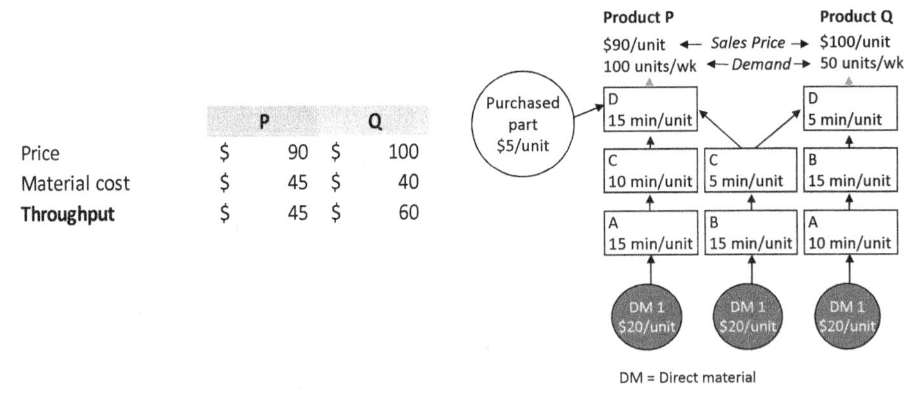

	P	Q
Price	$ 90	$ 100
Material cost	$ 45	$ 40
Throughput	$ 45	$ 60

LSSI
LEAN SIX SIGMA INSTITUTE

Supply all demand for Q and use the remaining capacity to produce P

Sales

	Quantity	Price	Subtotal	
Q	50	$ 100	$	5,000
P	60	$ 90	$	5,400
Total Sales			$	10,400

Cost of Material

Q	50	$ 40	$	2,000
P	60	$ 45	$	2,700
Total cost of material			$	4,700
Conversion Cost			$	6,000
Profit			$	(300)

Constraint	Used	Total	Remaining
30	**1500**	**2400**	**900**

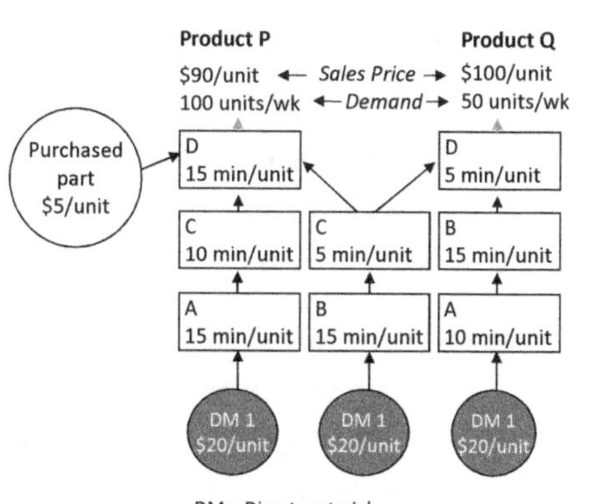

Supply all demand for P and use the remaining capacity to produce Q

Sales

	Quantity	Price	Subtotal	
Q	30	$ 100	$	3,000
P	100	$ 90	$	9,000
Total Sales			$	12,000

Cost of Material

Q	30	$ 40	$	1,200
P	100	$ 45	$	4,500
Total cost of material			$	5,700
Conversion Cost			$	6,000
Profit			$	300

Constraint	Used	Total	Remaining
15	**1500**	**2400**	**900**

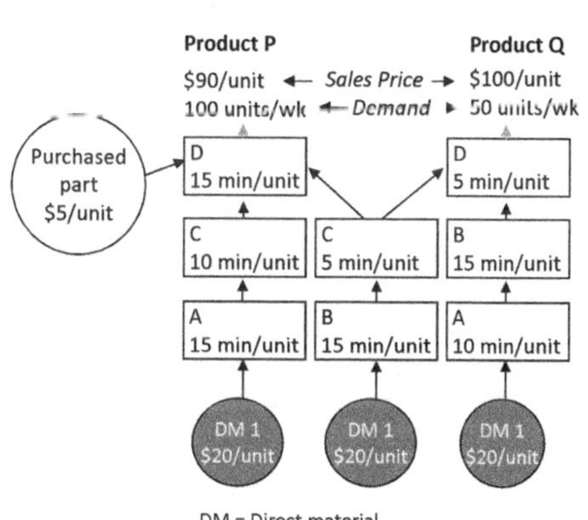

	P	Q
Price	$ 90	$ 100
Material cost	$ 45	$ 40
Throughput	$ 45	$ 60
Restriction (min)	15	30
Throughput / min	$ 3	$ 2

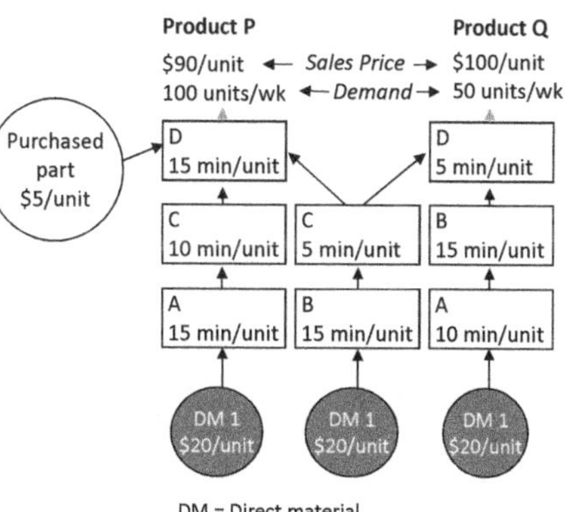

2. Increase in Capacity

- An increase in capacity of employees, equipment, and processes also increases the opportunity to satisfy increased demand with existing resources.

- It is important to note that increasing capacity positively impacts value creation potential even if these changes are not immediately reflected in a company's financial statements.

- However, an increase in capacity only translates to actual economic value creation when further steps are taken to increase profits.

Profit Model: Increase Capacity
Exercises 3 and 4

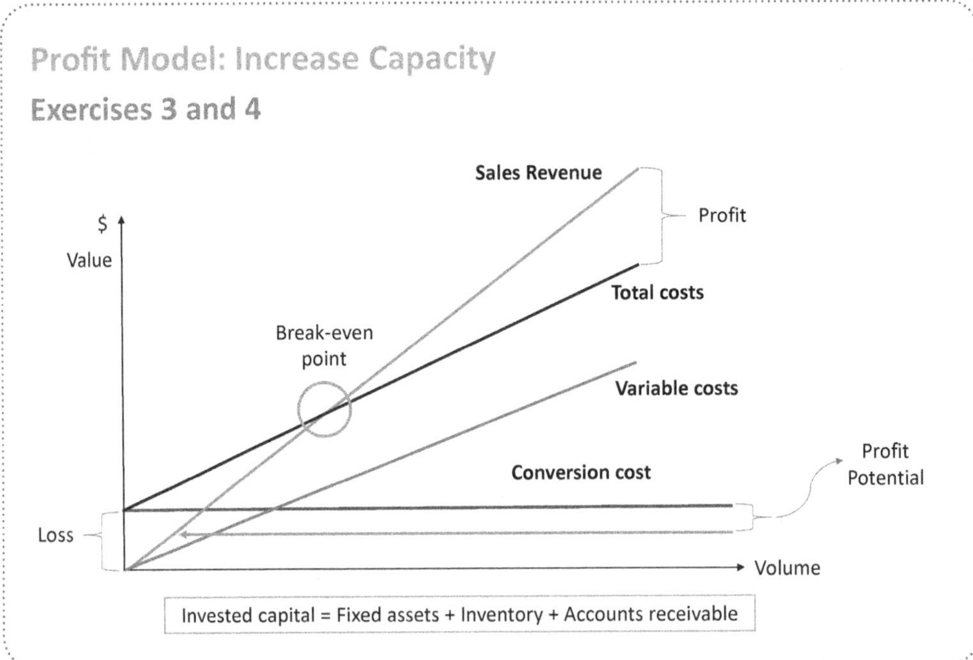

LSSI
LEAN SIX SIGMA INSTITUTE

Examples: Increase in Capacity

Setup time reduction:

- Produce more in order to satisfy customer demand without increasing costs.

- Reduce batch size which reduces finished goods (FG) and work-in-progress (WIP) inventory.

Space reduction:

- Reducing the space needed to work creates the opportunity to grow without having to invest in additional facilities.

- The space saved (no longer needed) can be utilized to increase capacity.

Reduction between 30 and 65%.

Reduction in service or product quality defects:

- This reduces the amount of rework.

- Time that was previously allocated to identifying and fixing product or service defects can now be used to meet customer needs.

Work time reduction:

- The essence of Lean Six Sigma is to eliminate activities that increase work time and unnecessary costs (non-value-added activities).

- Eliminating or decreasing non-value-added activities allows teams to provide more services or produce more goods while using the same amount of time and resources.

LSSI
LEAN SIX SIGMA INSTITUTE

3. Increase in Demand

- When there is an increase in demand, both sales and contribution margin increase as well.

- Strategies to increase sales facilitate the implementation of Lean Six Sigma improvements.

- Furthermore, Lean improvements can help attract more customers.

  For example: Reducing delivery time encourages customers to make purchases since value is being created for them without having to incur additional costs.

Profit Model: Increase in demand
Exercise 5

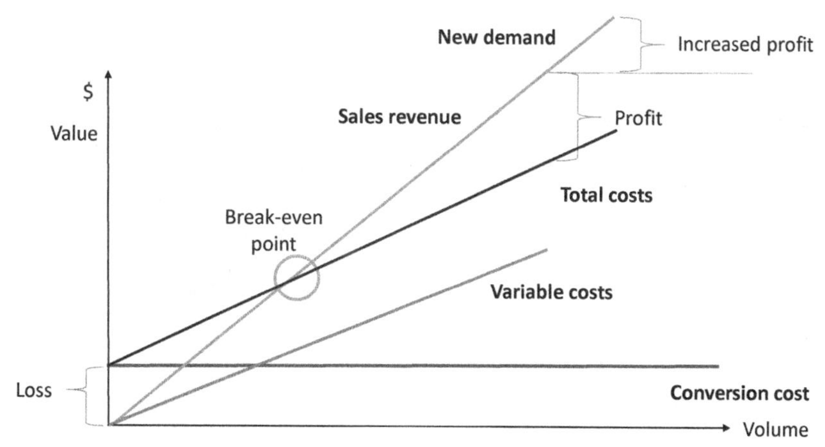

Increase in Demand

- An increase in demand and the additional capacity created by Lean Six Sigma projects, together increase profits.

- The benefits of Lean Six Sigma projects (i.e., increasing speed and improving quality) increase the level of customer satisfaction, which in turn increases demand further.

- Motivation increases when employees see increases in productivity without greater stress or having to work harder.

How does Lean Six Sigma help increase demand?

- Record-time services and deliveries.

- Excellent quality.

- Service and product customization.

- Outstanding customer service.

- Lower prices.

- Improved goodwill and company image.

LSSI
LEAN SIX SIGMA INSTITUTE

Case Study: **Packing Material Supplier**

- Initial lead time = 42-45 days.
- Final lead time = 12 days.

- Increase in capacity.
- Increase in demand.
- Increase in price.

Case Study: **Convenience Store Chain**

- Traditionally used a "Push system".
- Changed to a "Kanban system".
  - Began replenishing sold merchandise only.
  - Now only pays for what is sold.
  - Optimized store layout and shelf space.

4. Increase in Contribution Margin

- When the price and variable cost relationship increases, profits also increase (in an upward slope).

- Ways to increase contribution margin:

  - Increase price.

  - Reduce required materials.

  - Reduce variable costs (i.e., commissions, purchased parts, shipping, etc.).

Profit Model: Increase in contribution margin
Exercise 6

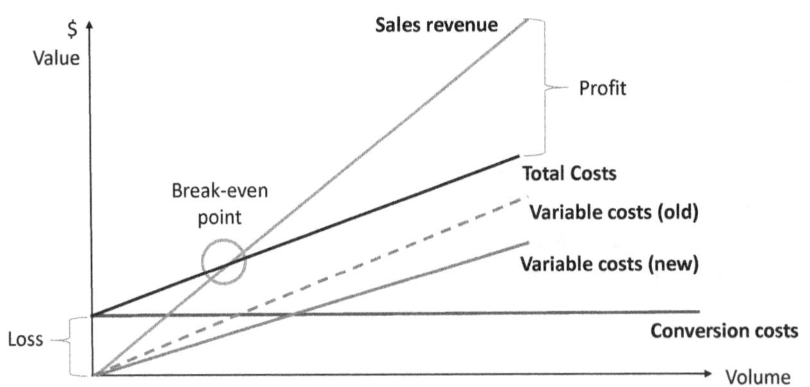

LSSI
LEAN SIX SIGMA INSTITUTE

How does Lean Six Sigma increase contribution margin?

Increase in value ➡ increase sales price:

- Develop significant competitive advantages over competitors: (e.g., outstanding customer service).

- Higher-quality products.

- Low customer complaints.

Increase sales price:

- Lean improvements help eliminate the barriers sales staff face when dealing with price increases.

- For example, develop a strategy for customizing products or services by improving capacity and increasing speed.

Reduce [direct] material content used:

- Avoid production errors by using only the direct material/resources required.

- Collaborate with suppliers to identify areas of opportunity.

Reduction in material cost

- Constantly hold product design meetings to sustain or improve value by reducing the cost of components.

Example: Material Content Reduction

Reduce cost of materials by modifying product designs

Design for Six Sigma &
Design for Manufacturing

Reduce the cost of materials by modifying product designs

Value Engineering

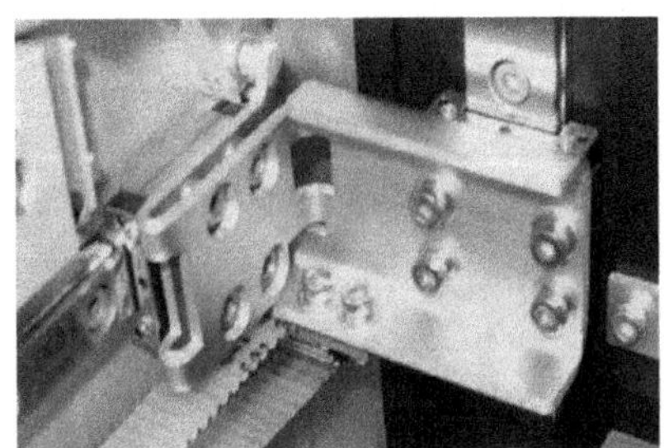

LSSI
LEAN SIX SIGMA INSTITUTE

5. Improvement in Capital Structure

- A reduction in the capital resources required to produce or deliver a certain quantity of products or services will cause an increase in the Return on Invested Capital (ROIC).

- Lean Six Sigma implementation mainly impacts the following aspects of capital structure:

  - Fixed assets (buildings, equipment, vehicles, etc.).
  - Inventory.
  - Accounts receivable.

Improvement in capital structure
ROI Calculation

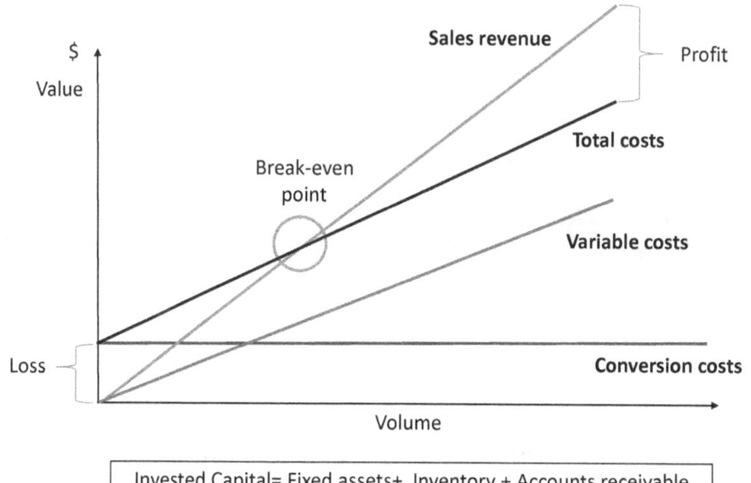

Invested Capital= Fixed assets+ Inventory + Accounts receivable

How does Lean Six Sigma improve capital structure?

Inventory:

- Less inventory reduces the need for time-intensive inventory counts.

- If WIP inventory is reduced and stabilized, then there is no need for a complex accounting system.

- When continuous flow is implemented, the first significant improvement is the reduction of inventory in stored materials, in process and in finished products.

- Kanban helps maintain low and stable inventory levels.

- Lean inventory management.

- Use 5S* to have only what is needed.

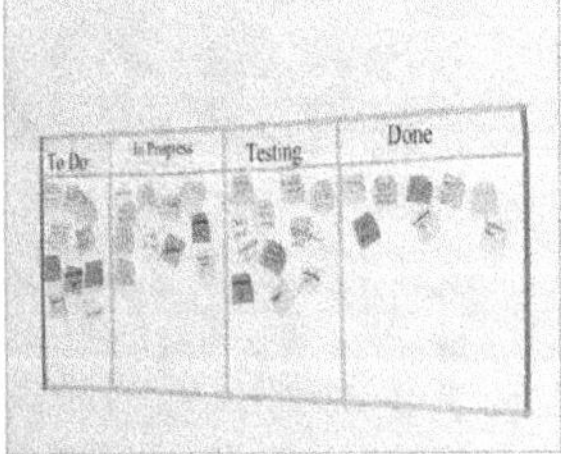

* L.V. Socconini, M. Barrantes: *Practical guide to improve quality and productivity.* Marge Books, 2023.

LSSI
LEAN SIX SIGMA INSTITUTE

Accounts receivable:

- Issue invoices upon service/product delivery.

- Invoice design (mistake-proof).

- Early payment discounts.

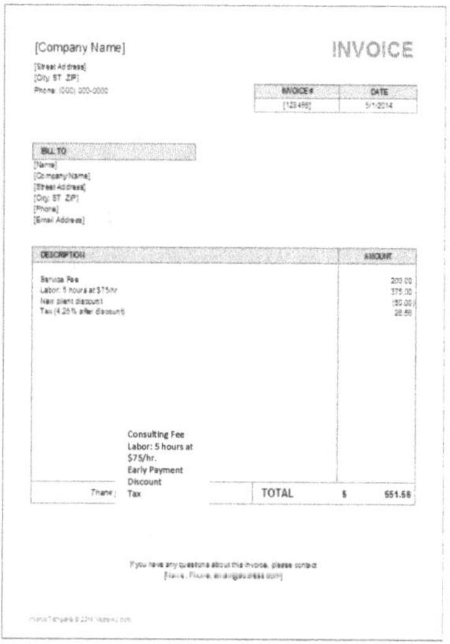

- Improve the account receivable processes by conducting Kaizen events and applying continuous flow from the point of receiving the clients' orders through the issuance of their invoices.

  - Record orders directly into the system.

  - Poka Yoke is used to eliminate errors when processing orders, collecting data, issuing invoices, etc. (e.g., bar codes).

Effective payment collection:

- Receiving advance payments.

- Collect payments as services/products are delivered to the customer (versus receiving full payment once a customer receives the full services or products).

- Prioritize invoices according to payment amounts.

- Maintain constant communication with sales personnel.

- Have teams dedicated to identifying internal issues and discrepancies.

Fixed assets: **"Everything that needs to be purchased to sustain work".**

Example: Buildings, Computers, Vehicles, Machinery, etc.

Lean companies don't require big or "monumental" facilities, assets and equipment. Everything is now purchased and used according to needs.

LSSI
LEAN SIX SIGMA INSTITUTE

Equipment

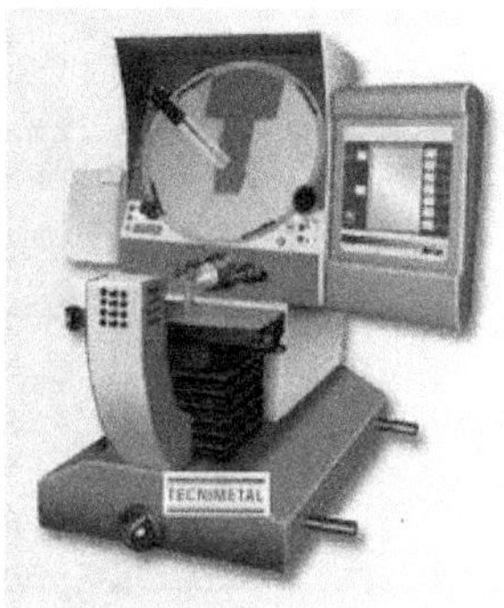

Optical comparator

Production line

5S, continuous flow, Kanban, etc., will help you significantly reduce space occupied by excess inventory, unused machinery, unnecessary tools, obsolete materials, etc.

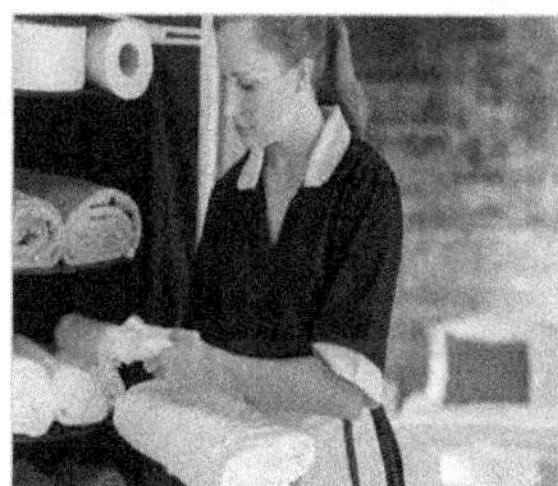

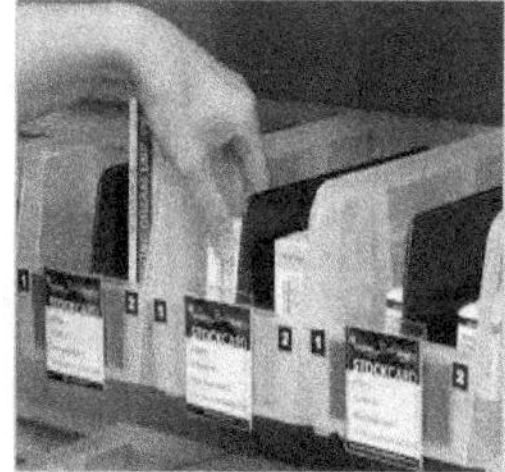

Traditional Metrics

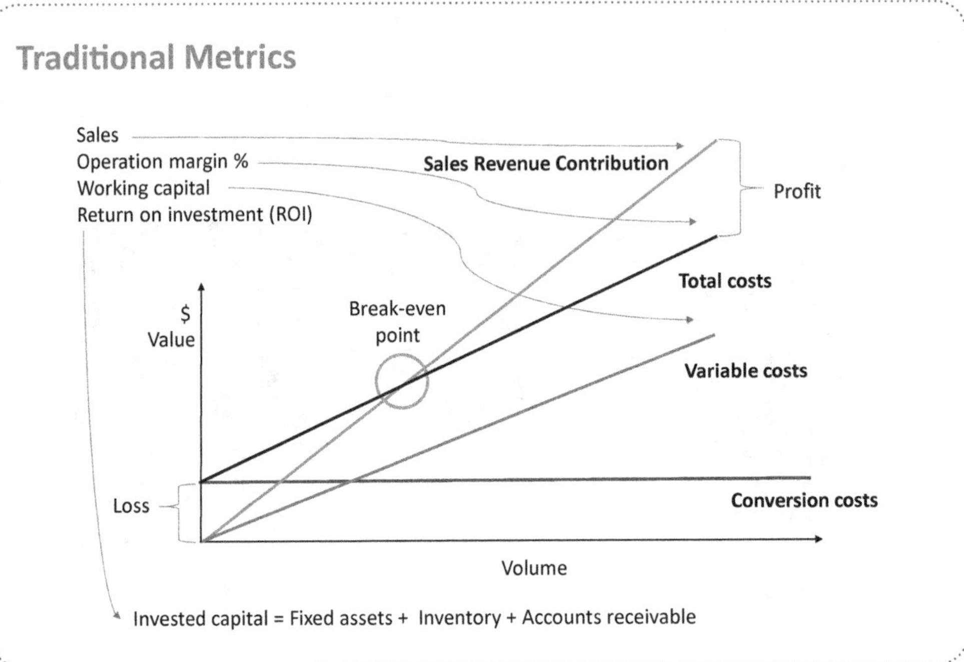

Profit Model

Exercise 7

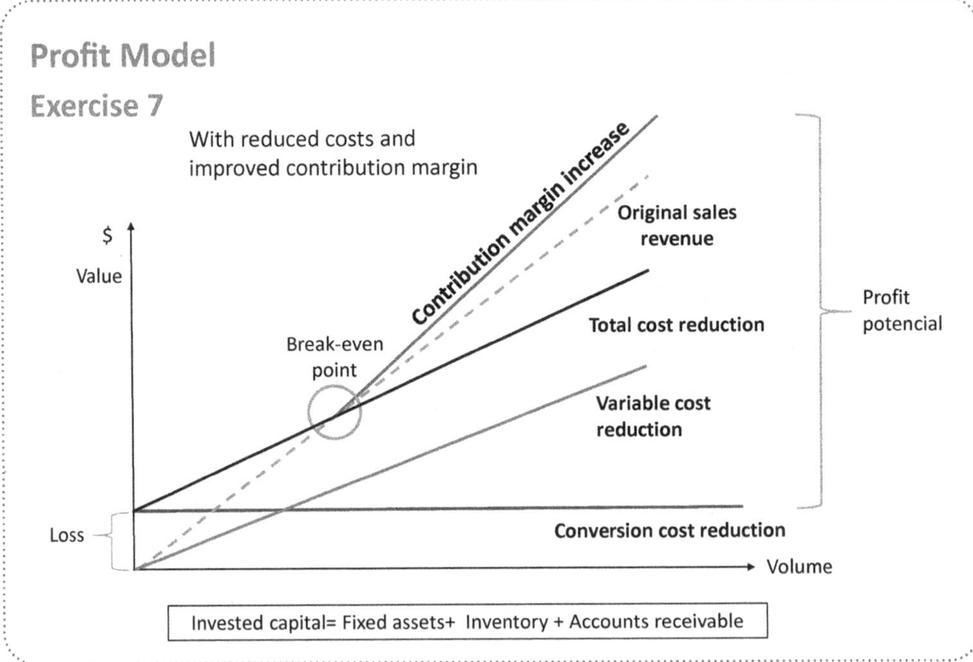

LSSI
LEAN SIX SIGMA INSTITUTE

Conclusions

Lean Six Sigma is not magic.

It is a proven way to improve a company's financial results through a *customer-focused approach*.

Accountants and Black Belts have the opportunity – and obligation – to use the profit model as a visual template to communicate and drive improvements in their organization.

Theory of Constraints

99% of problems can be solved by focusing on 1% of the resources

Learning objectives

1. Understand the basic concepts of Theory of Constraints (TOC).
2. Describe the benefits of implementing TOC.
3. Understand the procedure to identify and eliminate constraints.

Content

> Background
> What is TOC?
> What is it used for?
> Types of constraints
> Who participates?
> When is TOC used?
> Procedure
> Exercise

Background

* The **Theory of Constraints (TOC)** was created and developed by Eliyahu M. Goldratt in the 1980s.

* He is the author of the best-selling business novel *The Goal.*

* The Theory of Constraints helps companies understand where to make improvements through a systemic approach.

Luis Socconini with Rami Goldratt

A true increase in productivity results in increased profits.

What is a constraint?

* It is a *limiting factor* to the performance of a system and *prevents* an organization from achieving its full potential.

* It can be the slowest step that determines the pace of the process (bottleneck).

* The performance of any real system is limited by its constraints.

What is TOC

- An overall **management philosophy** used to establish priorities and improve areas, systems, processes, and/or activities that limit – or prevent – an organization from achieving its full potential.

- An **improvement methodology** that helps companies to continually achieve their goals by improving constraints that limit performance.

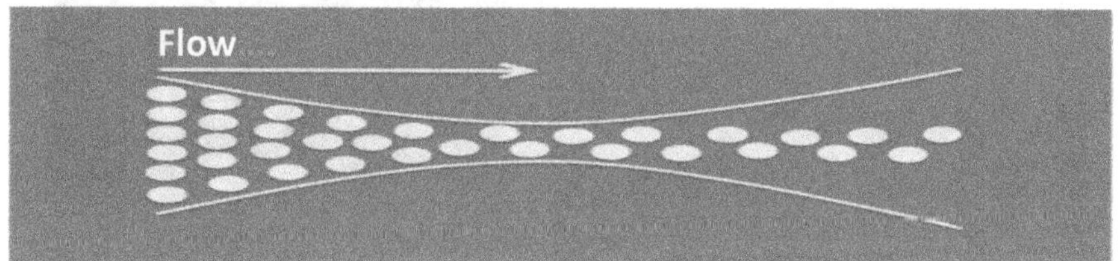

Theory of Constraints

In **traditional** companies, goals and indicators are specified by department. However, these are all interdependent – since they fulfill functions within the same system.

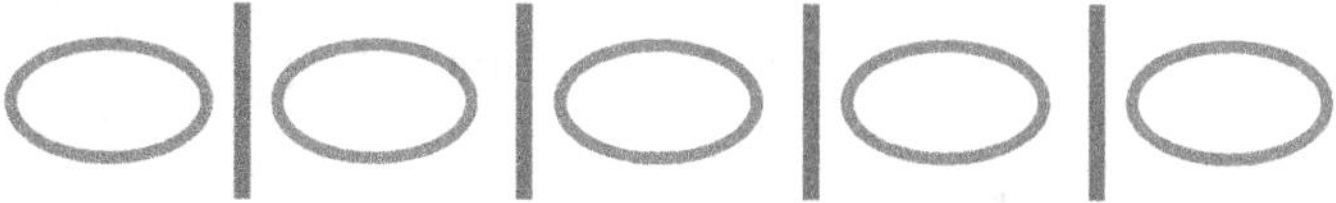

If we could bring together all managers and executives, and ask them:

- *"What is the main challenge your company faces?"*

...how likely is it that all members would provide the same response?

What is TOC used for?

- To increase the capacity of any system.

- To reduce inventory.

- To increase throughput.

- To improve teamwork performance.

- To reduce operating expenses.

Throughput = sales − direct cost

Where to implement TOC: examples

A Systemic approach:

- **Logistics** → Excess inventory.
- **Customer Service** → High number of customer complaints.
- **Finance** → Long payback periods.
- **Human Resources** → Poor internal interactions.
- **Operations** → Late deliveries and high costs.
- **Strategy** → Misaligned priorities.
- **Marketing** → Diminishing customer base.
- **Sales** → Poor sales.

Theory of Constraints

Physical

- Production capacity.
- Warehouse size.
- Number of employees.
- Materials and supplies (quantity).

Non-Physical

- Market demand.
- Procedures.
- Workplace policies.
- Management style and culture.

Who participates?

- **Business process leaders** who are responsible for increasing the capacity for any system, reducing inventories, improving activities, and increasing profits.

- **Company leaders and Champions** (business units) who identify opportunities and help develop the right implementation of TOC as a company strategy.

- **Team members** who develop ideas for improvement and propose the best ways to implement TOC.

- **Implementation leaders** (Black Belts/Master Black Belts) who guide teams through the correct implementation of Lean tools and ensure projects achieve results by optimizing resources.

When is TOC used?

- The Theory of Constraints is constantly used as part of the continuous improvement process to optimize the "weakest link" (constraint) and therefore achieve improvements in the internal activities of the organization.

- Use TOC in:

  - DEFINE phase: to define the current situation.

  - MEASURE and MAP phase: to identify the constraint.

  - ANALYZE phase: to determine the causes of the constraint and evaluate the best way(s) to optimize resources.

  - IMPROVE phase: to subordinate resources to the constraint and elevate it.

  - CONTROL phase: to ensure continuous identification and elimination of constraints.

Procedure

Identifying and eliminating constraints in 5 steps

LSSI
LEAN SIX SIGMA INSTITUTE

1. Identify the constraint

Constraints can be internal o external:

- If the capacity of the system is less than the market demand, then the constraint is *internal*.

- If the capacity of the system exceeds the market demand, then the constraint is *external*.

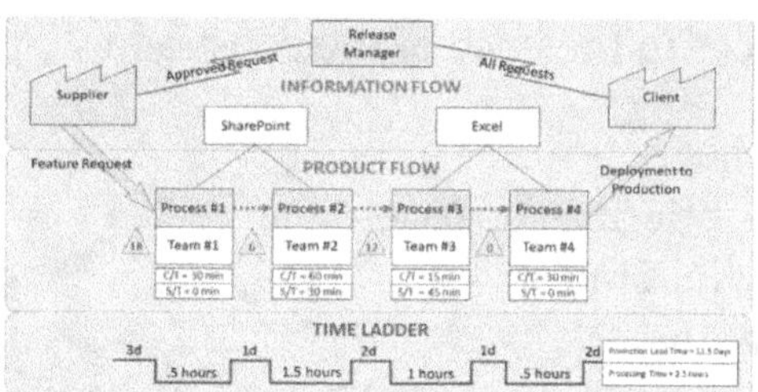

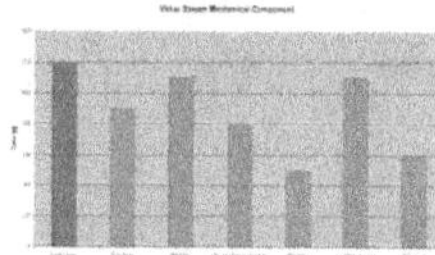

Use the Value Stream Map and Balance Graph to identify constraints in any system.

2. Exploit the constraint

Make the most out of what you have

- Ensure the constraint (bottleneck) is continuously operating by making the most out of the existing resources:
  - Personnel.
  - Information.
  - Material.
  - Maintenance.
- Always check quality immediately before the constraint.
- Maximize the time the constraint (bottleneck) creates value for the customer to increase throughput.

3. Subordinate to the constraint

Establish priorities

- Align non-constraint resources (people, equipment, material, etc.) to support the needs of the constraint and maintain a continuous flow of operations.

- Synchronize other resources to the pace of the constraint (bottleneck).

- If you have WIP inventory, prioritize turning WIP inventory into throughput rather than producing more inventory.

4. Elevate the constraint

- Consider what further actions can be taken to "break" or eliminate the constraint.

- Improve the performance of the constraint by increasing its capacity.

  - This might require investments in time and money (e.g., equipment, hiring, etc.).

  - Allocate people, equipment, resources, etc. to help the constraint achieve the capacity required to meet the demand.

LSSI
LEAN SIX SIGMA INSTITUTE

5. Repeat

Ensure that the procedure is not a one-time implementation, but rather a continuous improvement process.

- **If the constraint is broken**, recognize that there is a new constraint and restart at Step 1.
  - The new priority is to find and eliminate the new constraint.
- **If the constraints is not broken**, recognize that more work is required, and restart at Step 1.

At any given system – there will *always* be at least one constraint limiting its goal.

Roadrunner mentality

"Full speed or dead stop.

If there is work to be done, work on it at full speed.

Otherwise, use the time for learning, helping team members, or work on another activity that will help the organization."

Source: *Theory of Constraints and Lean Manufacturing: Friends or Foes?* Richard Moore, Ph.D. and Lisa Scheinkopf

DBR (Drum, Buffer, Rope) method

A method of synchronizing resources and increasing throughput

DRUM:

- The constraint/bottleneck.
- The speed, at which the constraint runs, sets the "beat" for the process and determines throughput.

BUFFER:

- Amount of inventory, time, or space needed to maintain consistent production.
- Ensures the fluctuations in non-constraints do not affect the "beat" set by the constraint.

ROPE:

- The "trigger" generated by the constraint to signal the next release [material/information] in the process.
- Maintains throughput consistency by avoiding an accumulation of excess inventory, time, space, etc.

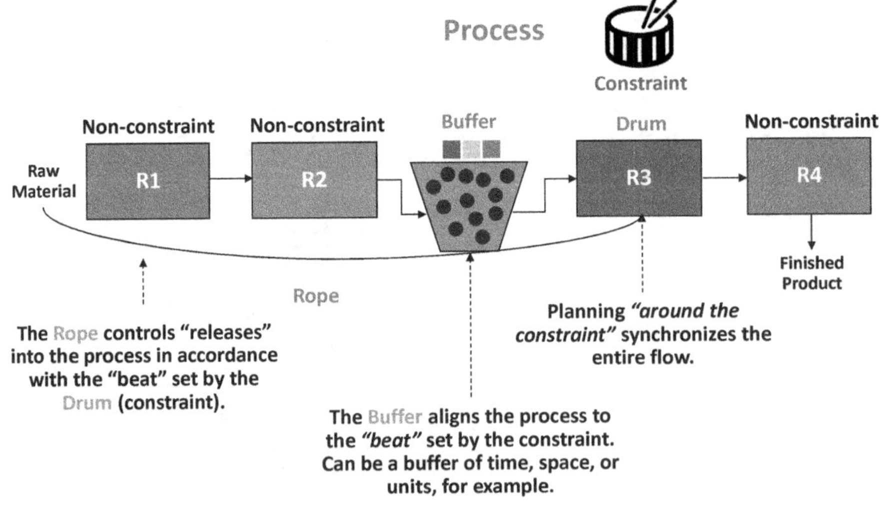

LSSI
LEAN SIX SIGMA INSTITUTE

Conclusion

- The Theory of Constraints is a process that starts and then continuous indefinitely (it never ends).

- It is very important to recognize that, at any given time, there will always be at least one constraint in a system that limits throughput – and it can be internal or external.

- Teams must work to identify constraints and continuously work to eliminate them.

> TOC is not a one-time implementation, but rather a continuous improvement process.

Exercise

Implement the 5-step procedure in a production, logistics or service process – or for a supporting activity.

1. Identify the system's constraint **(bottleneck)** and explain why it is the constraint. Assume that internal capacity is lower than demand.

2. Explain which existing **resources** can be utilized **(exploited)** along with the constraint.

3. Suggest **priorities** and ways to align/synchronize the resources of the process with the constraint.

4. Propose ways to **elevate the constraint.** (Elevate = "Break" or eliminate).

5. Identify the **new restriction.**

6

Distributions

Learning objectives

1. Understand different types of data.
2. Know the importance of data distributions in statistics.
3. Understand different types of service and product defects.
4. Learn how to apply the normal distribution model to determine the probability of defects.
5. Lean how to apply other distribution models.

Content

> Types of Data
> Measurement Scales
> Introduction to statistical distributions
> Distributions for continuous data
> Distributions for discrete data
> Transforming non-normal data to normal

Types of Data

The characteristic can be expressed in numbers:
- Distance traveled
- Number of services completed
- Number of satisfied customers
- Product X Cost

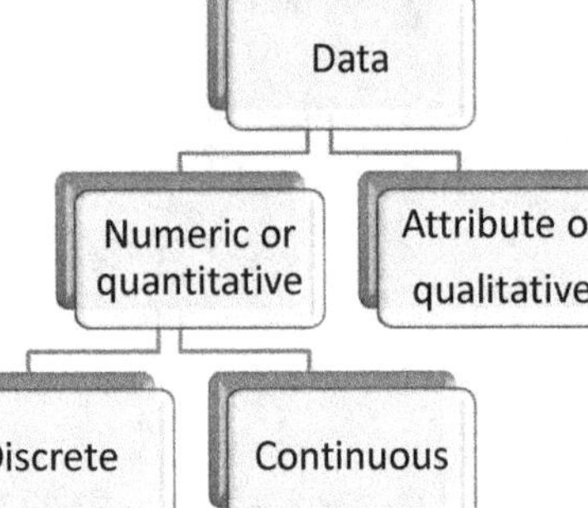

The characteristic is not numeric:
- Level of customer satisfaction (e.g., very satisfied, dissatisfied)
- Gender
- Religion
- Outcome of service (i.e., completed, in-progress, etc.)
- Birthplace
- Eye color

Are countable:
- Pass or not pass
- Number of broken parts
- Number of defective services

Are measurable:
- Time to complete a service
- Distance traveled
- Temperature

Measurement Scales

Scale	Description	Examples
Nominal	Data that can only be classified in categories without having any quantitative value (cannot be ordered)	Eye color, gender, pass/fail, countable data
Ordinal	Data that can be ordered, but differences between values cannot be determined or are inconsequential	Good/better/best small/medium/large Scale from 1 to 5
Interval	The interval scale has the same features as the ordinal scale, with the added feature that intervals between measurements are known and identical. However, there is no absolute zero	Temperature
Ratio	The ratio scale has the same features as the interval scale, but it also features an absolute zero	Money, NBA player heights, dimensions

LSSI
LEAN SIX SIGMA INSTITUTE

Introduction to statistical distributions

- The probability of a process to meet customer requirements, that is, the probability of producing products and providing services free of defects, is strongly connected to the distribution of the data obtained from the process.

- A high defect probability means relatively high levels of customer dissatisfaction.

- Conversely, a low defect probability means relatively high levels of customer satisfaction.

Statistical Distributions

- To facilitate data manipulation and analysis, data should follow a Normal Distribution. If the data follows a different type of distribution, there are a variety of mathematical transformations that can be used on the original data so that it becomes closer to a Normal Distribution.

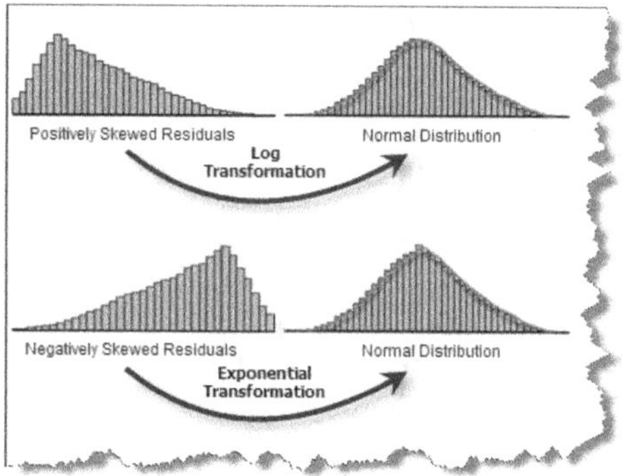

Distributions for continuous data

In statistics, the most important distribution of a continuous probability is the normal distribution (AKA Gaussian distribution).

The normal distribution is bell-shaped.

For a symmetrical bell distribution, the rule is:

- Approximately 68% of observations will be within +/- 1 σ from the mean.

- Approximately 95% of observations will be within + / - 2 σ from the mean.

- Approximately 99.7% of observations will be within + / - 3 σ from the mean.

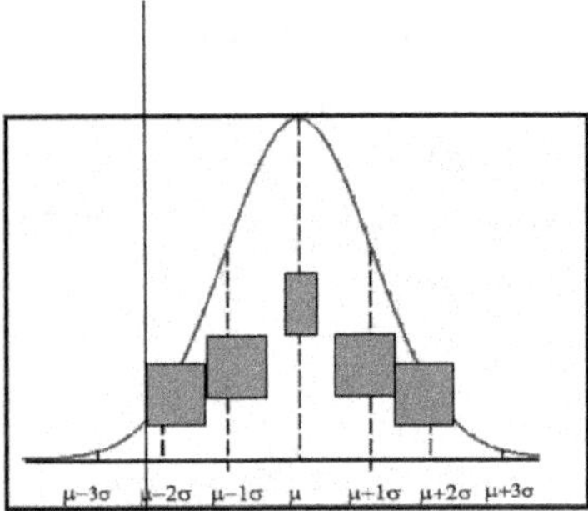

Normal Distribution

Definition

A Normal probability distribution is used to model continuous variables. It is characterized by its well-known bell shape. It is applied in a great number of situations where random data values have the same probability of occurring on both sides of an expected "midpoint" value (i.e., mean), and where the values on the ends are increasingly less frequent in their occurrence. The normal distribution is described perfectly by defining the mean and standard deviation.

Uses

It is used for most continuous data types. the first assumed probability distribution is the normal distribution.

Examples

- Height or weight of a group of people.
- Time for providing a service.
- Certain types of Key Performance Indicators.

LSSI
LEAN SIX SIGMA INSTITUTE

Six Sigma Quality Level
3.4 DPMO

0.00034% Out of Spec

99.99966% Within Spec

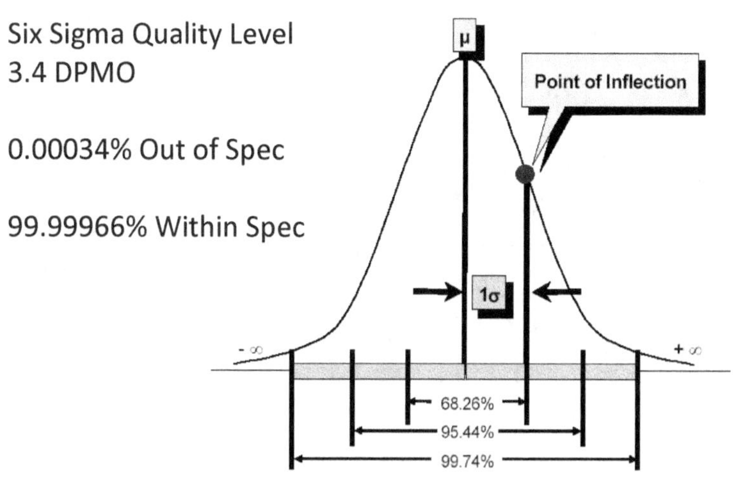

Empirical Rule

The following rules apply even when a set of data is not perfectly normally distributed.

Number of Standard Deviations	Theoretical Normal	Empirical (Almost any distribution)
± 1σ	68,27%	60 - 75%
± 2σ	95,45%	90 - 98%
± 3σ	99,73%	99 - 100%

Normal probability graphs

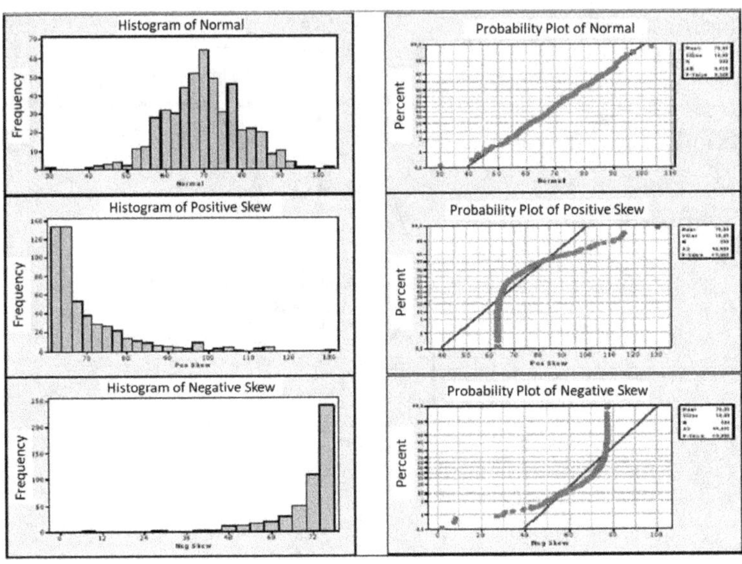

- **Property 1:** A distribution can be completely described by knowing its mean and standard deviation.

- **Property 2:** The area under the curve can be used to estimate the cumulative probability of the occurrence of a certain event.

- **Property 3:** The curve is perfectly symmetric around the mean (exactly 50% of data falls above the mean and the other 50% falls below the mean), which indicates that the mean and median are identical.

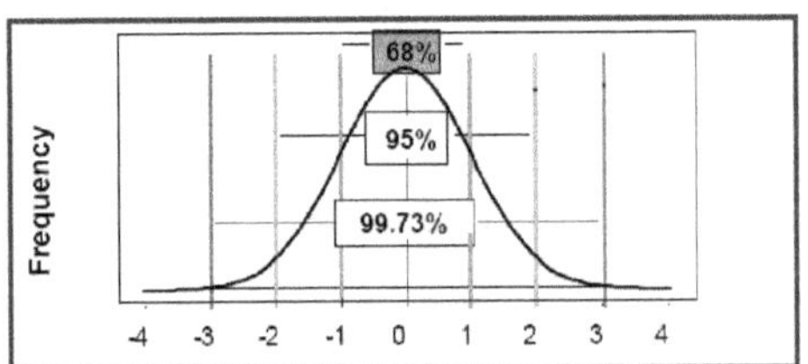

LSSI
LEAN SIX SIGMA INSTITUTE

Understanding the Z transformation

- This transformation produces a value of a distribution where the Mean $\mu = 0$ and $\sigma = 1$.

- The value indicates how far the data value is from the Mean measured in standard deviations.

- For example, if $Z = 2$, then the said value is 2 standard deviations away from the mean.

$$Z = \frac{(X - \overline{X})}{S} \quad \text{or} \quad Z = \frac{(X - \mu)}{\sigma}$$

Z Transformation - Example

- Predict the efficiency of a product.

- 150 measurements were collected that yielded the following results:

Mean = 1.03

SD = 0.0573

- Specifications are:

LSL = 0.90

USL = 1.10

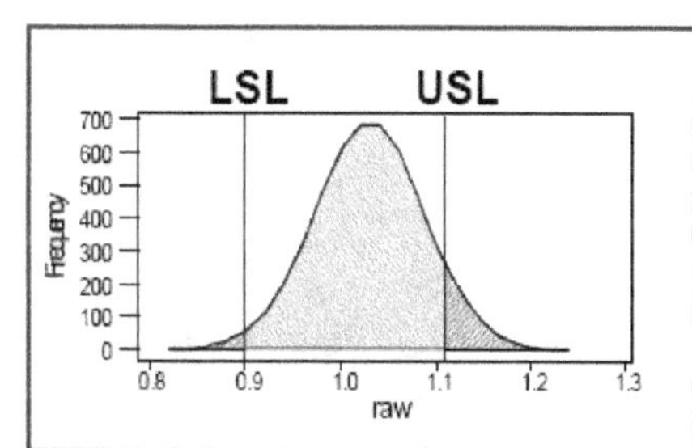

* LSL and USL are, respectively, the lower limit and the upper limit of specification.

The task is to determine the portion of the normal curve that is outside the upper and lower specification limits.

1. Calculate the *Z*-value for each specification limit:

$$Z_L = \frac{(LSL - \overline{X})}{SD} \qquad\qquad Z_L = \frac{(USL - \overline{X})}{SD}$$

$$= \frac{0.9 - 1.03}{0.0573} \qquad\qquad = \frac{1.1 - 1.03}{0.0573}$$

$$= -2.27 \qquad\qquad = 1.22$$

2. Identify the corresponding percentage for each *Z*-value (in Excel, use the Standard Normal Distribution):

- Standard Normal Distribution (−2.27) = 0.0116 = **1.16%**
- 1 − Standard Normal Distribution (1.22) = 0.1109 = **11.09%**

3. Add the two values. The result represents the percentage of data outside the specification limits:

- % Out of Specification Limits = 11.10% + 1.16 % = 12 .26%

LSSI
LEAN SIX SIGMA INSTITUTE

Exercise

The human IQ follows a normal distribution where $\mu = 100$ and $\sigma = 15$.

Question 1
What is the probability that a person will have an IQ equal to or greater than Albert Einstein's (Estimated IQ=180)?

Question 2
What percentage of humans have an IQ lower than Forrest Gump's (Estimated IQ = 75)?

Lognormal Distribution

Definition

The **Lognormal** distribution has a simple but critical relationship to the **normal distribution.** A variable is considered to follow this distribution if $Log_A(x)$ is normally distributed. In other words, we can say that if $y=A^x$, where x follows a normal distribution, then Y has a Lognormal distribution.

Uses

The **lognormal distribution** is often used when time is a critical variable affecting the process output. It models processes where the relationship between the process variable and time is progressive.

Examples

- Cycle times.

- Time needed to complete a service task.

- Difference between standard time and real time to execute an operation.

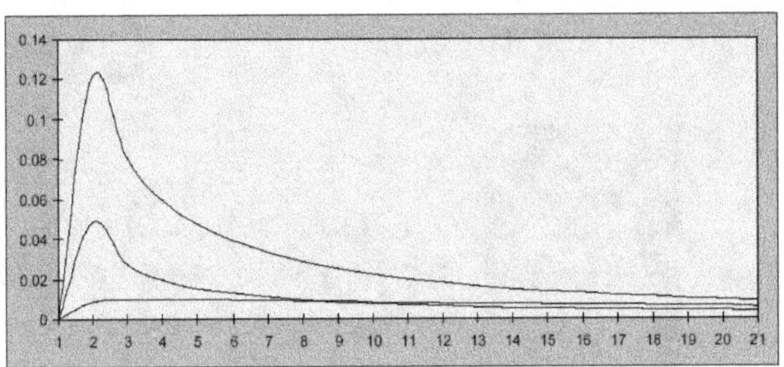

Exercise

Let's suppose that survival time (years) after a surgery (time elapsed between the surgery and the patient's death) on a certain population follows a lognormal distribution with a scale of 2.32 and a location of 0.20. Calculate the probability of survival at 12 years.

μ: Scale = 2.32

σ: location = 0.20

$P(x > 12) = ?$

Lognormal Distribution (12, 2.32, 0.2)

$P(x > 12) = 1 - 0.7951 = 20\%$

LSSI
LEAN SIX SIGMA INSTITUTE

Weibull Distribution

Definition

- Weibull is really a family of distributions, which can be used to calculate probabilities of a population. Typically, this type of distribution has two or three parameters", depending on the number of factors used to define the distribution mathematically.

Uses

- In practice, the Weibull distribution is applied extensively in *Reliability Engineering* to model complex system failure patterns.

Examples

- Nature of the equipment's failure patterns
- Expected number of failures in a given period, using historical data. This is used to estimate spare part requirements.

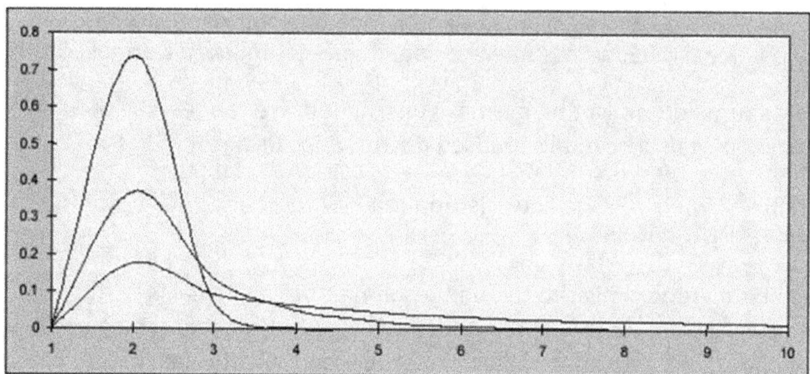

Examples

The Weibull distribution is used to model the failure distribution of an integrated circuit, using $\gamma = 0$, $\delta = 2{,}000$ and $\beta = 0.5$.

Calculate the probability that the life of the integrated circuit lasts less than 5,000 hrs:

WEIBULL (5000,0.5,2000,true)

$P\,(x < 5000) = 0.794$

Identifying the type of distribution

Normality Test

Minitab ⇨ Stat > Basic Statistics > Normality test.

If the p-value > 0.05, we assume the data follows a Normal Distribution.
If the p-value < 0.05, we assume the data does NOT follow a Normal Distribution.

If the data turns out to Not be normally distributed, we can test the data by graphing it against several supposed distributions using:

Minitab ⇨ Graph > Probability Distribution Plot (or Stat > Quality Tools> Individual Distribution ID).

The result is a graph similar to the one resulting from a normality test, but without considering the statistics nor the p-value. A visual test can be used by checking how closely the data follows the supposed distribution. In other words, how well the data follows a straight line. The more closely the data follows a straight line, the more we can say the data follows that kind of distribution.

LSSI
LEAN SIX SIGMA INSTITUTE

Binomial Distribution

Definition

- Probability distribution for discrete data. This applies when many independent tests are performed, where each test has two possible outcomes, such as: "pass" or "fail".

- Due to the fact that there are only two possible outcomes for each test, the probability of success is called *"p"* and the probability of failure is equal to *"1-p"*.

Uses

- The Binomial Distribution is used when events/occurrences are being counted and the population is not too large.

Applications

- Number of right or wrong answers on a multiple choice test.
- Number of warranty complaints paid out (vs. not paid).
- Number of services provided that are considered acceptable or unacceptable.

A Binomial Distribution has four required conditions:

1. The output of each sample or trial is classified into one or two mutually exclusive categories (pass or fail).

2. The probability of success is the same for each sample or trial.

3. Each of the samples or trials is independent of the other. Samples are random.

4. There are a fixed number of samples or trials, n

The formula is:

$$P(x) = \frac{n!}{x!(n-x)!} p^x (1-p)^{n-x}$$

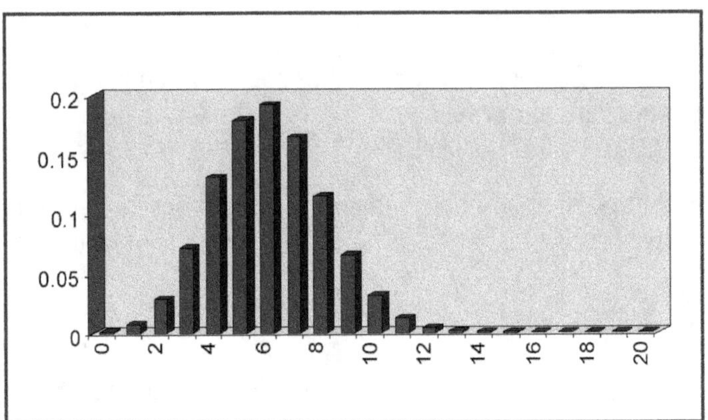

Binomial Distribution approximation using the Normal Distribution

This technique is valid as long as the *n* value is very large. When we have a large *n* and a high number of service, product or process defects, the expected effect appears to be continuous.

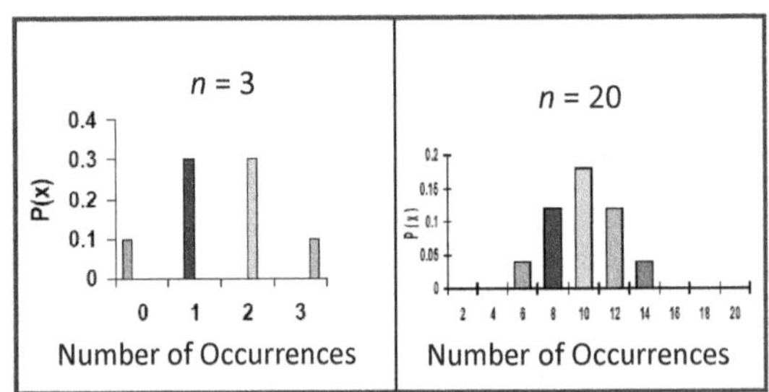

LSSI LEAN SIX SIGMA INSTITUTE

Exercise

Calculate the probability of finding 30 service defects out of 500 events. There is a historical defect rate of 5%:

BINOMDIST (30, 500, 0.05, false)
$P(x = 30) = 0.046$

BINOMDIST (30, 500, 0.05, true) $P(x \leq 30) = 0.869$

Poisson Distribution

Definition

- The Poisson Distribution is perhaps the most important probability distribution for discrete data. It includes the characteristics of the binomial distribution, and in some cases, it is considered an acceptable approximation of the binomial distribution. This approximation is critical for determining process performance, process capability and defects per unit/event.

Uses

- In practice, it is used when the number of opportunities for non-conformities is large and the probability of an event occurrence is low.

Examples

- Number of errors per page on a manual.
- Number of calls received by a call center.

As stated previously, the Binomial distribution requires that a given value is only classified as a pass or fail. When a service or unit can have more than one defect, using the binomial distribution to illustrate this situation, would result in a loss of information.

In such cases, it is useful to use the Poisson distribution.

$$P(x) = \frac{\mu^{x} e^{-\mu}}{x!}$$

The suitability conditions of the Poisson experiment are:

- An interval can be an interval of time, area, or volume.

- The interval is subdivided in a way that the probability of an occurrence during the subinterval is small.

- The probability of the event occurring is the same for any two subintervals of equal length.

- The probability of more than one event occurring during one sufficiently small subinterval is zero.

- The occurrence of an event within a subinterval is independent of the occurrence in another subinterval.

- The events occur at random.

LSSI
LEAN SIX SIGMA INSTITUTE

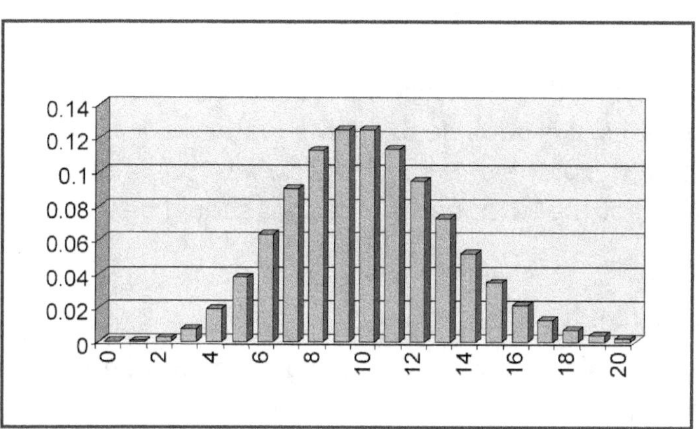

Exercise

Calculate the probability of an insurance customer enrollment representative receiving an enrollment form with exactly 5 missing fields, if there is an average of 3 customer-omissions (defects) per enrollment request.

POISSON (5, 3, false) $P(x = 5) = 0.101$

Central Limit Theorem

- Sometimes data does not follow a Normal distribution. In many of these cases, it is possible to apply a mathematical transformation of the data to produce a new set of data that is relatively "normal". The transformations should be used as a last option.

- The first step in analyzing a strange distribution, before applying a mathematical transformation, is to determine whether any physical effect has caused the data to be non-normal.

- Next, we analyze the data in terms of the means, rather than as individual data points. Thanks to the Central Limit Theorem, the samples' means approach a Normal distribution even if the population of values that we used to calculate the means does not follow a normal distribution. This type of transformation reveals interpretations, however, because it only applies to the means, not the original distribution.

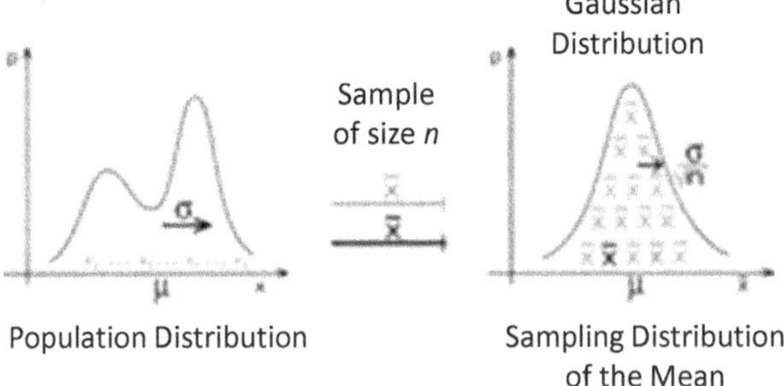

Population Distribution

Sampling Distribution
of the Mean

LSSI
LEAN SIX SIGMA INSTITUTE

If none of the non-mathematical transformation techniques render a favorable result, then we can apply a mathematical transformation to the distribution to transform it into a relatively normal one. To follow are some of the mathematical transformations that can be applied to non-normal data to transform them into relatively normal data:

- Calculate the square root of each observation.

- Calculate Log (base 10 or base e) for each observation (a transformation method recommended for a Lognormal distribution).

- Calculate the cubic root of each observation.

- Calculate the inverse sine of the square root of each observation.

- Use the Box-Cox Method (Minitab ⇨ Stat > Control Charts > Box-Cox Trans).

- It is very important to remember that when the data from the original distribution is transformed into a relatively normal one, the specification limits should also be mathematically transformed in the same way and using the same formula as the original distribution.

Fractional Factorial Designs

Learning objectives

1. Understand fractional factorial designs and their purpose.
2. Conduct fractional experiments to test factors and levels that optimize the process.

Content

> What are Fractional Factorial Designs?
> When are they used?
> Why are they used?
> Resolution
> Exercise

What are Fractional Factorial Designs?

A design of experiment in which only a fraction of the factorial treatments are selected in order to study the effects of the factors while using the least amount of experimental runs.

 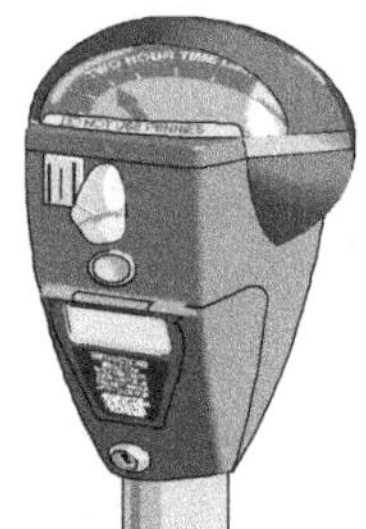

Fractional Factorial Designs

- It is likely that in the early stages of an investigation, we are interested in studying several factors.

- To accomplish this, we need a strategy that helps us reduce the number of experimental runs without loosing valuable results.

Fractional factorial designs!

LSSI
LEAN SIX SIGMA INSTITUTE

When they are used?

- In a full factorial design (2^k), as the number of factors increases, so do the number of treatments.

- For example, if k = 6 factors, one replicate of a general full factorial implies a total of 64 runs. If k= 7, then there would be a total of 128 runs.

- In practice, it may not be reasonable or cost effective to perform a large number of experimental runs.

Theory of Fractional Factorial Designs

The theory of fractional factorial designs is based on a hierarchical ordering of effects; the main effects are most important, followed by double, triple and quadruple interactions.

Design	Total Effects	Unignorable Effects	Ignorable Effects
k = 2	3	3	0
k = 3	7	6	1
k = 4	15	10	5
k = 5	31	15	16
k = 6	63	21	42
k = 7	127	28	99

It has been observed that for designs with 5 or more factors, k ≥ 5, the number of insignificant factors is greater than the number of significant factors, which means that these designs can be fractionated without loosing valuable information.

- The first type of factorial design that generates a large amount of excess information is the 2^5 full factorial design.

- This design estimates 31 effects of which 15 are potentially important (i.e., the 5 main effects and the 10 interactions between the factors). 16 effects consist of interactions between three or more factors, which for practical purposes can be ignored.

Design	Total Effects	Unignorable Effects	Ignorable Effects
k = 2	3	3	0
k = 3	7	6	1
k = 4	15	10	5
k = 5	31	15	16
k = 6	63	21	42
k = 7	127	28	99

2^{5-1} fractional factorial designs can essentially obtain the same information as full 2^k factorial designs, but at half the experimental cost.

2^{k-p} Fractional Factorial Designs

$$2^{K-p}$$

- Number of factors
- Number of design generators (size of the fraction)
- Number of levels

- When the number of factors is 5 or more (even for designs with 2 levels) the amount of experimental runs increases significantly.

- Fractional factorial designs are an alternative method for conducting experiments with many variables using fewer runs.

Half Fraction *(p = 1)*

- A 2^{5-1} experimental design can be done as follows:

$$\frac{1}{2}\,(2^5) = 2^{5-1}$$

- You can fully estimate the 15 important effects and ignore the information regarding the higher order interactions because these aren't really important.

  As an example, we will use a 2^{3-1} experimental design (even though it isn't recommended to fractionate it).

  $2^{3-1} = 2^2$ = four experimental runs with 3 factors. This correspond to half of a full factorial design with 8 runs:

$$\frac{1}{2}\,(2^3) = \frac{2^3}{2} = 2^3\,2^{-1} = 2^{3-1}$$

Which runs do you choose?

Run	A	B	C	AB	AC	BC	ABC
1	-1	-1	-1	1	1	1	-1
2	1	-1	-1	-1	-1	1	1
3	-1	1	-1	-1	1	-1	1
4	1	1	-1	1	-1	-1	-1
5	-1	-1	1	1	-1	-1	1
6	1	-1	1	-1	1	-1	-1
7	-1	1	1	-1	-1	1	-1
8	1	1	1	1	1	1	1

And how do you choose them?

- Using a 2^3 design you can estimate 7 effects: A, B, C, AB, AC, BC and ABC. According to their hierarchy, the least important effect is the triple interaction. The design generator is based on the ABC contrast: The + signs make up the main fraction and the – signs make up the alternate fraction.

A	B	C
-1	-1	-1
1	-1	-1
-1	1	-1
1	1	-1
-1	-1	1
1	-1	1
-1	1	1
1	1	1

Contrast

Design Generator
A relationship between factors that is used to generate a fractional factorial design.

ABC
-
+
+
-
+
-
-
+

Fraction 1		
A	B	C
1	-1	-1
-1	1	-1
-1	-1	1
1	1	1

Fraction 2		
A	B	C
-1	-1	-1
1	1	-1
1	-1	1
-1	1	1

- Using the tables, you can observe that for each factor, there are two + levels and two - levels.

- Moreover, by running either of the fractions you will not be able to estimate the effect of ABC. We can say that ABC's contrast is confounded or aliased with the rest of the data.

LSSI
LEAN SIX SIGMA INSTITUTE

Fractional Factorial Designs

- Fractional factorial designs are typically used for "screening experiments" because we can study a few important factors among a relatively large number of factors using fewer runs.

- Screening experiments are generally performed in the DMAIC Improve Phase.

Resolution

- Resolution is related to the level of confounding of effects when fractionating the experiment.

- The resolution of an experiment is equal to the number of "letters" of the generator, since it establishes the defining relationship of the experiment.

- Therefore, the fractions 2^{3-1}, 2^{4-1} and 2^{5-1}, have III, IV and V resolutions respectively, since the generators are composed of 3, 4 and 5 letters.

An experimental design with a higher resolution is better.

- The design resolution is the length of the shortest "word" in the design generator. The resolution indicates the confounding pattern of the design.
- Resolution III Designs – The main effects are confounded with two-factor interactions.
- Resolution IV Designs – The main effects are confounded with three-factor interactions and two-factor interactions are confounded with other two-factor interactions.
- Resolution V Designs – The main effects are confounded with four-factor interactions and two-factor interactions are confounded with three-factor interactions.

Confounded/Aliased:

Meaning they cannot be estimated separately from each other.

Fractional Factorial Design Notation

The general notation for a fractional factorial design is:

$$2_R^{k-p}$$

Where:

k = Number of factors.

2^{k-p} = Number of runs.

R = Design resolution (III, IV, V...).

Note:

If $p = 1$, then: Half fractional.

If $p = 2$, then: Quarter fractional.

LSSI
LEAN SIX SIGMA INSTITUTE

Constructing 2^{k-1} Half Fractional

The following is a 2-step method to construct a half fractional design with the highest possible design resolution:

1. List the full factorial designs for $k-1$ factors to determine the first $k-1$ columns of the desired fraction.

2. The level for the remaining blank column (k-th) is calculated by multiplying the levels of the previous columns from that same row.

Example Construction of a 2^{4-1} Half Fractional

1. List the full factorial design table:

A	B	C	D
-	-	-	
+	-	-	
-	+	-	
+	+	-	
-	-	+	
+	-	+	
-	+	+	
+	+	+	

$$2^{4-1} = 2^3$$

Leave the levels for factor D blank.

2. The missing levels of factor D can be obtained by multiplying columns A, B and C according to the generator. In this case, the generator is D = ABC, resulting in:

A	B	C	D=ABC
-	-	-	-
+	-	-	+
-	+	-	+
+	+	-	-
-	-	+	+
+	-	+	-
-	+	+	-
+	+	+	+

Number of factors	Design	Resolution	Number of Runs	Fraction	Generators
4	4-1	IV	8	1/2	D = ABC
5	5-1	V	16	1/2	E = ABCD
6	6-1	VI	32	1/2	F = ABCDE
6	6-2	IV	15	1/4	E = ABCD
7	7-1	VII	64	1/2	G = ABCDEF
7	7-2	IV	32	1/4	F = ABCD
7	7-3	IV	16	1/8	G = ABC
8	8-2	V	64	1/4	G = ABCD
8	8-3	IV	32	1/8	E=BCD
8	8-4	IV	16	1/16	E = BCD

Exercise

A semiconductor manufacturing plant wants to improve its yield. The factors that affect yield are the following:

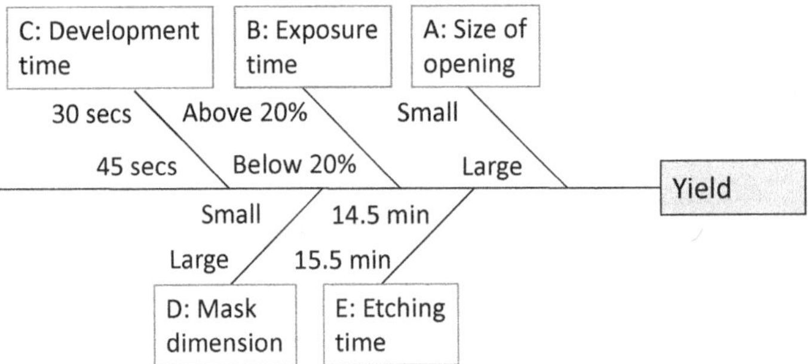

Determine which are the significant factors and in what levels of each one, the response is maximized.

Yates Notation	A	B	C	D	E	Yield %
(1)	-1	-1	-1	-1	-1	7
a	1	-1	-1	-1	-1	9
b	-1	1	-1	-1	-1	34
ab	1	1	-1	-1	-1	55
c	-1	-1	1	-1	-1	16
ac	1	-1	1	-1	-1	20
bc	-1	1	1	-1	-1	40
abc	1	1	1	-1	-1	60
d	-1	-1	-1	1	-1	8
ad	1	-1	-1	1	-1	10
bd	-1	1	-1	1	-1	32
abd	1	1	-1	1	-1	50
cd	-1	-1	1	1	-1	18
acd	1	-1	1	1	-1	21
bcd	-1	1	1	1	-1	44
abcd	1	1	1	1	-1	61

Yates Notation	A	B	C	D	E	Yield %
e	-1	-1	-1	-1	1	8
ae	1	-1	-1	-1	1	12
be	-1	1	-1	-1	1	35
abe	1	1	-1	-1	1	52
ce	-1	-1	1	-1	1	15
ace	1	-1	1	-1	1	22
bce	-1	1	1	-1	1	45
abce	1	1	1	-1	1	65
de	-1	-1	-1	1	1	6
ade	1	-1	-1	1	1	10
bde	-1	1	-1	1	1	30
abde	1	1	-1	1	1	53
cde	-1	-1	1	1	1	15
acde	1	-1	1	1	1	20
bcde	-1	1	1	1	1	41
abcde	1	1	1	1	1	63

Main Fraction	Alternate Fraction
e	(1)
a	ae
b	be
abe	ab
c	ce
ace	ac
bce	bc
abc	abce
d	de
ade	ad
bde	bd
abd	abde
cde	cd
acd	acde
bcd	bcde
abcde	abcd

Regression Analysis

Learning objectives

1. Apply multiple regression analysis to improve business decision-making.
2. Analyze and interpret the results of statistical programs for One-Factor, Multiple, and Polynomial regression models.
3. Evaluate the significance of independent variables in a regression model.

Content

> Regression Analysis
> One-Factor Regression Model
> Multiple Linear Regression
> Polynomial Regression
> Examples and exercises

Regression Analysis

Regression Analysis is a technique used to model the relationship between one or more independent variables and a dependent variable (response variable).

Uses for Regression:

1. Description: Represent the behavior of a process.

2. Prediction and estimation:

   - **Prediction** is based on a known x value.

   - **Estimation** is based on an unknown x value.

3. Control: Obtain a certain desired response from the process.

One-Factor Regression Model

$$y = \beta_0 + \beta_1 x + \varepsilon$$

Where:

- y = Dependent variable to model (response).

- x = Independent variable *(y predictor)*.

- e = Error component (measurement + natural error). Random variable.

- b_0 = Intersection. If data includes zero, then it represents **y**'s distribution mean when all **x = 0**. The intercept has no meaning if x never equals zero.

- b_1 = Slope. This is the change in **y** for every incremental change in **x**.

LSSI
LEAN SIX SIGMA INSTITUTE

1. Estimation of the model's parameters

We can calculate the parameters using the least squares method, which consists of minimizing the error of the model.

$$\hat{\beta}_1 = \frac{Sxy}{Sxx}$$

$$Sxy = \sum xy - \frac{(\sum x)(\sum y)}{n}$$

$$Sxx = \sum x^2 - \frac{(\sum x)^2}{n}$$

$$\hat{\beta}_0 = \bar{y} - \hat{\beta}_1 \bar{x}$$

$$\hat{y} = \hat{\beta}_0 + \hat{\beta}_1 \bar{x}$$

Example

At **Logistics Company**, the quantity of warehouse shortages is compared to the On-Time In-Full (OTIF) for the past 12 weeks:

Week	Shortages (X)	OTIF (Y)
7	10	88
8	6	93,9
9	5	95,5
10	8	90,5
11	7	92,6
12	3	96,3
13	0	99,8
14	1	99,1
15	2	97
16	7	92,2
17	11	85,8
18	8	90,9
	68	1.121,6

$$Sxy = \sum xy - \frac{(\sum x)(\sum y)}{n} = 6191.5 - \frac{68 \cdot 1121,6}{12} = -164.23$$

$$Sxx = \sum x^2 - \frac{(\sum x)^2}{n} = 522 - \frac{68^2}{12} = 136.67$$

$$\hat{\beta}_1 = \frac{Sxy}{Sxx} = \frac{-164.23}{136.67} = -1.202$$

$$\hat{\beta}_0 = \bar{y} - \hat{\beta}_1 \bar{x} = \frac{1121.6}{12} - (-1.202) \cdot \frac{68}{12} = 100.278$$

OTIF (Y) = 100.3 − 1.202 Shortages(X)

* OTIF: logistics performance indicator that calculates the total percentage of shipments that a supplier delivers on time and complete.

The scatter plot shows the following:

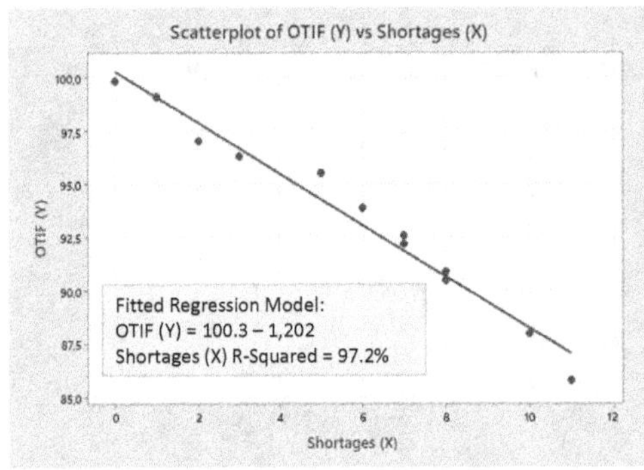

- There is a strong negative relationship.

- The regression model is:

  OTIF(Y) = 100.3 – 1,202 Shortages(X)

- For every incremental unit increase in Shortages, OTIF decreases by 1,202 units, on average.

- Given that zero is included in the interval, OTIF will have a value close to 100% when there are 0 shortages.

2. Statistical tests for the model

Before the one-factor regression model is used, the following tests must be performed:

2.1 Test for significance of regression.

2.2 Test for significance of the variable X.

2.3 Coefficient of determination, R^2.

2.4 Correlation coefficient, R.

2.5 Normality test (of residuals).

2.6 Constant variance test.

2.7 Test for independence (of residuals).

2.8 Lack-of-Fit.

2.9 PRESS/SSE relationship.

2.10 Durbin-Watson test.

LSSI
LEAN SIX SIGMA INSTITUTE

2.1. Test for significance of regression

Ho: $\beta_1 = 0$ There is no linear relationship between **x** and **y**.
Regression has no significance.

Ha: $\beta_1 \neq 0$ **x** can be useful in explaining the variation in **y**.

Elements needed to obtain a **test statistic**:

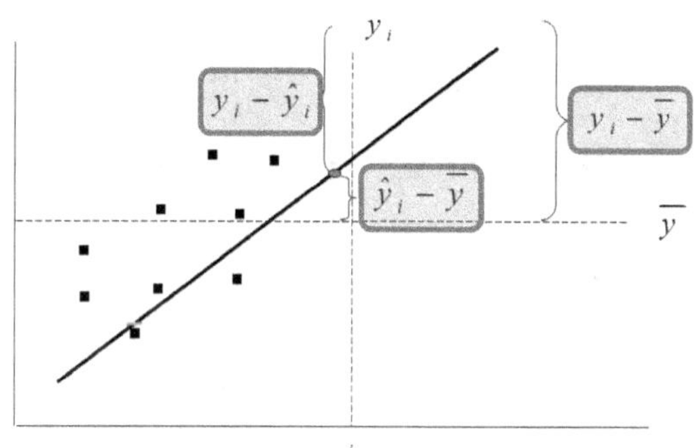

Take the following key relationships into consideration:

$$\sum (y_i - \overline{y})^2 = \sum (\hat{y}_i - \overline{y})^2 + \sum (y_i - \hat{y}_i)^2$$

$$\text{SST} = Syy = \text{SSR} + \text{SSE}$$

SST = Syy = Total variation in data.

SSR = Variation represented by the regression model.

SSE = Residual variation not represented by regression.

$$\text{SST} = Syy = \sum_i y_i^2 - \frac{(\sum y_i)^2}{n}$$

$$\text{SSR} = \hat{\beta}_1 \cdot Sxy$$

$$\text{SSE} = Syy - \text{SSR}$$

Anova Table

Source of Variation	Df	SS	MS	F
Regression	1	SSR	MSR = SSR/1	MSR/MSE
Error	$n-2$	SSE	MSE = SSE/($n-2$)	
TOTAL	$n-1$	SST		

Reject Ho if $F > F$ (tables) $= F_{\alpha;1;n-2}$ or if the value $p < 0.05$

Ho: $\beta_1 = 0$

Ha: $\beta_1 \neq 0$

That is, the regression makes sense and is fulfilled **Ha: $\beta_1 \neq 0$**

Plotted results of the test:

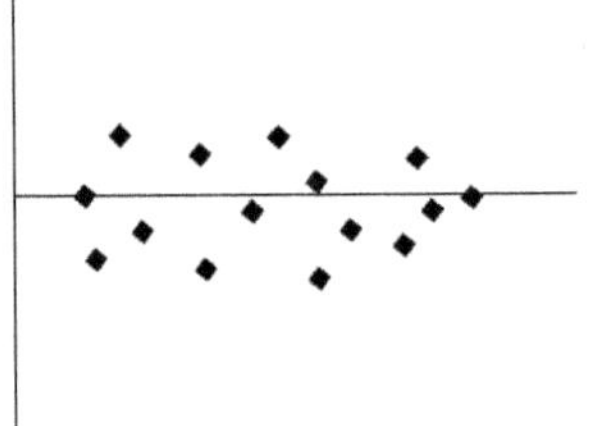

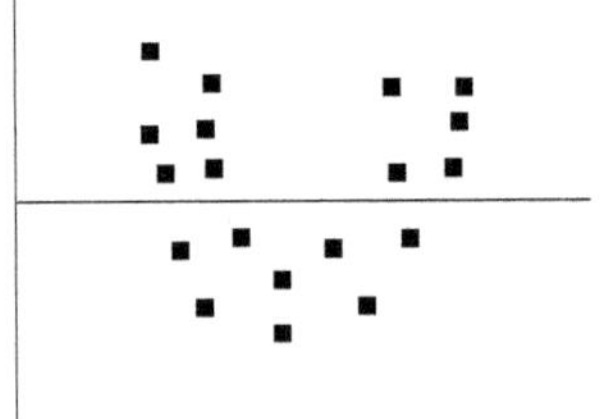

$\beta_1 = 0$. Regression has **no** significance.

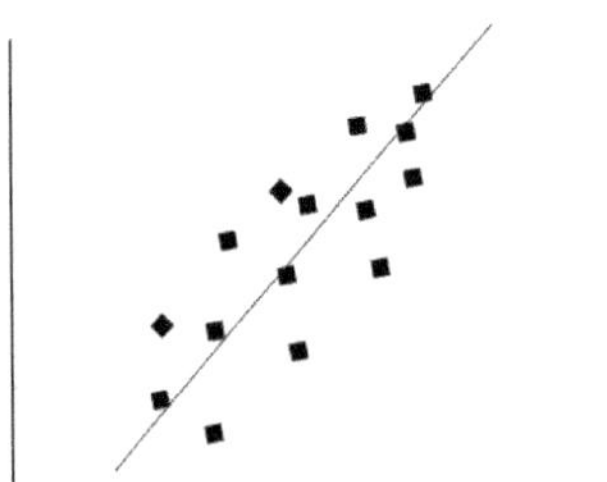

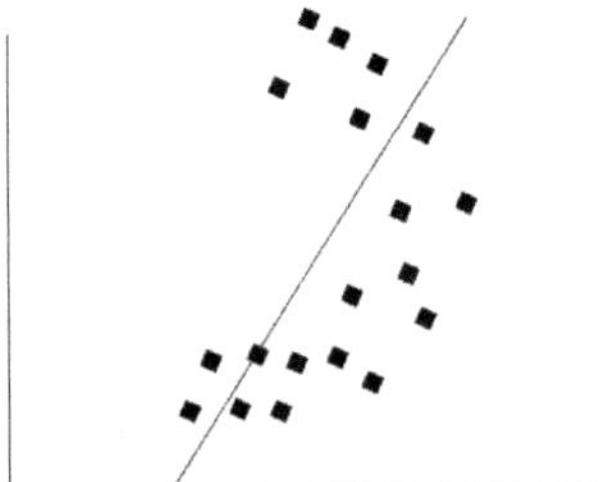

$\beta_1 \neq 0$. Regression **has** significance.

LSSI — LEAN SIX SIGMA INSTITUTE

Example

In the **Logistics Company** case:

$$\text{SST} = Syy = \sum_i y^2 - \frac{(\sum y_i)^2}{n} = 105{,}035.3 - \frac{(1{,}121.6)^2}{12} = 203.087$$

$$\text{SSR} = \hat{\beta}_1 \cdot Sxy = -1.202 \cdot (-164.23) = 197.306$$

$$\text{SSE} = Syy - \text{SSR} = 203.087 - 197.404306 = 5.726$$

Source of Variation	Df	SS	MS	F
Regression	1	197.360	197.360	344.66
Error	10	5.726	0.573	
TOTAL	11	203.087		

$$F_{\alpha;\ df(R);\ df(E)} = F_{0.05;\ 1;\ 10} = 4.965$$

Given 344.66 > 4.965, the regression **has** significance.

The ANOVA table built with Minitab shows the following:

Analysis of Variance

Source	Df	Adj. SS	Adj. MS	F-Value	P-Value
Regression	1	197.360	197.360	344.66	0.000
Shortages (X)	1	197.360	197.360	344.66	0.000
Error	10	5.726	0.573		
Lack-of-Fit	8	5.566	0.696	8.70	0.107
Pure Error	2	0.160	0.08		
Total	11	203.087			

Given that p-value 0.000 < 0.05, we conclude that the regression has significance. F-value is the same as that which was previously calculated.

2.2. Test for significance of variable X

We can determine if variable X must remain in the regression model or not through its corresponding p-value.

P-value must be less than 0.05 (α).

Example

The ANOVA table built with Minitab shows the following:

Coefficients

Term	Coef.	SE Coef.	T-Value	P-Value	VIF
Constant	100.276	0.427	234.88	0.000	
Shortages (X)	-1.2017	0.0647	-18.56	0.000	1.00

For Shortages(X), p-value = 0.000 < 0.05; in which case X must remain in the model.

2.3. Coefficient of determination

$$R^2 = r^2 = \frac{SSR}{SST} \qquad 0 \leq R^2 \leq 1 \qquad R^2 = \frac{197.360}{203.087} = 0.9718$$

The coefficient of determination is the proportion of total variation that is explained (represented) by the regression model.

In the case of **Logistics Company**, 97.18% of the variation in **OTIF** is explainable by **Shortages**.

The **determination coefficient** is considered appropriate or acceptable when it is greater than 80%.

LSSI
LEAN SIX SIGMA INSTITUTE

2.4. Correlation coefficient

$$r = \frac{S_{xy}}{\sqrt{S_{yy} \cdot S_{xx}}} = \frac{n\sum xy - \sum x \sum y}{\sqrt{\left[n\sum x^2 - (\sum x)^2\right]\left[n\sum y^2 - (\sum y)^2\right]}} = \sqrt{R^2}$$

$-1 \leq r \leq 1$

Correlation coefficient measures the degree of linear association between **x** and **y**. In the case of **Logistics Company**:

$$r = \frac{-164.23}{\sqrt{(203.087) \cdot (136.67)}} = -0.986$$

With this result, we can confirm that the relationship is strong and negative.

A [positive or negative] **correlation** is adequate or acceptable if its absolute value is greater than 0.8 (Wheeler, 1995).

Assumptions of the model

The model of consideration includes an error term, and it is assumed that said errors follow a normal distribution with constant variance and are independent from each other.

The non-compliance of these assumptions can produce an unstable model where different samples can result in different models with opposite or contradicting conclusions.

Residuals represent the error term in the model (ε):

- Regular: $e_i = y_i - \hat{y}_i$
- Standardized: $d_i = \dfrac{e_i}{\sqrt{MSE}}$ $d_i = \dfrac{e_i}{\sigma_i \,(estimate)}$

- Studentized: $r_i = \dfrac{e_i}{\sqrt{MSE\left[1 - \left(\frac{1}{n} + \frac{(x_i - \bar{x})^2}{S_{xx}}\right)\right]}}$ $|d_i| > 2 \rightarrow$ Outliers

$r_i = y_i - \hat{y}_i$ $\hat{y}_i = fitted\ value\ in\ a\ model\ that\ omits\ the\ ith\ observation\ from\ its\ calculations.$
$|r_i| > 2 \rightarrow$ Outliers.

2.5. Normality test

If residuals follow an approximately linear pattern, then **normality** is accepted.

In the case of **Logistics Company**:

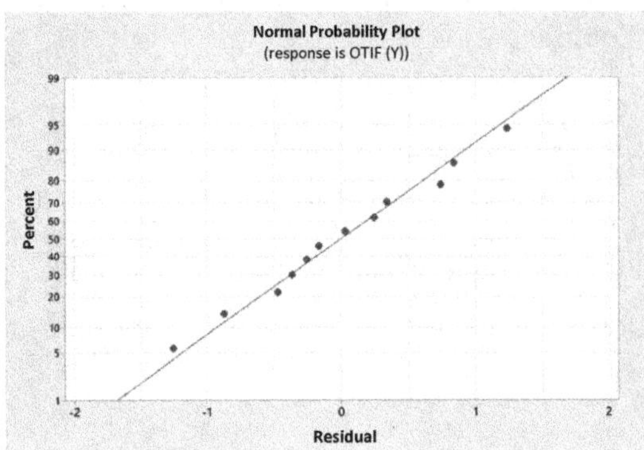

Normality is accepted.

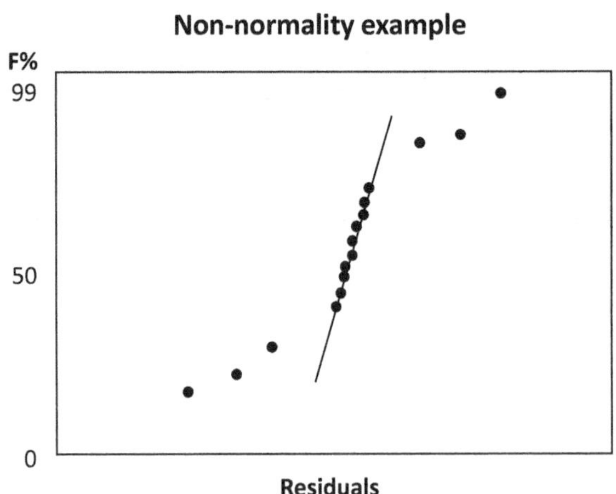

Non-normality example

LSSI
LEAN SIX SIGMA INSTITUTE

2.6. Constant variance test

1. Plot the residuals vs. $\hat{y}$.

2. The variance is considered to be constant if the spread of the points is approximately the same (i.e., similar number of points distributed randomly) above and below the center line.

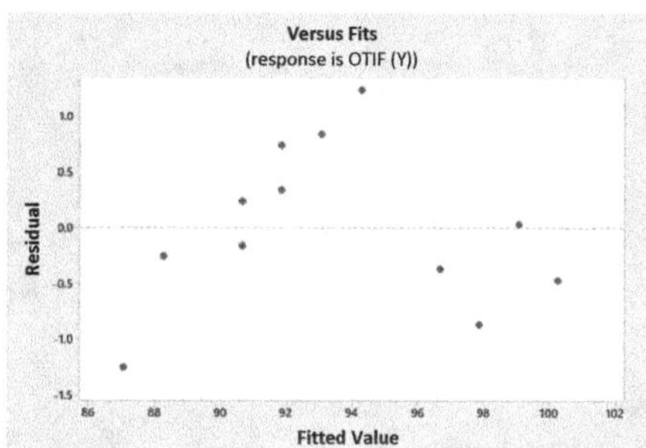

In the **Logistics Company** case, **constant variance** is accepted.

2.7. Test for independence

- When conducing experiments, the order in which they are performed must be documented.

- The **independence test** consists of plotting the residuals vs. the order of each experiment.

- If random fluctuations in a horizontal band are observed, then **independence** is accepted.

- Otherwise – if a pattern is observed – the experiment should be repeated while being mindful of the randomness of tests.

- In cases where the study is not performed as a controlled experiment, it is important to know the order in which the observations were obtained.

In the **Logistics Company** case:

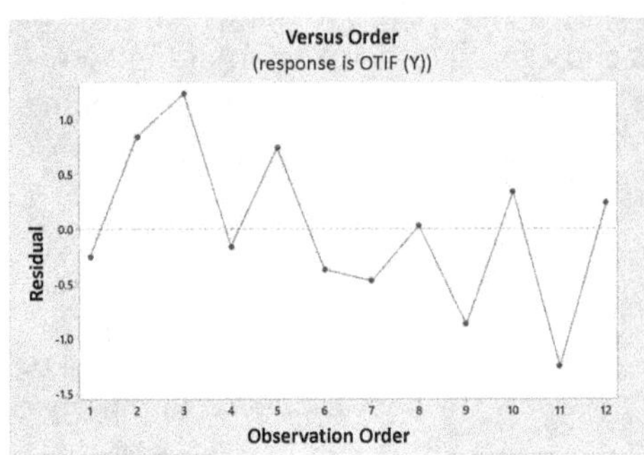

Independence is not rejected.

Example: Lack of independence

Example: Lack of independence

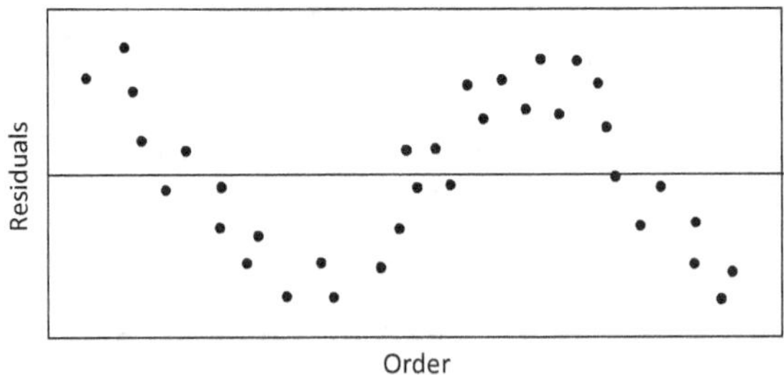

LSSI
LEAN SIX SIGMA INSTITUTE

2.8. Lack-of-Fit of the model test

- This test assumes that the assumptions of the model are true.

- We aim to test:

$$\text{Ho: } y = \beta_0 + \beta_1 x + \varepsilon \qquad\qquad \text{Ha: } y \neq \beta_0 + \beta_1 x + \varepsilon$$

(This linear model is appropriate)   (This linear model is not appropriate)

To perform this test, it is necessary to repeat observations (replicates) for **y** for at least one level of **x**.

In this case, we want to **"ACCEPT"** Ho: that the **linear model is appropriate.** Therefore, we look for **$p > 0.05$**.

Procedure

The test develops as follows:

- **m** is the total number of levels for **x** (in this case, $m = 11$, since there is one repeated value).

- n_i is the number of observations for x_i ($i = 1 \ldots m$).

- y_{ij} is the j-the observation in x_i ($j = 1 \ldots n_i$).

- **n** is the total number of observations $\quad n = \sum_{1}^{m} n_i$

The basic principle is to partition the error into two components:

- Lack-of-Fit (LOF).

- Pure Error (PE).

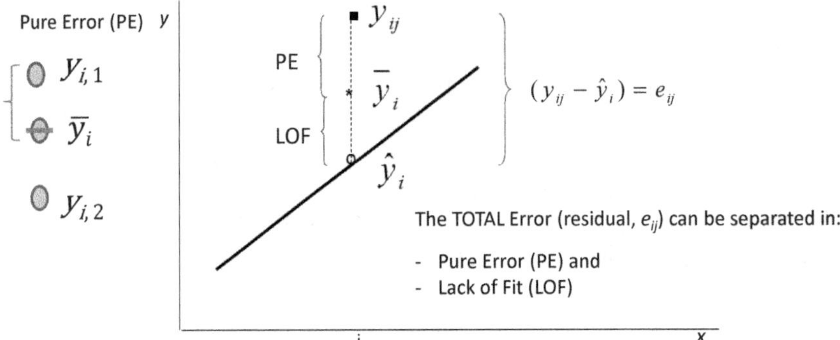

The TOTAL Error (residual, e_{ij}) can be separated in:

- Pure Error (PE) and
- Lack of Fit (LOF)

The residual, e_{ij}, is the difference between the observed value y_{ij} and the expected value $\hat{y}_i$ and can be divided in 2:

1. **PE**: Pure Error: difference between each observation and the average (of the repetitions) : $y_{ij} - \overline{y}_i$

2. **LOF**: Lack of Fit: difference between the average and the expected value (regression) : $\overline{y}_i - \hat{y}_i$

Analysis of Variance

Source	Df	Seq. SS	Contribution	Adj. SS	Adj. MS	F-Value	P-Value
Regression	1	197.360	97.18%	197.360	197.360	344.66	0.000
Shortages (X)	1	197.360	97.18%	197.360	197.360	344.66	0.000
Error	10	5.726	2.82%	5.726	0.573		
Lack-of-Fit	8	5.566	2.74%	5.566	0.696	8.70	0.107
Pure Error	2	0.160	0.08%	0.160	0.080		
Total	11	203.087	100.00%				

$$\text{ST:} \quad F = \frac{MS(LOF)}{MS(PE)} = \frac{0.696}{0.080} = 8.70$$

Ho: $y = \beta_0 + \beta_1 x + \varepsilon$ (The linear model is appropriate)

Ha: $y \neq \beta_0 + \beta_1 x + \varepsilon$ (The linear model is not appropriate)

Reject Ho if $F > F_{\alpha;m-2;n-m} = F_{0.05;9;1} = 250.54$ or if **p-value < 0.05**.

Given that 8.70 is not greater than 250.54 and that p-value = 0.107 > 0.05; the proposed linear model is **not rejected.**

If F < F tables ($p > 0.05$) we do not reject Ho: the liner model proposed is appropriate (LOF < PE).

2.9. PRESS/SSE relationship

PRESS (Predicted Residual Error Sum of Squares):

- PRESS evaluates the **prediction capability** of the model.
- **PRESS** is compared against **SSE.** If the relationship is less than **2,** you can assume that **the model is good at predicting**.

In the **Logistics Company** case:

Summary of the model

S	R-Squared	Adj. R-Squared	PRESS	Pred. R-Squared	AICc	BIC
0.756721	97.18%	96.90%	8.62965	95.75%	34.18	32.63

Analysis of Variance

Source	Df	Seq. SS	Contribution	Adj. SS	Adj. MS	F-Value	P-Value
Regression	1	197.360	97.18%	197.360	197.360	344.66	0.000
Shortages (X)	1	197.360	97.18%	197.360	197.360	344.66	0.000
Error	10	5.726	2.82%	5.726	0.573		
Lack-of-Fit	8	5.566	2.74%	5.566	0.696	8.70	0.107
Pure Error	2	0.160	0.08%	0.160	0.080		
Total	11	203.087	100.00%				

$$\text{PRESS/SSE} = \frac{8.62965}{5.726} = 1.507 < 2$$

The model has adequate predictive capabilities.

2.10. Durbin-Watson test

The Durbin-Watson test detects **autocorrelation** between errors (lack of independence). This test assumes that errors follow a normal distribution:

Ho: There is no positive autocorrelation, $p = 0$

Ha: There is positive autocorrelation, $p > 0$

The following can also be tested:

Ho: There is no negative autocorrelation, $p = 0$

Ha: There is negative autocorrelation, $p < 0$

The test's statistical model is: $\text{EP} : d = \dfrac{\sum\limits_{t=2}^{n} (e_t - e_{t-1})^2}{\sum\limits_{t=1}^{n} e_t^2}$

Find **dL** and **dU** on the **Durbin-Watson** tables and come to a decision based on the following figure:

Autocorrelation is often present when one of the variables is time.

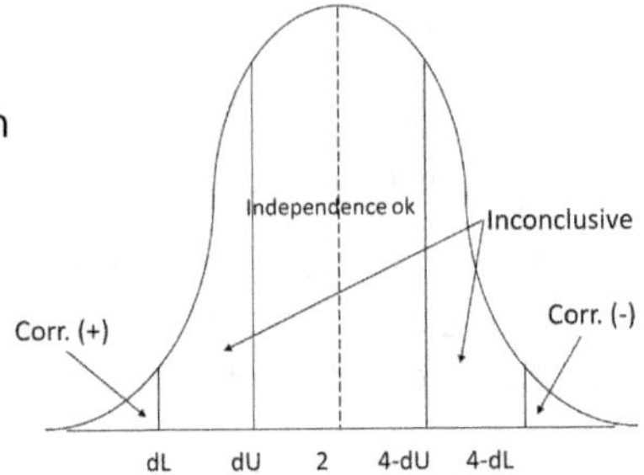

To use the **Durbin-Watson (DW)** tables, it is necessary to know **n** (if it is lower than 6, then use n = 6), define *p (p* = number of parameters, *βs*, including the constant term), and set the level of **α** (normally to 5%).

Example

In the **Logistics Company** case, we obtain the following using **Minitab**:

Durbin-Watson statistic = 2.20640

With $n = 12$, $p = 2$, and using α = 5%, we obtain from the DW table: dL = 0,97076 and dU = 1,33137.

We can determine that 4 − dU = 2,66863 and 4 − dL = 3,02924. Therefore, we can conclude that there is NO **autocorrelation** among the errors.

Autocorrelation can also be detected when plotting the residuals against the observation order (**test for independence**) and by observing groups of data points on the same side of the center line.

Autocorrelation is generally **caused** when one or more important variables are not included in the model; For example, when evaluating annual sales against advertising expenses, the population growth variable (within time) should be included.

The effects of **autocorrelation** are:

- Inefficient model estimators,
- Underestimation of error, and
- Inaccurate hypothesis testing and confidence interval results.

LSSI
LEAN SIX SIGMA INSTITUTE

3. Prediction of new observations

Before using the regression model for predictions, verify that it has passed all tests:

2.1 Test for significance of regression. ✓

2.2 Test for significance of variable X. ✓

2.3 Coefficient of determination, R^2. ✓

2.4 Correlation coefficient, R. ✓

2.5 Normality test (of residuals). ✓

2.6 Constant variance test. ✓

2.7 Test for independence (of residuals). ✓

2.8 Lack-of-Fit. ✓

2.9 PRESS/SSE relationship. ✓

2.10 Durbin-Watson test. ✓

To **"predict" the outcome of a new observation** (different value of **x** – within the range – or a value of the original data), we have two intervals: one for the individual observation, and one for the prediction average.

$$x_0 \rightarrow \hat{y}_0$$

- **Individual prediction interval (PI)**   For an individual value

$$\hat{y}_0 \pm t_{\alpha/2\,;\,n-2} \sqrt{MSE \left(1 + \frac{1}{n} + \frac{(x_0 - \bar{x})^2}{Sxx} \right)}$$

- **Confidence interval (CI)**   For the average

$$\hat{y}_0 \pm t_{\alpha/2\,;\,n-2} \sqrt{MSE \left(\frac{1}{n} + \frac{(x_0 - \bar{x})^2}{Sxx} \right)}$$

Example

In **Logistics Company**, a team wants to predict the OTIF value for a shortage quantity of 9:

Settings

Variable	Setting
Shortages (X)	9

Prediction

Fit	SE Fit	95% CI	95% PI
89.4610	0.307041	(88.7768, 90.1451)	(87.6414, 91.2806)

- For the **average**, the interval is between 88.7768 and 90.1451.
- For an **individual** value, the interval is between 87.6414 and 91.2806.
- Confidence level: 95%.

Exercise

At **Chelsea Footwear,** tests are performed with different solidification time and shoe sole hardness measurements:

T-Solid (X)	Hardness (Y)
10	4.5
11	4.2
12	3.8
13	3.6
14	3.4
15	3.0
16	2.9
17	2.4
18	2.2
19	2.1
20	1.8

- Graph – Build a scatter plot diagram and determine the type and degree of relationship between the input and output variables.

1. Build a regression model and interpret its results.

2. Perform the 10 applicable tests on the model and interpret each result.

3. Predict the confidence interval for hardness that would be obtained with a solidification time of 10.5 minutes.

Multiple Linear Regression

Multiple linear regression consists of building regression models with more than one independent variable *(Xs)*.

$$y = \beta_0 + \beta_1 x_1 + \beta_2 x_2 + \cdots + \beta_k x_k + \varepsilon$$

- n = Sample size.

- p = number of parameters (βs).

- k = number of variables (Xs).

- ε = error component.

The relationship between the number of parameters and the number of variables is:

$$p = k + 1$$

β_i (i = 1..k) represents the expected change in the response *y* when x_i changes one unit, while maintaining all other **Xs** constant.

Betas (βs) are referred to as **partial correlation coefficients**.

β_0 represents the intersection of the regression hyperplane.

If the range of data (**Xs**) includes $x_1 = x_2 = \ldots = x_k = 0$, then β_0 represents the mean of *y* when $x_1 = x_2 = \ldots = x_k = 0$.

The model in matrix form is:

$$\vec{y} = \vec{X}\vec{\beta} + \vec{\varepsilon}$$

1. Estimation of the model parameters

Where:

$$\vec{y} = \begin{bmatrix} y_1 \\ y_2 \\ \cdots \\ y_n \end{bmatrix} \qquad \vec{x} = \begin{bmatrix} 1 & x_{11} & x_{12} & \cdots & x_{1k} \\ 1 & x_{21} & x_{22} & \cdots & x_{2k} \\ \cdots & \cdots & \cdots & \cdots & \cdots \\ 1 & x_{n1} & x_{n2} & \cdots & x_{nk} \end{bmatrix} \qquad \vec{\beta} = \begin{bmatrix} \beta_0 \\ \beta_1 \\ \cdots \\ \beta_k \end{bmatrix} \qquad \vec{\varepsilon} = \begin{bmatrix} \varepsilon_1 \\ \varepsilon_2 \\ \cdots \\ \varepsilon_n \end{bmatrix}$$

The matrix solution is: $\hat{\vec{\beta}} = (\vec{X}'\vec{X})^{-1}\vec{X}'\vec{y}$

Resulting in the model: $\hat{\vec{y}} = \vec{x}\hat{\vec{\beta}}$

Example

In **Chemical Manufacturing**, tests are performed at different temperature levels (in °C), stirring speeds (in rpms), and pressure levels (in psi), and the effects on filtration flow are measured (in liters/hour):

Temperature (X1)	Speed (X2)	Pressure (X3)	Filtration Flow (Y)
101	848	10	49
120	845	12	44
115	847	26	46
140	837	34	38
123	844	23	43
107	847	11	47
130	840	32	41
135	838	12	38
105	846	21	47
110	845	23	45
118	845	32	44
138	836	25	37
125	845	31	44
132	840	19	40

Where:

$$\vec{y} = \begin{bmatrix} 49 \\ 44 \\ \cdots \\ 40 \end{bmatrix} \qquad \vec{x} = \begin{bmatrix} 1 & 101 & 848 & 10 \\ 1 & 120 & 845 & 12 \\ \cdots & \cdots & \cdots & \cdots \\ 1 & 132 & 840 & 19 \end{bmatrix} \qquad \hat{\vec{\beta}} = \begin{bmatrix} \hat{\beta}_0 \\ \hat{\beta}_1 \\ \cdots \\ \hat{\beta}_k \end{bmatrix}$$

$$\hat{\vec{y}} = \vec{x}\hat{\vec{\beta}}$$

Regression equation

Filtration Flow(Y) = $- 360.7 - 0.1455$ Temperature(X_1) + 0.4994 Speed (X_2) + 0.0177 Pressure (X_3)

LSSI LEAN SIX SIGMA INSTITUTE

2. Statistical tests for the model

For **multiple** linear regression, the following tests must be performed:

2.1 Test for significance of regression.

2.2 Test for the significance of variable X.

2.3 Stepwise regression (variable selection).

2.4 Best subsets (variable selection).

2.5 Coefficient of determination, R^2.

2.6 Adjusted multiple coefficient of determination.

2.7 Normality test (of residuals).

2.8 Constant variance test.

2.9 Test for independence (of residuals).

2.10 PRESS/SSE relationship.

2.11 Durbin-Watson test.

2.12 Multicollinearity.

2.1. Test for significance of regression

$$\text{Ho: } \beta_1 = \beta_2 = \dots = \beta_k = 0$$

$$\text{Ha: } \beta_j \neq 0 \text{ for at least one } j$$

The test statistic is:

$$\text{EP} : F = \frac{\text{SSR}/k}{\text{SSE}/(n-k-1)} = \frac{\text{MSR}}{\text{MSE}}$$

- p = number of parameters (βs).
- k = number of variables (Xs).
- $p = k + 1 \qquad n - k - 1 = n - p \qquad k = p - 1$

$$\boxed{\text{Reject Ho if} \quad F > F_{\alpha\,;\,k\,;\,n-k-1}}$$

2.2. Test for significance of variable X

$$\text{Ho: } \beta_j = 0$$

$$\text{Ha: } \beta_j \neq 0$$

The test statistical model is:

$$EP : t = \frac{\hat{\beta}_j}{se(\hat{\beta}_j)} = \frac{\hat{\beta}_j}{\sqrt{\hat{\sigma}^2 c_{jj}}}$$

C_{jj} are the elements of the diagonal of the matrix $(\vec{X}'\vec{X})^{-1}$

Reject Ho if $|t| > t_{\alpha/2;\,n-k-1}$

Results for tests 2.1 and 2.2 in the example

Results and interpretation using **Minitab**:

Analysis of Variance

Source	Df	Seq. SS	Contribution	Adj. SS	Adj. MS	F-Value	P-Value	
Regression	3	180.513	98.68%	180.513	60.1710	249.10	0.000	←
Temperature (X1)	1	171.700	93.86%	5.637	5.6370	23.34	0.001	←
Speed (X2)	1	8.590	4.70%	7.425	7.4249	30.74	0.000	←
Pressure (X3)	1	0.223	0.12%	0.223	0.2230	0.92	0.359	←
Error	10	2.415	1.32%	2.415	0.2415			
Total	13	182.929	100.00%					

- Regression has significance: p-value = 0.000 < 0.05.

- Temperature(X1) has significance: p-value = 0.001 < 0.05.

- Speed(X2) has significance: p-value = 0.000 < 0.05.

- Pressure(X3) apparently does not have significance: p-value = 0.359 > 0.05 and must be removed from the model.

LSSI LEAN SIX SIGMA INSTITUTE

2.3. Stepwise regression

- Stepwise regression is a method used to determine the variables that should remain in the model.

- Start with an empty model except for β_0, and then begin to add variables one at a time, starting with the variables that have the greatest correlation with **y**.

- A variable is included in the model if its **F-value** is greater than a given, pre-defined value (**F-to-enter**).

- The second variable selected is the one with the greatest partial correlation to **y**.

- For every step that a variable is added, all the other ones previously included are re-evaluated through partial **F** tests in order to determine whether it is of value to keep them in the model given the incorporation of the other variables.

- This way, we also obtain an **F-to-remove** value.

Example

In the **Chemical Manufacturing** case:

Stepwise selection

Candidate terms: Temperature (X1), Speed (X2), Pressure (X3)

	-------Step 1-------		-------Step 2-------	
	Coef	P	Coef	P
Constant	-724.1		-379.6	
Speed (X2)	0.9099		0.5207	0.000
Temperature (X1)		0.000	-0.1343	0.001
S		0.831090		0.489763
R-Sq.		95.47%		98.56%
R-Sq. (Adj.)		95.09%		98.30%
Mallows' Cp		24.31		2.92
AICc		40.79		28.81
BIC		40.31		26.92

α to enter = 0.15, α to remove = 0.15

Regression equation

Filtration Flow (Y) = -379.6 − 0.1343 Temperature (X1) + 0.5207 Speed (X2)

Coefficients

Term	Coef	SE Coef.	95% CI	T-Value	P-Value	VIF
Constant	-379.6	76.5	(-547.9, -211.3)	-4.96	0.000	
Temperature (X1)	-0.1343	0.0277	(-0.1952, -0.0734)	-4.85	0.001	6.66
Speed (X2)	0.5207	0.0870	(0.3292, 0.7122)	5.98	0.000	6.66

We validate that Pressure (X3) should **not** be included in the model.

2.4. Best subsets

It is also used to determine the variables that should remain in the model.

This method develops the best regression model based upon the best combination (subset) of input variables, and it calculates the following performance measures:

R^2, $R^2\text{adj}$, Cp (Mallows)

$$Cp = \frac{SSE}{MSE} - n + 2p$$

- p = number of parameters in the particular subset model.
- Use the SSE of the model based on the particular subset.
- Use the MSE of the complete model (containing all variables).

Example

In the **Chemical Manufacturing** case:

The response is Filtration Flow (Y)

Vars	R-Sq	Adj. R-Sq	Pred. R-Sq	Mallows'Cp	S	Temperature (X1)	Speed (X2)	Pressure (X3)
1	95.5	95.1	93.9	24.3	0.83109		X	
1	93.9	93.4	91.9	36.5	0.96732	X		
2	98.6	98.3	97.6	2.9	0.48976	X	X	
2	95.6	94.8	92.7	25.3	0.85559		X	X
3	98.7	98.3	97.4	4	0.49148	X	X	X

Using Best Subsets, we validate that Pressure (X3) should **not** be included in the model.

LSSI
LEAN SIX SIGMA INSTITUTE

2.5. Estimation of the model parameters

Based on the previous results, the regression model is adjusted, eliminating the Pressure (X3) variable:

Regression equation

Filtration Flow (Y) = -379.6 – 0.1343 Temperature (X1) + 0.5207 Speed (X2)

Subsequent tests will be performed for this model only.

It is no longer necessary to repeat tests:

> 2.3. Stepwise regression (variable selection).

> 2.4. Best subsets (variable selection).

Results for tests 2.1, 2.2 and 2.5 in the example

Results and interpretation using **Minitab**:

Coefficients

Term	Coef	SE Coef.	95% CI	T-Value	P-Value	VIF
Constant	-379.6	76.5	(-547.9, -211.3)	-4.96	0.000	
Temperature (X1)	-0.1343	0.0277	(-0.1952, -0.0734)	-4.85	0.001	6.66
Speed (X2)	0.5207	0.0870	(0.3292, 0.7122)	5.98	0.000	6.66

Summary of the model

S	R-Squared	Adj. R-Squared	PRESS	Pred. R-Squared	AICc	BIC
0.489763	98.56%	98.30%	4.32217	97.64%	28.81	26.92

- Regression has significance: p-value = 0.000 < 0.05.
- Temperature (X1) has significance: p-value = 0.001 < 0.05.
- Speed (X2) has significance: p-value = 0.000 < 0.05.
- The coefficient of determination, R^2, is appropriate: 98.56% > 80%. 98.56% of the variation in Filtration Flow can be explained by the variation in Temperature and in Stirring Speed.

2.6. Adjusted multiple coefficient of determination

Defined by: $R^2\text{adj} = 1 - \dfrac{\text{MSE}}{\text{MST}} = 1 - \dfrac{n-1}{n-p}(1 - R^2)$

Given:

- n = number of observations.
- p = number of parameters (βs).
- R^2 = SSR/SST.

Model Summary

S	R-sq	R-sq(adj)	R-sq(pred)
0,489763	98,56%	98,30%	97,64%

If both values **R²adj** and **R²** are highly different, then this means that the model is over-adjusted.

R²adj penalizes you by adding variables that are not important to the model.

In this case, R²adj = 98.30% is nearly equal to R² = 98.56%.

2.7. Normality test

In the **Chemical Manufacturing** case:

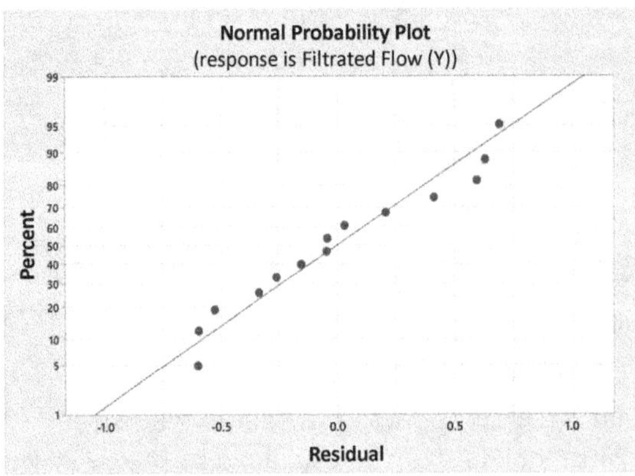

Normality is accepted.

LSSI
LEAN SIX SIGMA INSTITUTE

2.8. Constant variance test

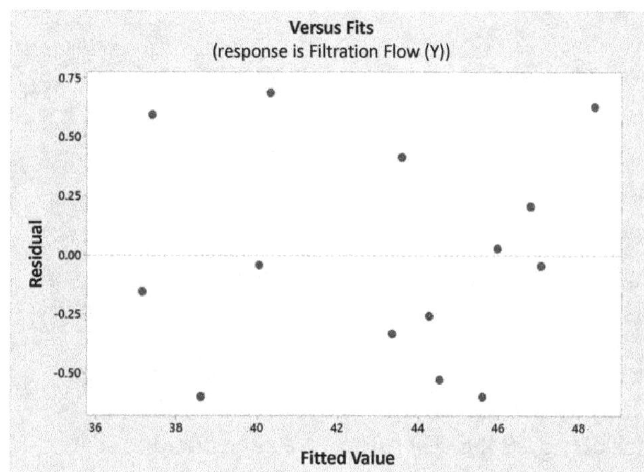

In the **Chemical Manufacturing** case, **constant variance** is accepted.

2.9. Test for independence

For **Chemical Manufacturing**:

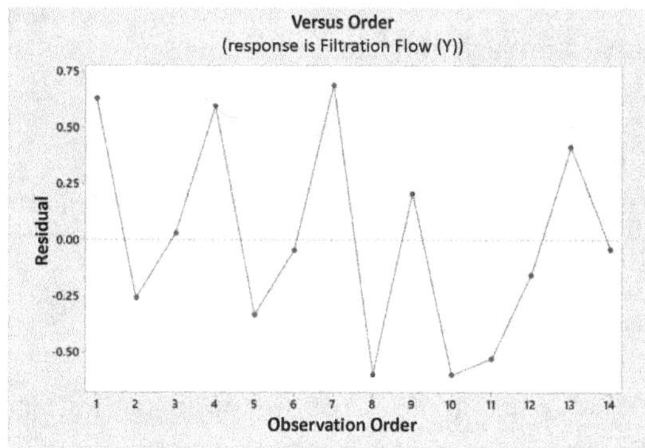

Independence is not rejected.

Results for tests 2.10 and 2.11 for Chemical Manufacturing

PRESS/SSE relationship and Durbin-Watson test

Model Summary

S	R-sq	R-sq(adj)	PRESS	R-sq(pred)	AICc	BIC
0.489763	98.56%	98.30%	4.32217	97.64%	28.81	26.92

Durbin-Watson Statistic

Durbin-Watson Statistic = 2.38858

Analysis of Variance

Source	DF	Seq SS	Contribution	Adj SS	Adj MS	F-Value	P-Value
Regression	2	180.290	98.56%	180.290	90.1450	375.81	0.000
Temperature (X1)	1	171.700	93.86%	5.650	5.6500	23.55	0.001
Speed (X2)	1	8.590	4.70%	8.590	8.5900	35.81	0.000
Error	11	2.639	1.44%	2.639	0.2399		
Total	13	182.929	100.00%				

- The model has strong prediction capability, since PRESS/SSE = 4.32217/2.639 = 1.638 < 2.

- The Durbin-Watson statistic = 2.38858. With n = 14, p = 3, and using α = 0.05, we obtain from the DW table: dL = 0,90544; dU = 1,55066; 4–dU = 2,44934 and 4-dL = 3,09456. Therefore, we can conclude that there is no autocorrelation.

2.12. Multicollinearity

Multicollinearity means that two or more predictor variables (Xs) are correlated with each other.

Indications of **multicollinearity** include the following:

1. Significant correlation between pairs of **Xs**.

2. The signs (+,-) of some of the parameters of the model are opposite of what is expected.

3. VIF_i (Variance Inflation Factor) > 10.

$$\mathrm{VIF}_i = \frac{1}{1 - \mathrm{R}_i^2} \quad i = 1...k \quad \mathrm{R}_i^2 \text{ of the model without including } x_i$$

VIF: Variance Inflation Factor.

LSSI
LEAN SIX SIGMA INSTITUTE

Solutions to multicollinearity:

1. Eliminate one or more variables from the model (the **stepwise** method could be used).

2. If you decide to leave in all variables, then avoid establishing cause-effect relationships between **Xs** and **y**.

The multicollinearity test is considered approved or passed **if the VIF values for all variables are less than 10.**

For Chemical Manufacturing, VIF = 6.66 for the variables, temperature and speed, which indicates that **there is no multicollinearity.**

Coefficients

Term	Coef	SE Coef.	95% CI	T-Value	P-Value	VIF
Constant	-379.6	76.5	(-547.9, -211.3)	-4.96	0.000	
Temperature (X1)	-0.1343	0.0277	(-0.1952, -0.0734)	-4.85	0.001	6.66
Speed (X2)	0.5207	0.0870	(0.3292, 0.7122)	5.98	0.000	6.66

3. Prediction of new observations

Before using the regression model for predictions, verify that it has passed all tests:

    2.1 Test for significance of regression. ✓
    2.2 Test for the significance of variable X. ✓
    2.3 Stepwise regression (variable selection). ✓
    2.4 Best subsets (variable selection). ✓
    2.5 Coefficient of determination, R^2. ✓
    2.6 Adjusted multiple coefficient of determination. ✓
    2.7 Normality test (of residuals). ✓
    2.8 Constant variance test. ✓
    2.9 Test for independence (of residuals). ✓
    2.10 PRESS/SSE relationship. ✓
    2.11 Durbin-Watson test. ✓
    2.12 Multicollinearity. ✓

Example

A team at **Chemical Manufacturing** wants to predict the value for Filtration Flow for a Temperature of 125°C and a Stirring Speed of 840 rpm:

Settings

Variable	Value
Temperature (X1)	125
Speed (X2)	840

Prediction

Fit	SE Fit	95% CI	95% PI
40.9830	0.221455	(40.4956, 41.4704)	(39.8000, 42.1660)

- For the average, the interval is: between 40.4956 and 41.4704.

- For an individual value, the interval is: between 39.8000 and 42.1660.

- Confidence level: 95%.

Exercise

A team at a production company is performing tests with different quantities of solvent (in ml), reaction volume (in liters) and catalyst (in grams) – in order to measure their effect on yield (measured as a percentage):

Solvent (X1)	Volume (X2)	Catalyst (X3)	Yield (Y)
25	100	3	62
40	120	8	90
35	140	4	43
40	130	5	78
80	200	6	98
48	130	2	58
60	150	8	90
38	160	9	76
67	170	1	65
56	200	6	81
33	180	3	32
29	160	7	56

1. Build a regression model and interpret its results.

2. Perform the 12 applicable tests on the model and interpret each result. Remember to only keep the significant factors in the model.

3. Predict the confidence interval for yield with a solvent quantity of 50 ml, a reaction volume of 110 liters, and a catalyst quantity of 5 grams.

LSSI
LEAN SIX SIGMA INSTITUTE

Polynomial Regression

Polynomial regression is a particular case of the regression model in which the parameters (βs) are not linear.

The Polynomial model of 2nd order and **one** variable is:

$$y = \beta_0 + \beta_1 x + \beta_2 x^2 + \varepsilon$$

The polynomial model of 2nd order and two variables is:

$$y = \beta_0 + \beta_1 x_1 + \beta_2 x_2 + \beta_{11} x_1^2 + \beta_{22} x_2^2 + \beta_{12} x_1 x_2 + \varepsilon$$

$$y = \beta_0 + \beta_1 x + \beta_2 x^2 + \varepsilon$$

- β_0 = Value of E(y) when x = 0 (only if x = 0 is in the interval).

- β_1 = parameter of parable translation (right, left).

- β_2 = curvature ratio (upwards or downwards).

Notes:

- Keep the polynomial order as low as possible (try transformations first).

- Always use the simplest model possible (parsimony).

- Using extrapolation could be very risky.

- It is best to use the revised version of the model to increase precision of the estimates and avoid potential multicollinearity.

Procedure

1. First, test a linear model. It is recommended to build a scatter diagram to observe its shape (linear or curvature).

2. Swiftly perform the following tests:

    2.1. Coefficient of Determination, R^2.
    2.2. Durbin-Watson test.
    2.3. Multicollinearity (VIFs).

3. If autocorrelation (Durbin-Watson in the rejection region) or multicollinearity (VIFs greater than 10) are observed, then try a model of second order.

4. If values within the acceptance criteria are not obtained, but if improvements are observed, then try with a model of third order.

5. Continue raising the order until you observe that the three initial tests have been passed (see steps 2.1, 2.2 and 2.3).

6. If the order is raised and the test parameters are not within the acceptance criteria, then try a transformation of the independent variable.

7. Repeat Step 2 (perform the three initial tests for the model of first order with the transformed variable) and, if necessary, continue raising the order until obtaining a model that passes the three initial tests.

8. If by raising the order with the transformed variable you observe that the parameters are still not found within the acceptance criteria, then try another transformation.

9. Once a model that passes all three initial tests is obtained, perform all other applicable tests.

LSSI
LEAN SIX SIGMA INSTITUTE

Example

Consider the existing relationship between the **carbon content** and the **resistance to tension** of a metal.

Carbon	Resistance
10	3
12	8
14	12
15	18
18	25
22	28
25	30
28	32
30	36
35	37
40	40
45	44
50	45
55	46
60	49

Scatter diagram

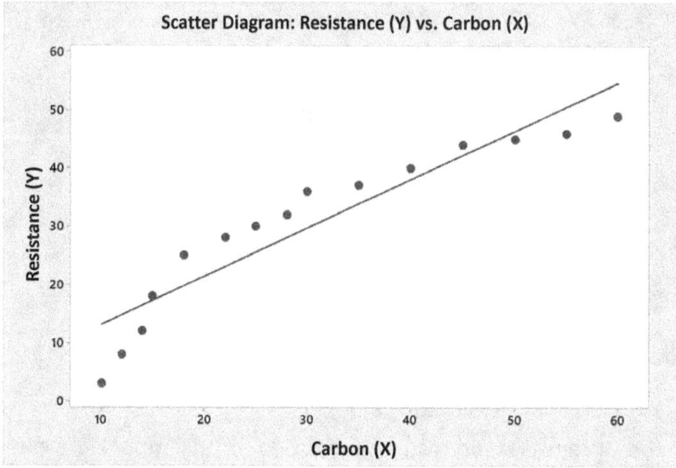

Initial tests with a linear model

Regression equation

Resistance (Y) = 4.73 + 0.8323 Carbon (X)

Coefficients

Term	Coef	SE Coef.	95% CI	T-Value	P-Value	VIF
Constant	4.73	2.99	(-1.74, 11.20)	1.58	0.138	
Carbon (X)	0.8323	0.0870	(0.6444, 1.0203)	9.57	0.000	1.00

Summary of the model

S	R-Squared	Adj. R-Squared	PRESS	Pred. R-Squared	AICc	BIC
5.30043	87.56%	86.61%	515.766	82.44%	98.64	98.58

Durbin-Watson statistic

Durbin-Watson statistic = 0.280176

This model shows **autocorrelation** (low Durbin-Watson statistic). A model of second order will be tested.

Initial tests with a model of second order

Regression equation

Resistance (Y) = -13.35 + 2.206 Carbon (X) − 0.02024 Carbon2 (X2)

Coefficients

Term	Coef	SE Coef.	95% CI	T-Value	P-Value	VIF
Constant	-13.35	3.31	(-20.55, -6.15)	-4.04	0.002	
Carbon (X)	2.206	0.2270	(1.711, 2.701)	9.71	0.000	26.24
Carbon2 (X2)	-0.02024	0.00328	(-0.02740, -0.01309)	-6.17	0.000	26.24

Summary of the model

S	R-Squared	Adj. R-Squared	PRESS	Pred. R-Squared	AICc	BIC
2.70196	97.02%	96.52%	161.659	94.49%	81.04	79.87

Durbin-Watson statistic

Durbin-Watson statistic = 0.811808

Although the Durbin-Watson statistic increased for this model, we can observe multicollinearity (VIFs > 10). Nevertheless, it will be tested with a model of third order.

LSSI
LEAN SIX SIGMA INSTITUTE

Initial tests with a model of third order

Regression equation

Resistance (Y) = -30.95 + 4.315 Carbon (X) − 0.0903 Carbon2 (X2) + 0.000679 Carbon3 (X3)

Coefficients

Term	Coef	SE Coef.	95% CI	T-Value	P-Value	VIF
Constant	-30.95	4.87	(-41.67, -20.23)	-6.36	0.000	
Carbon (X)	4.315	0.542	(3.121, 5.508)	7.96	0.000	341.08
Carbon2 (X2)	-0.0903	0.0174	(-0.1287, -0.0519)	-5.18	0.000	1690.37
Carbon3 (X3)	0.000679	0.000168	(0.000310, 0.001048)	4.05	0.002	560.15

Summary of the model

S	R-Squared	Adj. R-Squared	PRESS	Pred. R-Squared	AICc	BIC
1.78895	98.80%	98.47%	61.4123	97.91%	72.03	68.91

Durbin-Watson statistic

Durbin-Watson statistic = 1.38187

Although the Durbin-Watson statistic improved, the FIV values are too high. This will be the trend as we continue to raise the order. Therefore, the model will be tested with the transformed variable.

Transformation of the independent variable

In these cases, a very useful transformation involves subtracting the average of all the values of X from the values of X themselves. The following table reflects the results of doing so:

Resistance (Y)	Carbon-m (X)
3	-20.6
8	-18.6
12	-16.6
18	-15.6
25	-12.6
28	-8.6
30	-5.6
32	-2.6
36	-0.6
37	4.4
40	9.4
44	14.4
45	19.4
46	24.4
49	29.4

- The table shows that approximately half of the values are negative while the other half are positive values.

- The three initial tests will be performed for the model of first order with the transformed variable.

Initial tests with a linear model

Regression equation

Resistance (Y) = 30.20 + 0.8323 (Carbon-m) (X)

Coefficients

Term	Coef	SE Coef.	95% CI	T-Value	P-Value	VIF
Constant	30.20	1.37	(27.24, 33.16)	22.07	0.000	
(Carbon-m) (X)	0.8323	0.0870	(0.6444, 1.0203)	9.57	0.000	1.00

Summary of the model

S	R-Squared	Adj. R-Squared	PRESS	Pred. R-Squared	AICc	BIC
5.30043	87.56%	86.61%	515.766	82.44%	98.64	98.58

Durbin-Watson statistic

Durbin-Watson statistic = 0.280176

This model shows **autocorrelation** (low Durbin-Watson statistic).
A model of second order will be tested.

Initial tests with a model of second order

Regression equation

Resistance (Y) = 35.21 + 0.9624 (Carbon-m) (X) − 0.02024 (Carbon-m)2(X2)

Coefficients

Term	Coef	SE Coef.	95% CI	T-Value	P-Value	VIF
Constant	35.21	1.07	(32.88, 37.54)	32.88	0.000	
(Carbon-m) (X)	0.9674	0.0495	(0.8596, 1.0752)	19.56	0.000	1.24
(Carbon-m)2 (X2)	-0.02024	0.00328	(-0.02740, -0.01309)	-6.17	0.000	1.24

Summary of the model

S	R-Squared	Adj. R-Squared	PRESS	Pred. R-Squared	AICc	BIC
2.70196	97.02%	96.52%	161.659	94.49%	81.04	79.87

Durbin-Watson statistic

Durbin-Watson statistic = 0.811808

The Durbin-Watson statistic increased for this model (although it is still found within the region of autocorrelation), but we do not observe multicollinearity. It will be tested with a model of third order.

LSSI
LEAN SIX SIGMA INSTITUTE

Initial tests with a model of third order

Regression equation

Resistance (Y) = 35.995 + 0.6966 (Carbon-m) (X) − 0.02795 (Carbon-m)2(X2) + 0.000679 (Carbon-m)3(X3)

Coefficients

Term	Coef	SE Coef.	95% CI	T-Value	P-Value	VIF
Constant	35.995	0.735	(34.377, 37.613)	48.97	0.000	
(Carbon-m) (X)	0.6966	0.0745	(0.5327, 0.8606)	9.35	0.000	6.44
(Carbon-m)2 (X2)	-0.02795	0.00289	(-0.03431, -0.02159)	-9.67	0.000	2.20
(Carbon-m)3 (X3)	0.000679	0.000168	(0.000310, 0.001048)	4.05	0.002	9.12

Summary of the model

S	R-Squared	Adj. R-Squared	PRESS	Pred. R-Squared	AICc	BIC
1.78895	98.80%	98.47%	61.4123	97.91%	72.03	68.91

Durbin-Watson statistic

Durbin-Watson statistic = 1.38187

The team should analyze in which region the Durbin-Watson statistic is found, since VIF values are now closer to 10 (still in the acceptance region).

- The Durbin-Watson statistic = 1.38187. With n = 15, p = 4, and using α = 0.05, we obtain the DW table: dL = 0,81396 and dU = 1,75014. The value is found within the inconclusive region. In this case, it is recommended to examine the diagram of independence:

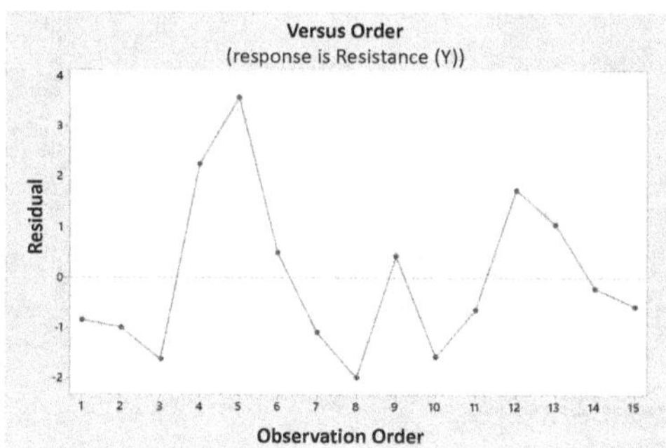

Given that no patterns are detected in the diagram, the model passes both the independence and the Durbin-Watson tests.

1. Estimation of the final model's parameters

The final model is:

Regression equation

Resistance (Y) = 35.995 + 0.6966 (Carbon-m) (X) − 0.02795 (Carbon-m)2(X2)
+ 0.000679 (Carbon-m)3(X3)

The remaining tests will be performed for this model; they are the same that were performed for multiple regression. It is not necessary to repeat the test that have already been performed.

2. Statistical tests for the final model

When it comes to polynomial regression, the following tests must be performed:

2.1 Test for significance of regression.
2.2 Test for the significance of variable X.
2.3 Stepwise regression (variable selection).
2.4 Best subsets (variable selection).
2.5 Coefficient of determination, R^2. ✓
2.6 Adjusted multiple coefficient of determination.
2.7 Normality test (of residuals).
2.8 Constant variance test.
2.9 Test for independence (of residuals). ✓
2.10 PRESS/SSE relationship.
2.11 Durbin-Watson test. ✓
2.12 Multicollinearity. ✓

Results for tests 2.1 and 2.2

Results and interpretation using **Minitab**:

Analysis of Variance

Source	Df	Seq. SS	Contribution	Adj. SS	Adj. MS	F-Value	P-Value
Regression	3	2901.20	98.80%	2901.20	967.065	302.17	0.000
(Carbon-m)(X)	1	2571.17	87.56%	279.84	279.835	87.44	0.000
(Carbon-m)2(X2)	1	277.62	9.45%	299.38	299.382	93.55	0.000
(Carbon-m)3(X3)	1	52.40	1.78%	52.40	52.403	16.37	0.002
Error	11	35.20	1.20%	35.20	3.200		
Total	14	2936.40	100.00%				

- Regression has significance: p-value = 0.000 < 0.05.

- The term (Carbon-m)(X) has significance: p-value = 0.000 < 0.05.

- The term (Carbon-m)2(X2) has significance: p-value = 0.000 < 0.05.

- The term (Carbon-m)3(X3) has significance : p-value = 0.002 < 0.05.

Result for test 2.3

Stepwise selection

Candidate terms: (Carbon-m)(X), (Carbon-m)2(X2), (Carbon-m)3(X3)

	-------Step 1-------		-------Step 2-------		-------Step 3-------	
	Coef	P	Coef	P	Coef	P
Constant	30.20		35.21		35.995	
(Carbon-m)(X)	0.8323	0.000	0.9674	0.000	0.6966	0.000
(Carbon-m)2(X2)			-0.02024	0.000	-0.02795	0.000
(Carbon-m)3(X3)					0.000679	0.002
S		5.30043		2.70196		1.78895
R-Sq.		87.56%		97.02%		98.80%
R-Sq. (Adj.)		86.61%		96.52%		98.47%
Mallows' Cp		103.12		18.37		4.00
AICc		98.64		81.04		72.03
BIC		98.58		79.87		68.91

α to enter = 0.15, α to remove = 0.15

From these results, it is verified that the three terms must remain in the model.

Result for test 2.4

From these results, it is verified that the three terms must remain in the model.

The response is Resistance (Y)

Vars	R-Sq	Adj. R-Sq	Pred. R-Sq	Mallows'Cp	S	(Carbon-m)(X)	(Carbon-m)2(X2)	(Carbon-m)3(X3)
1	87.6	86.6	82.4	103.1	5.3004	X		
1	63.2	60.4	23.0	326.3	9.1129			X
2	97.0	96.5	94.5	18.4	2.7020	X	X	
2	89.3	87.5	75.8	89.4	5.1238		X	X
3	98.8	98.5	97.9	4.0	1.7890	X	X	X

Results for tests 2.6 and 2.10

- In this case, R^2adj = 96.52% and is nearly equal to R^2 = 97.02%.

- The value for PRESS/SSE = 61.4123/35.20 = 1.745 < 2. Therefore, the model has good predictive capability.

- Keep in mind that when it comes to predictions, it is necessary to perform the same transformation on the value for "Carbon" in order to find the appropriate model (i.e., subtract the value from the average).

2.7. Normality test

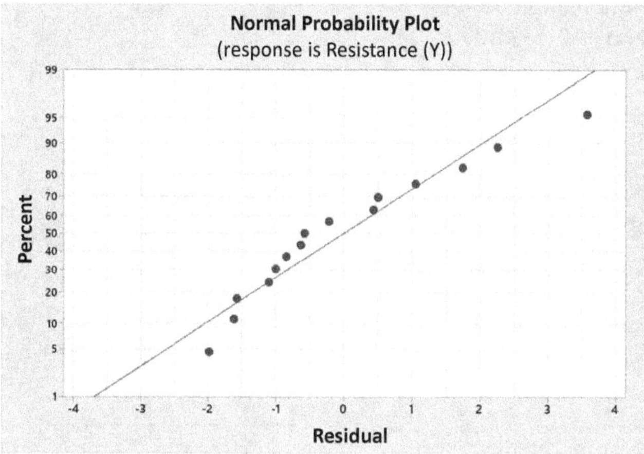

Normality is accepted.

2.8. Constant variance test

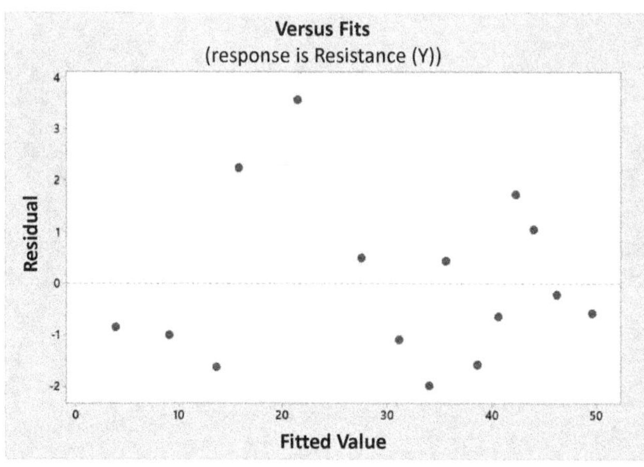

Constant variance is accepted.

Exercise

Analyze the relationship between the **pressure of a gas (Y)** and its **temperature (X)**.

Temperature	Pressure
100	50
110	40
120	30
130	25
140	21
150	22
160	21
170	27
180	30
190	40
200	47
210	50
220	60
230	70
240	80

LSSI
LEAN SIX SIGMA INSTITUTE

Response Surface Design 

Learning objectives

1. Understand how to use Response Surface Design to obtain an optimal operating region (response).
2. Learn how to define the factors that optimize the value of the response variable.

Contenidos

> Definition
> Procedure
> Example
> Design with center points
> Steepest ascent/descent method
> Central composite design (CCD)
> Obtaining a stationary point
> Exercise

Response Surface Design

Response Surface Methodology

Response Surface Design is a modeling technique of the behaviors of process characteristics.

Objective

To obtain an *optimal operating region* (response) for a process characteristic.

Procedure

- A. Apply a first-order model (factorial design).
- B. Add center point experiments to the model.
- C. Apply a steepest ascent/descent model.
- D. Propose a central composite design.
- E. Obtain a stationary point.

Source: Box and Draper (1987); Montgomery (1997); Myers and Montgomery (1995).

A. Apply a first-order model (factorial design).

1. Build a factorial design to define significant factors and interactions, and to obtain the corresponding first-order regression model.

2. Conduct all tests for the model.

3. Define the final regression model.

4. Build factorial plots to define levels for each significant factor in which we obtain the best response.

5. Build a contour plot to establish the direction in which new experiments should be conducted in order to optimize the response variable.

LSSI
LEAN SIX SIGMA INSTITUTE

B. Add center point experiments to the model in order to determine that no curvature exists within the observed region.

   6. Demonstrate lack of significance in the curvature.

C. Apply a steepest ascent /descent model to find the nearest optimal point.

   7. Determine the proximity of the optimal point.

D. Propose a central composite design to define the second-order model in the optimal point region.

   8. Conduct all tests on the second-order model.

   9. Build a contour plot to establish a visual approximation of the optimal point.

E. Obtain a stationary point.

Example

Time is represented in seconds and hundredths of a second. E.g., 176 represents 1 sec and 76 hundredths.

This first design was made with 2 genuine replicates in the order indicated by the RunOrder column.

StdOrder	RunOrder	Wings	Body	Width	Time
1	14	2	2	1	176
2	9	3	2	1	225
3	12	2	3	1	159
4	6	3	3	1	211
5	3	2	2	1.5	171
6	7	3	2	1.5	224
7	11	2	3	1.5	158
8	5	3	3	1.5	195
9	2	2	2	1	161
10	16	3	2	1	212
11	10	2	3	1	159
12	4	3	3	1	197
13	15	2	2	1.5	186
14	13	3	2	1.5	227
15	1	2	3	1.5	154
16	8	3	3	1.5	215

Factorial Regression: Time versus Wings, Body, Width

Analysis of Variance

Source	DF	Adj SS	Adj MS	F-Value	P-Value
Model	7	10403.7	1486.25	19.18	0.000
Linear	3	10298.8	3432.92	44.30	0.000
Wings	1	9120.3	9120.25	117.68	0.000
Body	1	1122.3	1122.25	14.48	0.005
Width	1	56.2	56.25	0.73	0.419
2-Way Interactions	3	92.7	30.92	0.40	0.758
Wings*Body	1	2.2	2.25	0.03	0.869
Wings*Width	1	0.3	0.25	0.00	0.956
Body*Width	1	90.2	90.25	1.16	0.312
3-Way Interactions	1	12.3	12.25	0.16	0.701
Wings*Body*Width	1	12.3	12.25	0.16	0.701
Error	8	620.0	77.50		
Total	15	11023.7			

Coded Coefficients

Term	Effect	Coef	SE Coef	T-Value	P-Value	VIF
Constant		189.38	2.20	86.05	0.000	
Wings	47.75	23.87	2.20	10.85	0.000	1.00
Body	-16.75	-8.38	2.20	-3.81	0.005	1.00
Width	3.75	1.88	2.20	0.85	0.419	1.00
Wings*Body	-0.75	-0.37	2.20	-0.17	0.869	1.00
Wings*Width	0.25	0.13	2.20	0.06	0.956	1.00
Body*Width	-4.75	-2.38	2.20	-1.08	0.312	1.00
Wings*Body*Width	1.75	0.88	2.20	0.40	0.701	1.00

Regression Equation in Uncoded Units

Time = -73 + 94 Wings + 55 Body + 140 Width - 19.0 Wings*Body - 34.0 Wings*Width - 54.0 Body*Width + 14.0 Wings*Body*Width

LSSI
LEAN SIX SIGMA INSTITUTE

Pareto Chart of the standardized effects

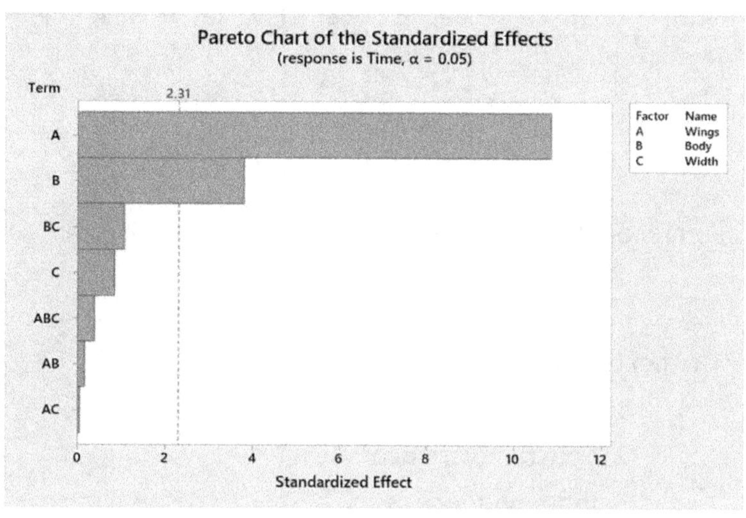

Final model after analysis

Analysis of Variance

Source	DF	Adj SS	Adj MS	F-Value	P-Value
Model	2	10242.5	5121.25	85.22	0.000
Linear	2	10242.5	5121.25	85.22	0.000
Wings	1	9120.3	9120.25	151.76	0.000
Body	1	1122.3	1122.25	18.67	0.001
Error	13	781.3	60.10		
Lack-of-Fit	5	161.3	32.25	0.42	0.825
Pure Error	8	620.0	77.50		
Total	15	11023.7			

Model Summary

S	R-sq	R-sq(adj)	R-sq(pred)
7.75217	92.91%	91.82%	89.26%

Coded Coefficients

Term	Effect	Coef	SE Coef	T-Value	P-Value	VIF
Constant		189.38	1.94	97.71	0.000	
Wings	47.75	23.87	1.94	12.32	0.000	1.00
Body	-16.75	-8.38	1.94	-4.32	0.001	1.00

Final model for the experiment in coded units is:

Time = 189.38 + 23.87 Wings − 8.38 Body

The next step is to verify:

1. Normality Test
2. Constant variance
3. Independence

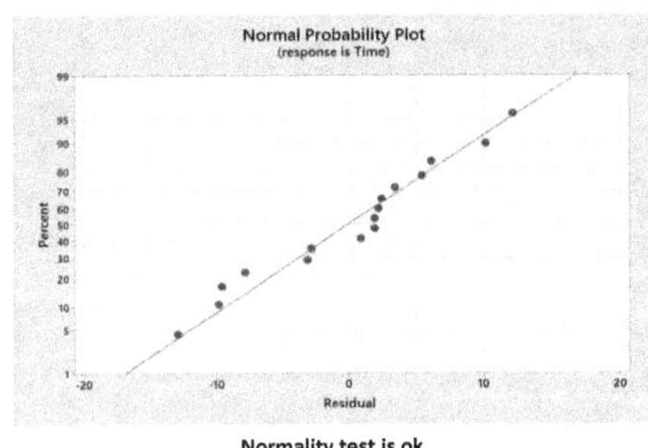

Normality test is ok.

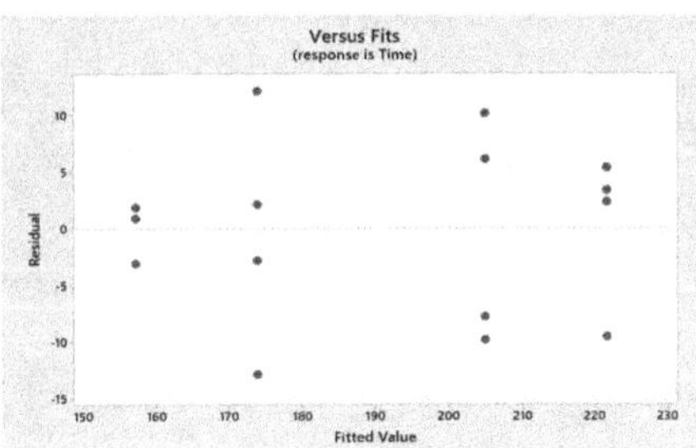

Constant Variance is ok.

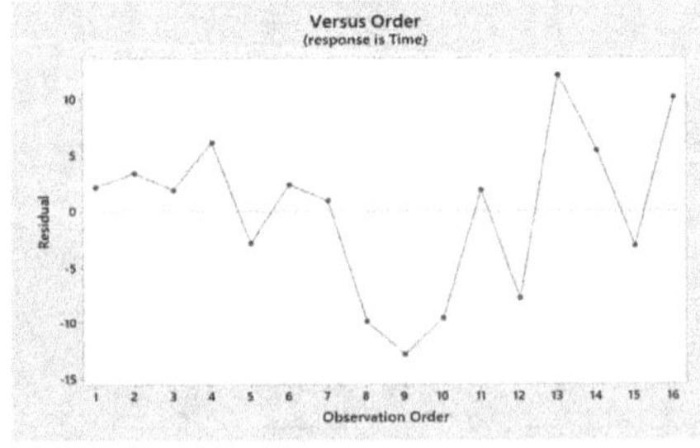

Independence is ok.

LSSI — LEAN SIX SIGMA INSTITUTE

Regression model with significant effects

Coefficients

Term	Coef	SE Coef	T-Value	P-Value	VIF
Constant	111.9	13.8	8.08	0.000	
Wings	47.75	3.88	12.32	0.000	1.00
Body	-16.75	3.88	-4.32	0.001	1.00

The final model for the experiment in uncoded units is:

Time = 111.9 + 47.75 Wings − 16.75 Body

Next step is verification with all regression tests

Regression Analysis: Time versus Wings, Body

Model Summary

S	R-sq	R-sq(adj)	PRESS	R-sq(pred)	AICc	BIC
7.75217	92.91%	91.82%	1183.43	89.26%	119.26	118.71

Analysis of Variance

Source	DF	Seq SS	Contribution	Adj SS	Adj MS	F-Value	P-Value
Regression	2	10242.5	92.91%	10242.5	5121.25	85.22	0.000
Wings	1	9120.3	82.73%	9120.3	9120.25	151.76	0.000
Body	1	1122.3	10.18%	1122.3	1122.25	18.67	0.001
Error	13	781.3	7.09%	781.3	60.10		
Lack-of-Fit	1	2.3	0.02%	2.3	2.25	0.03	0.855
Pure Error	12	779.0	7.07%	779.0	64.92		
Total	15	11023.8	100.00%				

Durbin-Watson Statistic

Durbin-Watson Statistic =   1.52128

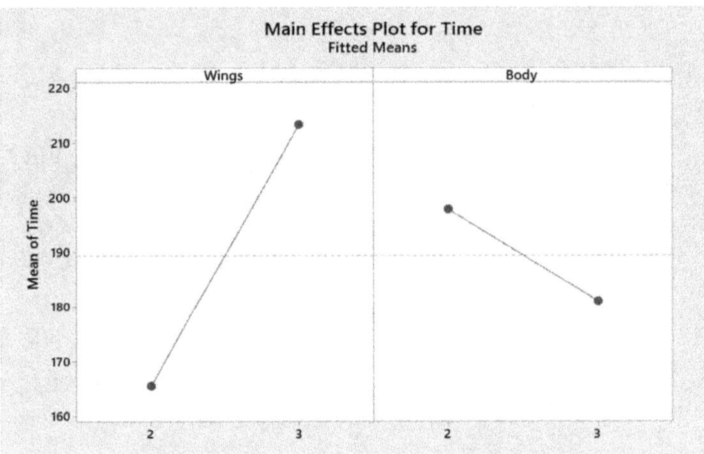

The values to maximize our response (Flight Time) are:
Wings = 3" and **Body = 2"**.

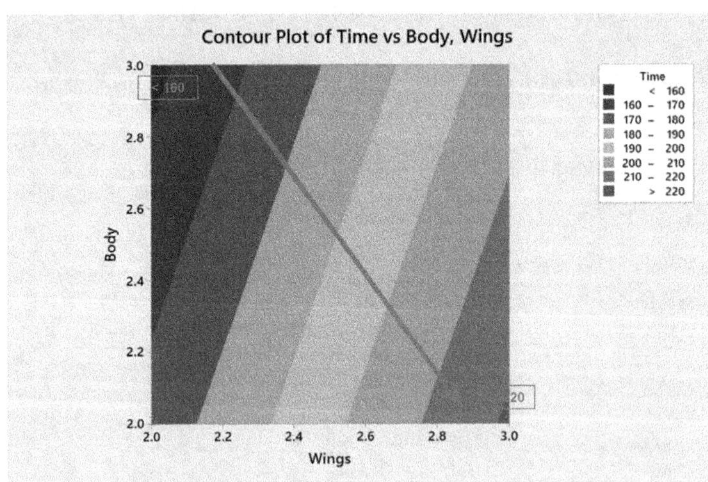

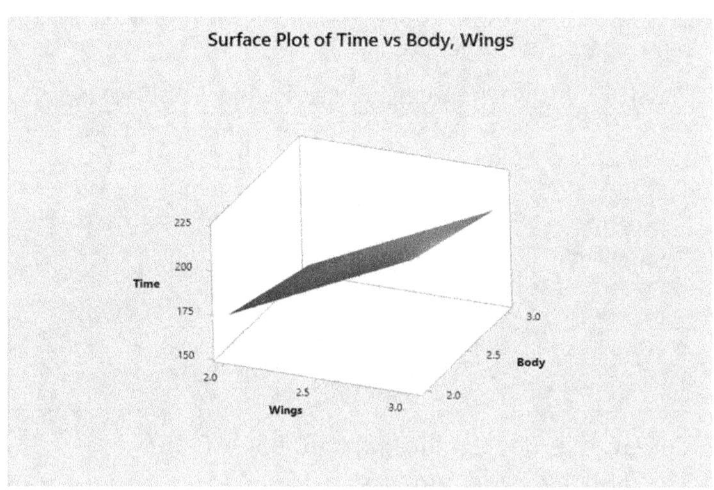

Design with Center Points

To maximize the response, more experiments need to be conducted while **increasing Wing length and decreasing Body length**.

Three runs with center points will be added to our original design (Wing length = 2.5", Body length = 2.5" and Body Width = 1.25") to evaluate curvature.

CenterPt	Wings	Body	Width	Time
1	2.00	2.00	1.00	176
1	3.00	2.00	1.00	225
1	2.00	3.00	1.00	159
1	3.00	3.00	1.00	211
1	2.00	2.00	1.50	171
1	3.00	2.00	1.50	224
1	2.00	3.00	1.50	158
1	3.00	3.00	1.50	195
1	2.00	2.00	1.00	161
1	3.00	2.00	1.00	212
1	2.00	3.00	1.00	159
1	3.00	3.00	1.00	197
1	2.00	2.00	1.50	186
1	3.00	2.00	1.50	227
1	2.00	3.00	1.50	154
1	3.00	3.00	1.50	215
0	2.50	2.50	1.25	195
0	2.50	2.50	1.25	189
0	2.50	2.50	1.25	185

Factorial Regression: Time vs. Wings, Body, Center Pt.

Significance of curvature

Source	DF	Adj SS	Adj MS	F-Value	P-Value
Model	3	10242.7	3414.24	61.56	0.000
Linear	2	10242.5	5121.25	92.34	0.000
Alas	1	9120.2	9120.25	164.44	0.000
Cuerpo	1	1122.3	1122.25	20.23	0.000
Curvature	1	0.2	0.21	0.00	0.951
Error	15	831.9	55.46		
Lack-of-Fit	5	161.3	32.25	0.48	0.783
Pure Error	10	670.7	67.07		
Total	18	11074.6			

Curvature is not significant $p = (0.951 > 0,05)$.
The model in coded units is:

Time = 189.38 + 23.88 Wings − 8.38 Body.

Steepest Ascent/Descent Method

To move into the direction of the response's optimal point (maximize):

1. Define the increment (ΔX_i) for the variable with the largest coefficient $\hat{\beta}_i$ in our model (absolute value).

   Xs are coded variables (their levels are -1 and 1 instead of *real* or *original* levels).

2. The increasing value for the rest of the variables will be:

$$\Delta X_j = \frac{\hat{\beta}_j \Delta X_i}{\hat{\beta}_i} \quad \forall j, j \neq i$$

To **minimize** the response, change the signs (i.e., positive and negative) of βs.

LSSI
LEAN SIX SIGMA INSTITUTE

3. Convert the increments of the coded values into increments of the uncoded (original) values (O_i).

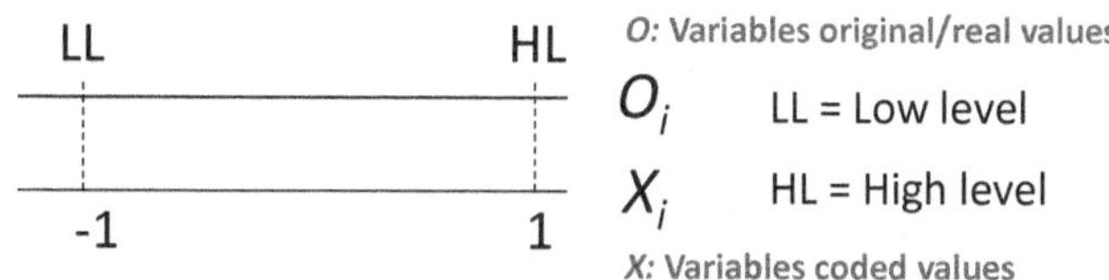

Equivalency:

HL - LL ----- 2

ΔO_i --------- ΔX_i

$$\Delta X_i = \frac{2\Delta O_i}{(HL - LL)}$$

$$\Delta O_i = \frac{(HL - LL)\Delta X_i}{2}$$

Our model in coded units is:

Time = 189.38 + 23.87 Wings − 8.38 Body.

Steepest ascent method:

Variable 1 is Wings (largest coefficient)

1. Increment for $\Delta O_1 = 0,5$. Therefore ΔX_1 (for Wings) is:

$$\Delta X_1 = \frac{2 \cdot \Delta O_1}{HL - LL} = \frac{2 \cdot 0,5}{3 - 2} = 1$$

2. Increment ΔX_2 for variable Body is:

$$\Delta X_2 = \frac{\hat{\beta}_2 \cdot \Delta X_1}{\hat{\beta}_1} = \frac{-8.38 \cdot 1}{23.87} = -0.351$$

To maximize the response, we have to move **23.87** units in **Wings** for each **−8.38** units in **Body**. To minimize, the direction would be the opposite.

3. Change the increments to the original values (O_i), with $\Delta O_1 = 0.5\,''$:

$$\Delta O_2 = \frac{(HL - LL) \cdot \Delta X_2}{2} = \frac{(3 - 2) \cdot (-0.351)}{2} = -0.176$$

Because **Width** is not significant, we will leave it at a level of **1**.

	X_1	X_2	O_1	O_2	
Central Points	0.000	0.000	2.500	2.500	
Delta	1	-0.351	0.500	-0.176	Time
1 Delta	1	-0.0351	3.000	2.324	224.67
2 Delta	2	-0.0702	3.500	2.148	247.33
3 Delta	3	-0.1053	4.000	1.972	282.33
4 Delta	4	-0.1404	4.500	1.796	229.67

The response **time** is the average of three launches. In 4 Delta, the helicopter presents considerable variation, as well as an unstable flight.

Vecinity of the optimal point

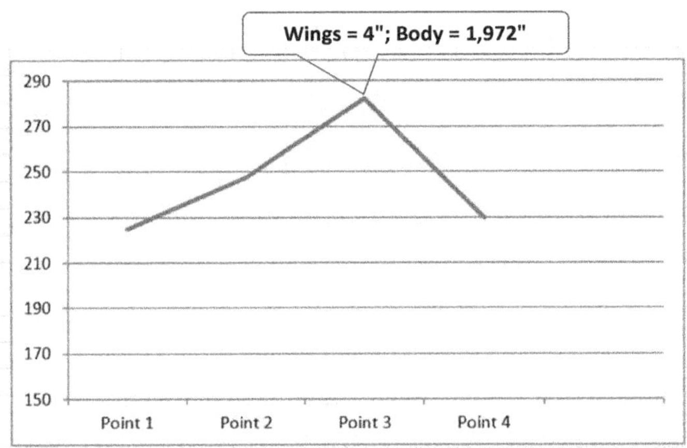

In the vicinity of **4" Wings** and a **1.972" Body (Step 3)** we find the best operating conditions to maximize flight time.

LSSI
LEAN SIX SIGMA INSTITUTE

Central Composite Design (CCD)

A second order model will be applied (**Central Composite Design, CCD**)

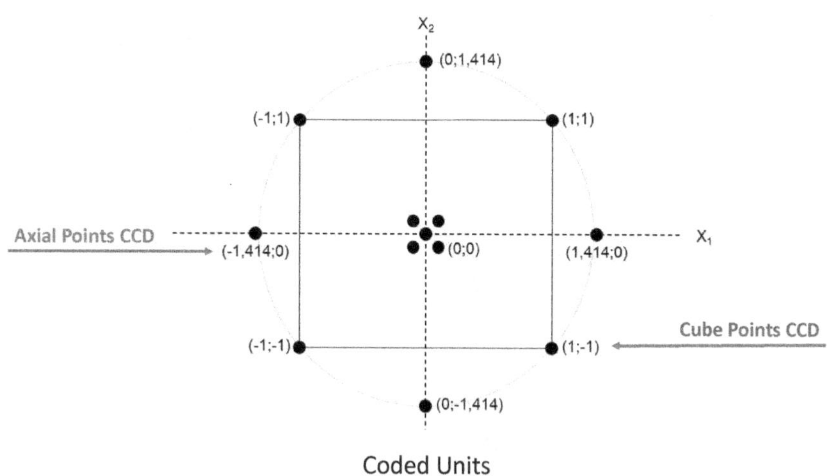

Axial Points

StdOrder	RunOrder	PtType	Blocks	Wings	Body	Time
13	1	0	1	4.0000	1.9720	288
7	2	-1	1	4.0000	1.7960	268
5	3	-1	1	3.5000	1.9720	262
2	4	1	1	4.3536	1.8475	258
1	5	1	1	3.6464	1.8475	255
12	6	0	1	4.0000	1.9720	285
8	7	-1	1	4.0000	2.1480	268
6	8	-1	1	4.5000	1.9720	270
4	9	1	1	4.3536	2.0965	260
3	10	1	1	3.6464	2.0965	255
10	11	0	1	4.0000	1.9720	282
9	12	0	1	4.0000	1.9720	278
11	13	0	1	4.0000	1.9720	287

Response Surface Regression: Time vs. Wings, Body

Analysis of Variance

Source	DF	Adj SS	Adj MS	F-Value	P-Value
Model	5	1541.36	308.272	8.06	0.008
Linear	2	47.13	23.564	0.62	0.567
Wings	1	46.63	46.627	1.22	0.306
Body	1	0.50	0.500	0.01	0.912
Square	2	1493.23	746.615	19.51	0.001
Wings*Wings	1	920.00	920.000	24.04	0.002
Body*Body	1	766.96	766.957	20.04	0.003
2-Way Interaction	1	1.00	1.000	0.03	0.876
Wings*Body	1	1.00	1.000	0.03	0.876
Error	7	267.87	38.268		
Lack-of-Fit	3	201.87	67.291	4.08	0.104
Pure Error	4	66.00	16.500		
Total	12	1809.23			

Quadratic terms for the **Wings** and **Body** are significant.

2-Way interaction term is not significant. Therefore, it will be eliminated and the experiment will be run and analyzed again.

Analysis of Variance

Source	DF	Adj SS	Adj MS	F-Value	P-Value
Model	4	1540.36	385.090	11.46	0.002
Linear	2	47.13	23.564	0.70	0.524
Wings	1	46.63	46.627	1.39	0.273
Body	1	0.50	0.500	0.01	0.906
Square	2	1493.23	746.615	22.21	0.001
Wings*Wings	1	920.00	920.000	27.37	0.001
Body*Body	1	766.96	766.957	22.82	0.001
Error	8	268.87	33.609		
Lack-of-Fit	4	202.87	50.718	3.07	0.151
Pure Error	4	66.00	16.500		
Total	12	1809.23			

Coded Coefficients

Term	Coef	SE Coef	T-Value	P-Value	VIF
Constant	284.00	2.59	109.54	0.000	
Wings	3.41	2.90	1.18	0.273	1.00
Body	0.35	2.90	0.12	0.906	1.00
Wings*Wings	-23.00	4.40	-5.23	0.001	1.02
Body*Body	-21.00	4.40	-4.78	0.001	1.02

Model Summary

S	R-sq	R-sq(adj)	R-sq(pred)
5.79733	85.14%	77.71%	40.20%

Regression Equation in Uncoded Units

Time = -3856 + 743 Wings + 2676 Body - 92.0 Wings*Wings - 678 Body*Body

Next step is to perform Normality, Constant Variance, and Independence Tests.

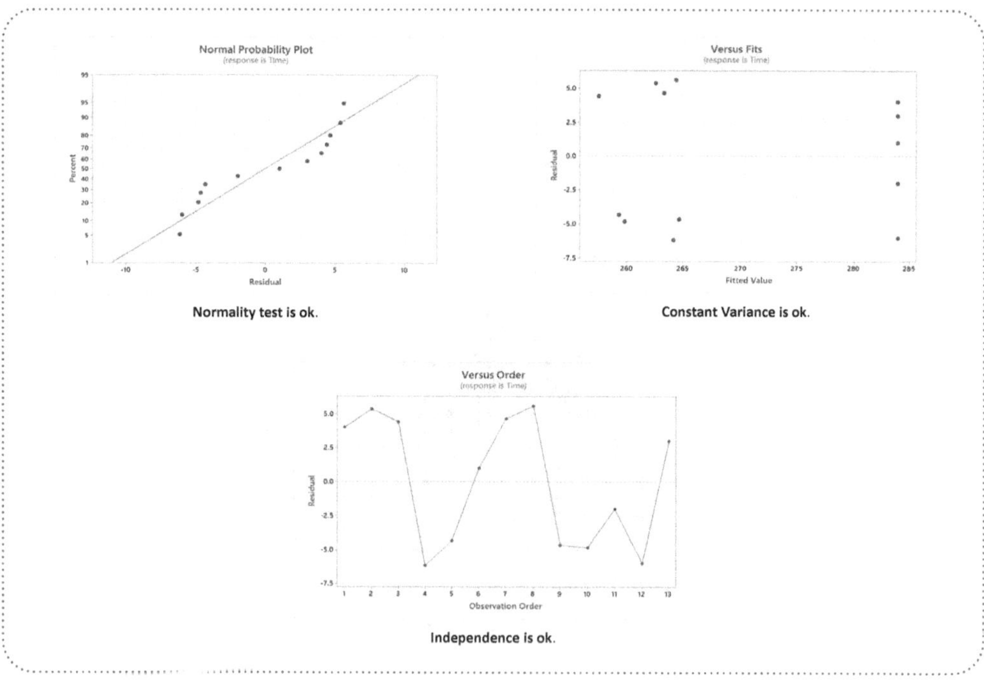

Normality test is ok.

Constant Variance is ok.

Independence is ok.

Contour Plot

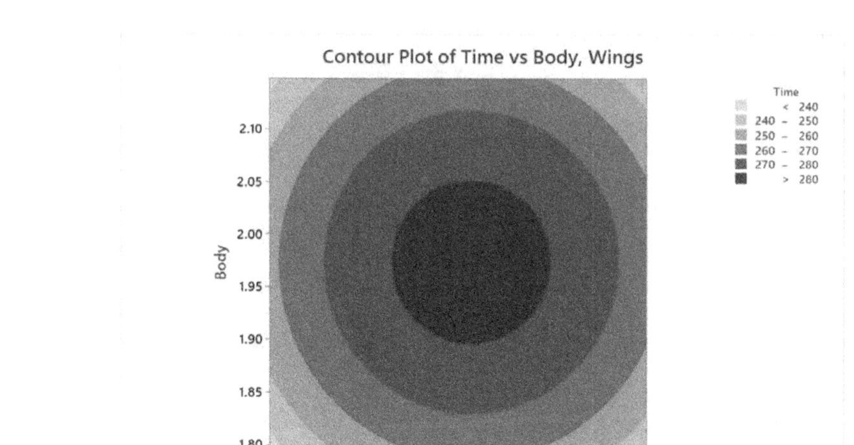

Optimal point is close to **4.05" Wings** and **1.975" Body.**

Surface Plot

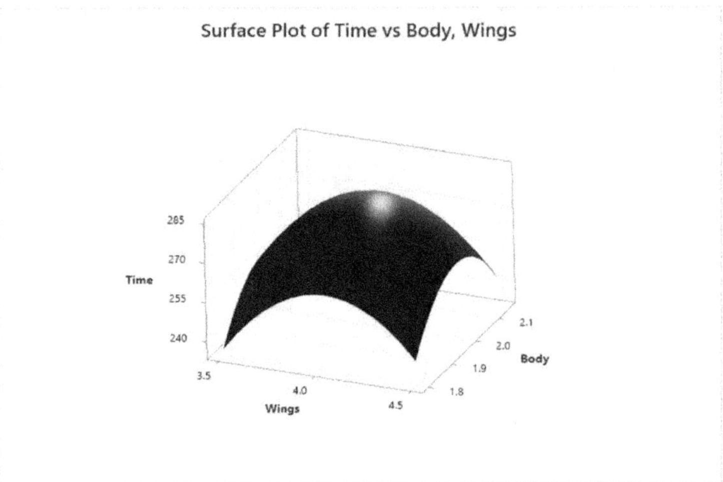

Optimal point is close to **4" Wings** and **2" Body.**

Obtaining a Stationary Point

Using response optimizer in Minitab we obtain:

Time = 284.1279, Wings = 4.0354" and Body = 1.9737".

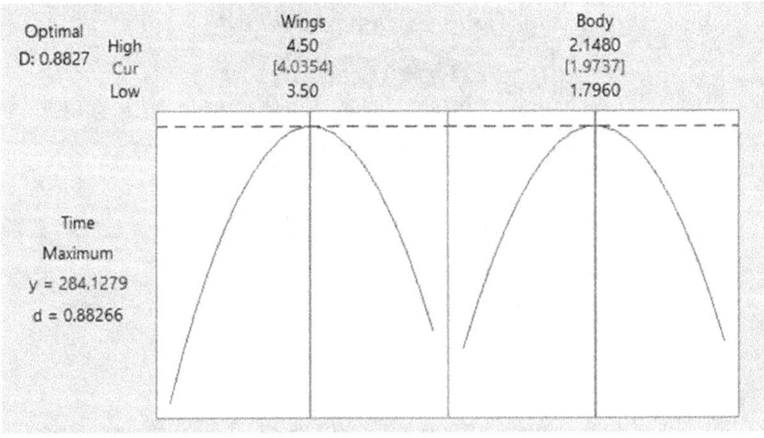

LSSI LEAN SIX SIGMA INSTITUTE

An exercise will be provided by the instructor. **Calculate the optimal point** by following all the steps shown in the previous slides.

Lean Company

Beyond manufacturing

Learning objectives

1. Understand how the philosophy of speed and quality work as an integral systematic model.
2. Determine how to implement Lean methodologies and tools in all functional areas of an organization.
3. Analyze all elements of an organization to integrate them into a single system to improve decision-making.

Content

> Background
> What is Lean Company?
> How is Lean Company implemented?
> Lean Company assessment
> Transformation process by function

Background

Common challenges businesses face

- Late delivery of products and services.
- Poor communication.
- Low inventory turnover.
- Poor inventory accuracy.
- Deficient communication.
- Inaccurate minimum order quantities.
- Constant reprogramming.
- Unknown real demand.
- Unreliable forecasts.
- Shortage of materials, supplies or products.
- Excess of materials, supplies or products.

Traditional companies

Imagine asking the following questions to different managers in the same company:

- What is the real demand for the products / services?
- What is the company's operating capacity?
- Where are the main bottlenecks?
- Are you making or losing money?
- What do customers think about the quality of the products/services?

LSSI
LEAN SIX SIGMA INSTITUTE

Example of traditional structure

How the project was documented

Source: http://www.projectcartoon.com/cartoon/3

How do traditional companies work?

Management makes decisions on behalf of all areas, which significantly reduces strategic planning.

- **Management and decision-making**
- **Business planning**
- **Strategic planning**
- **Project development**
- **Meetings**
- **Measures**
- **Structure**
- **Talent development**

- Design & engineering
- Marketing
- Sales
- Logistics
- Procurement
- Warehouse & storage

- Delivery
- Manufacturing
- Accounting
- Quality
- Maintenance
- Information systems

The 3 enemies of productivity in every functional area

Beyond manufacturing

What is Lean Company?

- Integrates all elements of an organization into a single system.

- Measures and evaluates processes, not people.

- Multi-disciplinary teams.

- Focuses on talent development and results.

- Improvement as a way of life.

- External competition, not internal.

- Everyone wins!

LSSI
LEAN SIX SIGMA INSTITUTE

Key elements

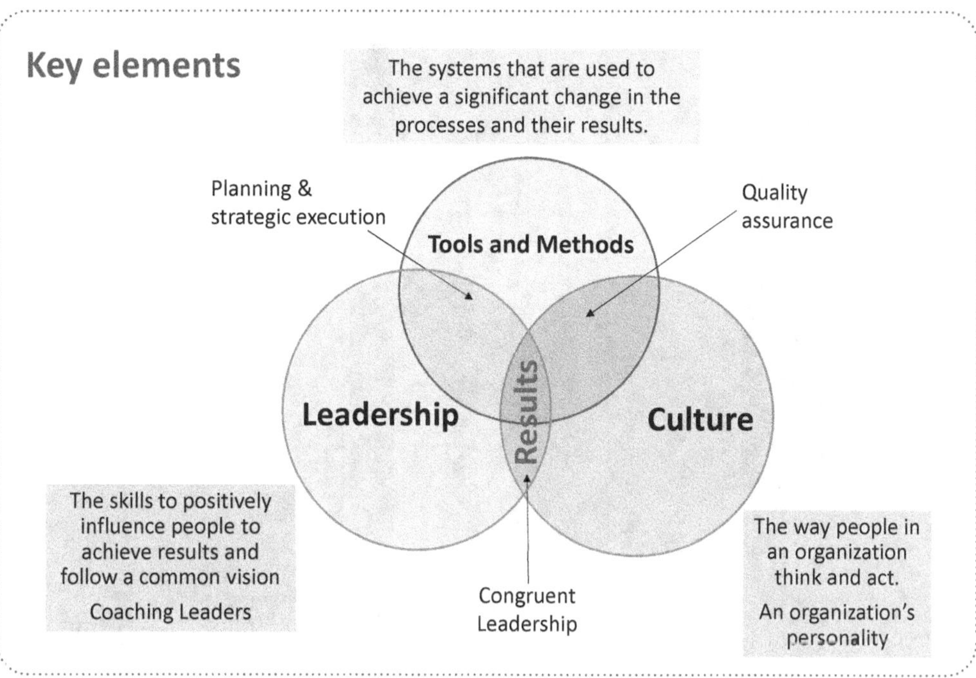

Lean Company

Lean Six Sigma is applied throughout the organization

	LEAN SIX SIGMA COMPANY											
	Upper Management	Human Resources	Research & Development	Sales & Marketing	Accounting & Finance	Procurement	Service	Manufacturing	Maintenance	Logistics	Quality	IT

STRATEGIC TOOLS
- Hoshin Kanri
- Value Stream Structure
- Value Stream Map
- Talent Development
- Agile Project Management
- Standard Work for Leaders
- Kata
- Gemba Walks

Strategic Tools

All areas use management tools to define, execute and follow up on strategies.

BASIC TOOLS
- 5S Housekeeping
- Visual Management (Andon)
- Standardize Work
- Personal (Self) Management

Tactical Tools

All areas use basic tools to support identification, development and sustainment of improvements.

LEAN	SIX SIGMA											
	Upper Management	Human Resources	Research & Development	Sales & Marketing	Accounting & Finance	Procurement	Service	Manufacturing	Maintenance	Logistics	Quality	IT

DMAIC

Tool Set

Upper Management	Human Resources	Research & Development	Sales & Marketing	Accounting & Finance	Procurement	Service	Manufacturing	Maintenance	Logistics	Quality	IT
Planning	Talent Attraction	Product Development	Mktg. Campaigns	Budget Cost Acct.	Supplier Development	Lean Service	Lean Manufacturing	Autonomous	Incoming Warehouse	Quality Deployment	Hardware
Strategic Mgmt.	Talent Development	Lean Startup	Surveys	Inventory Payroll	Purchasing			Preventive	Routing Loading	Quality System	Software
Decision Making		Design for Six Sigma	Pricing	Invoicing Credit Acct. Payable	Warehouse			Predictive	Transportation	Calibration	Communication
			Lean Retail	Financial Statements				Energy			Help Desk

How is Lean Company implemented?

1 Preparation	2 Pilot phase	3 Value Streams	4 Lean Company
1 - 3 months	*4 - 6 months*	*1 - 2 years*	*1 - 2 + years*

1 Preparation (*1 - 3 months*)
- Development of:
  - Strategy
  - Structure
  - Talent
- Project launch

2 Pilot phase (*4 - 6 months*)
- Management team
- Define pilot value streams and implementation teams
- Implementation of Lean Six Sigma tools
- Develop adaptation cycles
- Develop improvement cycles
- Certify pilot value stream

3 Value Streams (*1 - 2 years*)
- Deployment to all value streams
- Deployment to all processes
- Certification

4 Lean Company (*1 - 2 + years*)
- Certify:
  - ✓ Processes
  - ✓ Value streams
  - ✓ Company

Lean Company Assessment

Helps us understand on what Lean Company level the organization is operating.

Lean Company Assessment

	Dec-17	Dec-18	Dec-19	Comments
Results (250)	86	164	229	
Management (150)	56	76	136	
Value Stream (150)	95	130	140	
Functions (300)	97	170	271	
Culture (150)	56	90	150	
Total	390	630	925	

600 to 699	Bronze
700 to 799	Silver
800 to 899	Gold
900 to 1000	Platinum

	Dec-17	Dec-18	Dec-19
Results	34%	66%	92%
Management	37%	51%	91%
Value Stream	63%	87%	93%
1 Research & Development	46%	51%	77%
2 Sales	25%	54%	81%
3 Marketing	32%	57%	87%
4 Logistics	29%	51%	86%
5 Production / Service	29%	64%	91%
6 Accounting & Finance	29%	57%	92%
7 Maintenance	25%	66%	90%
8 Quality Management	36%	57%	91%
9 IT Systems	31%	51%	85%
Culture	37%	60%	100%

Activity   Internal Team   LSSI Coaches

Benefits:
- Identify areas of improvement.
- Define the master implementation plan.
- Define Lean system requirements.
- Evaluate progress [towards Lean Six Sigma] as company, value streams, and processes.

Lean Talent Management

What is it?

The process of developing knowledge and commitment in people, in order to perform their functions well, and deliver high quality products and services for customers at target cost and in the shortest amount of time possible.

Benefits

Nourishes high capacity and quality, and provides building blocks for:

- Committed teams.
- Valuable knowledge sharing and creation.
- Value creation and delivery.
- Continuous learning culture.

Limitation	Lean Talent Management
Overburden	Tasks are dangerous and complicated when people lack adequate knowledge to perform them
Variability	Poor training is one of the main causes of variability
Overproduction	More courses and training take place than needed
Excess inventory/ Resources	A lack of knowledge of real demand, as well as a lack of knowledge of Lean methods, which results in organizations using excess inventory to cover up inefficiencies
Waiting & Searching	During training, much time is wasted searching for conference rooms and materials. Similarly, much time is wasted waiting for both trainees and coaches
Defects/Errors	Poor training results in defects and avoidable mistakes and errors
Unnecessary Transportation & Movement	People having to attend training sessions in other cities instead of participating remotely (online) or having the training come to their location
Overprocessing	A lack of knowledge when it comes to functions and poor training results in people engaging in a great deal of rework and non-value-added tasks
Non-utilized talent	People with specific knowledge and experience are not encouraged to train colleagues

LSSI
LEAN SIX SIGMA INSTITUTE

Improving the hiring process

Interviews: During the initial interview, valuable time and effort can be saved if the interviewers help candidates learn more about the company as well as the position they are interviewing for; this way, they can identify if the job is going to be the right fit for them.

Assessments: Knowledge and experience are evaluated using tests and challenges similar to those that the candidate will face as part of the role he or she is applying for. It is necessary to create an environment that emulates the one the candidate will experience if hired; this includes situations that assess initiative, attitude, and teamwork.

Kanban – candidate files: Helps keep candidate files updated and readily available for whenever they need to be called upon for the selection process. Furthermore, it facilitates overall candidate management.

Lean Design
Product and service design

What is it?

A philosophy used to design and redesign innovative products and services that the competition finds hard to overcome in terms of value, price, cost, and development time.

Benefits:

- Improved design of products and services.

- Improved time and quality in the design process.

- Eliminated waste and variation in processes.

- Higher quality products and services – both on time and at a low-cost.

Limitations to Productivity	Lean Design
Overburden	Stress created during development More time needed to fulfill tasks
Variability	Cost variability Discrepancy between the original concept and the final product/service
Overproduction	Adding unnecessary design features/elements Overengineering
Excess inventory/ Resources	Saturated email inbox and paper trays
Waiting & Searching	Management approval Waiting for customer's input/requirements
Defects/Errors	Design errors Late engineering changes due to errors
Unnecessary Transportation & Movement	Emailing: excess messaging and irrelevant information Circulating paperwork and chasing approvals
Overprocessing	Input the same information multiple times Unnecessary reports/paperwork
Non-utilized talent	Limited or lack of decision-making power Not involving the manufacturing team during design

LSSI
LEAN SIX SIGMA INSTITUTE

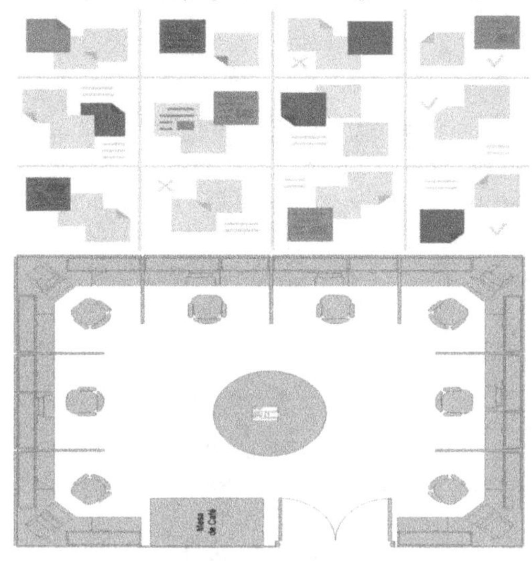

Kanban boards for project management. Provides a visual display of all planned activities

Work cell design to integrate key design personnel (design leaders) with test specialists and project managers in a continuous flow of communication and prioritization of activities.

Lean Design: example
Product design

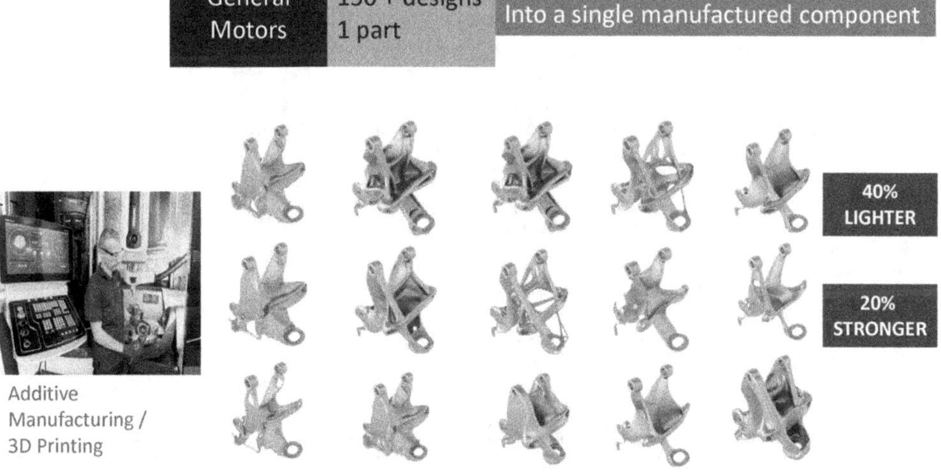

Additive Manufacturing / 3D Printing

Lean Commerce
Marketing & Sales

What is it?

- **Lean Commerce** is a philosophy that brings Lean Marketing and Lean Sales together in a collaborative process between the value stream elements.
- Lean Marketing aims to improve the process of brand development and creation as well as increase market share.
- Lean Sales aims to improve sales and benefits of the products and services offered, developing better negotiation methods.

Benefits

- Sales based on customer needs.
- Identification of real demand to synchronize value stream processes with customer needs.
- Development of creative marketing and sales strategies to gain market share and increase sales.
- Elimination of overbearing tasks that derive from internal and external business politics that turn sales into a stressful, challenging job.
- Optimization of sellers' time by eliminating unnecessary transportation and movement, defects, errors, etc.

Limitations to Productivity	Lean Commerce
Overburden	Work-related stress Significant amount of analysis and no real benefit Customer confrontations
Variability	Constant changing market trends and customer needs
Overproduction	Investing in inefficient campaigns that lack specific goals
Excess inventory/ Resources	Accumulation of irrelevant information or survey responses Storing excessive amount of products
Waiting & Searching	Management approval Slow data analysis for strategic decision-making Approvals, meetings, input for decision-making
Defects/Errors	Errors in data analysis and purchase orders Change in strategy and project prioritization High-cost, low-impact projects and campaigns
Unnecessary Transportation & Movement	Unnecessary or redundant emails and communication Displaying poor-performing products/services in catalogs
Overprocessing	Input the same information multiple times Fulfilling wrong orders
Non-utilized talent	Limited or lack of decision-making power Not involving Sales, Quality Assurance, Design, and Marketing teams Sellers with no guidance or specific goals and objectives

LSSI
LEAN SIX SIGMA INSTITUTE

Lean Marketing

Background

▸ Isolated planning.
▸ Completion takes too long.
▸ Unfocused campaigns.
▸ Unnecessary expenses.
▸ Little to no interaction with Sales and no review of results.

Transformation process

▸ Before
  ◦ Define target market
  ◦ Clear message
  ◦ Means / channels to reach target market
▸ During
  ◦ System to identify new leads
  ◦ Leads tracking
  ◦ Conversion strategy
▸ After
  ◦ How to provide a great customer experience
  ◦ Increase CLV (Customer Lifetime Value)
  ◦ Boost referrals

Results

• Reduction of marketing costs.
• Reduction of waste through extensive planning.
• Significant customer attraction VS traditional models.

Marketing Plan

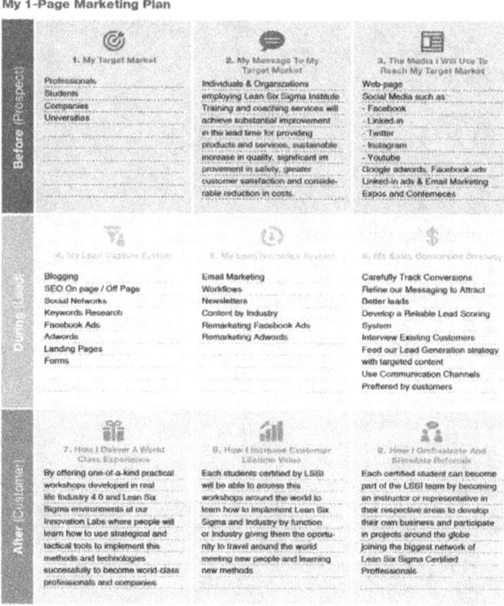

My 1-Page Marketing Plan

Sales routes

Background

	Initial Situation	Objetive	# of Visits
A Stores	5.54	6.00	Weekly
B Stores	4.05	4.50	Weekly
C Stores	3.08	3.00	Weekly

Kaizen – Sales route optimization

- ▶ Stores were classified in 3 types, according to their sales potential: A, B, and C.
- ▶ Sale routes were redefined using sales reps' input.
- ▶ A sales rep was assigned to every A store.
- ▶ All C stores are now managed by 4 sales reps with the purpose of decreasing the number of visits per week in order to cause an increase in the number of visits to B stores.

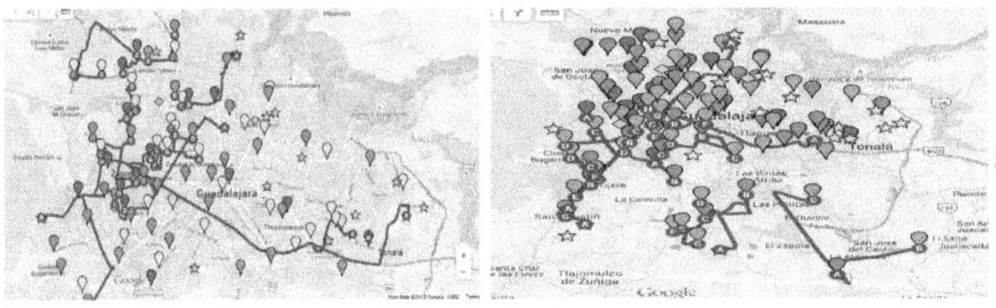

Results

Sales in Metropolitan Area

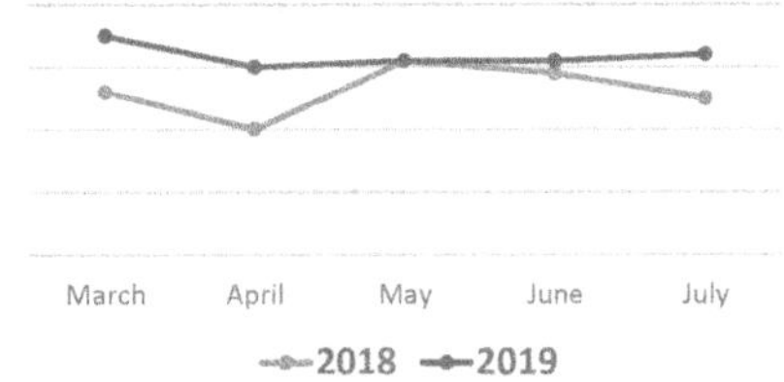

SALES INCREASED BY
16.5 %

LSSI
LEAN SIX SIGMA INSTITUTE

Kanban Consignment

Background

- High variability in sales.
- Customers with low disposable income.
- Sales per brand.
- Isolated efforts by sellers.
- Products were not properly displayed.
- High number of product returns.

Top Sales

	Product description	Sales	% of total sales
1	White bread 470g TT BIM	$ 7,428,750.00	22%
2	White bread 350g TAT BIM	$ 6,655,950.00	19%
3	White bread 600g BIM	$ 2,377,764.00	7%
4	Whole wheat 500g BIM	$ 2,337,500.00	7%
5	White bread 730g BIM	$ 1,911,668.00	6%
6	Pound cake 60g DAN	$ 1,861,110.00	5%
7	Pound cake 230g BIM	$ 1,753,485.00	5%
8	Super bread 6p 405 BIM	$ 1,609,086.00	5%
9	Pound cake A1 230g BIM	$ 1,470,608.00	4%
10	Whole wheat XL 570g GUA	$ 1,305,000.00	4%
11	Super bread 6p 205g BIM	$ 1,179,276.00	3%
12	Butter bread XL 550g GUA	$ 1,178,775.00	3%
13	Super burger bread 4p 350g BIM	$ 1,135,251.00	3%
14	White bread 580g BIM	$ 1,060,896.00	3%
15	Butter bread A1 460g BIM	$ 956,080.00	3%

Top Returns

Product description	% of return
White bread 470g TT BIM	18.60%
White bread 600g BIM	16.54%
White bread 350g TAT BIM	16.53%
Super bread 6p 205g BIM	6.80%
Whole wheat XL 570g GUA	6.64%
Super bread 6p 405 BIM	3.68%
Super burger bread 4p 350g BIM	3.68%
White bread 730g BIM	3.54%

Transformation Process

- Analysis of sales and returns patterns.
- Replenishment system for Kanban on consignment.
- Retailers pay only for the products they sell.
- Best shelf placement is negotiated — middle shelf, at eye level.
- Delivery routes are defined by store instead of by product line (1-2 deliveries per day instead of 4-6).
- Continuous analysis of buying patterns to maintain an updated Kanban.

Results

- Sales increased by 54%.
- Reduction of product returns by 82%.
- Reduction of delivery cost by 62%.

Lean Commerce

Establish Kanban system for marketing strategies to be used as needed. Examples:

- Scripts.
- Articles.
- Videos.
- Publications/Bulletins.
- Advertisements.
- Social media.
- Conferences.
- Print material.

Improve pricing strategy: Define the price that maximizes profit and reflects the true value the customer places on the benefits delivered.

Conduct statistical analysis to determine price variation and define price ranges that maximize profits.

LSSI
LEAN SIX SIGMA INSTITUTE

Lean Service

What is it?

Lean Service aims to develop highly effective organizations that provide customers with high quality services at a low cost by eliminating waste, overbearing tasks, and variability. This way, excellent services can be delivered at a reasonable cost and the value provided is greater than that of competitors.

Benefits

- High customer satisfaction.
- Improved customer service.
- Increased operational capacity.
- Increased employee job satisfaction.
- Cost reduction.
- Increase in market share.
- Increase in referrals.

Limitations to Productivity	Lean Service
Overburden	Poor time management Unsafe workplace, lack of safety equipment
Variability	Inconsistency in cost, delivery time, and quality
Overproduction	Performing activities the customers do not need Analysis that does not provide valuable insight
Excess inventory/ Resources	Excess material and/or resources Poor resource allocation
Waiting & Searching	Management approval Customer wait times
Defects/Errors	Errors in set up/preparation: registrations, reservations Services do not meet customers' expectations and requirements
Unnecessary Transportation & Movement	Unnecessary transportation of customers and/or resources Redundant processes when providing the service
Overprocessing	Unnecessary meetings, reports, and paperwork Requesting the same information multiple times
Non-utilized talent	Assigning employees to non-value-added activities Poor training and coaching

Lean Service: Banking (loan processing)

Before

▸ Capacity = 120 loans processed per month.
▸ Low earnings.
▸ High fixed costs per processed loans.
▸ Constant re-work caused by human error.
▸ Excessive waiting time.
▸ Deficient communication between departments.

Transformation Process

• Creation of a Hoshin Kanri and box score.
• Implementation of 5S Housekeeping workshops.
• Design and installation of Andon boards in the workplace.
• Implementation of talent development system conducting cross-training and compensation models.
• Redesign of areas by continuous flow, rather than by departments.
  • Simple loans pod/work cell.
  • Complex loans pod/work cell.

Results

• Capacity = 312 processed loans per month.
• Cost per loan decreased by more than 40%.
• The same resources were able to perform 3x faster.
• Earnings increased more than 22% per loan.

LSSI
LEAN SIX SIGMA INSTITUTE

Lean Maintenance

What is it?

- Lean Maintenance aims to enable and achieve continuity of business and ensure optimal conditions to perform functions in the most effective and efficient manner.

- Furthers the development of best practices in the maintenance process to ensure continuity across the value streams and achieve objectives in terms of quality, costs, delivery time, and safety for both customers and employees.

Benefits

- Optimized use of equipment, material, and facilities
- Significant risk reduction
- Improved product and services quality
- Increased safety
- Reduction in costs associated with repairs, down time, etc.
- Maximize effectiveness of the organization
- Increase in useful life
- Elimination of forced or unnecessary wear and tear
- Elimination of waste in equipment and material
- Reduced energy consumption

Limitations to Productivity	Lean Maintenance
Overburden	High risk when repairing or operating equipment Unsafe workplace, lack of safety equipment Poor time management
Variability	Inconsistent, unpredictable maintenance costs Variability in processing times
Overproduction	Replacing parts when unnecessary
Excess inventory/ Resources	Excess tools and spare parts Inefficient allocation of personnel
Waiting & Searching	Waiting for instructions and material Searching for documents, spare parts, tools, etc.
Defects/Errors	Human errors in operating equipment
Unnecessary Transportation & Movement	Unnecessary transportation of tools and equipment
Overprocessing	Confusing or unclear instructions Requesting unnecessary spare parts or reports/documents/information
Non-utilized talent	Employees limited to specific tasks due to a lack of knowledge or training

Lean Maintenance: Maintenance

Before

- Delivery time = 2-3 days.
- Insufficient capacity.
- Constant customer complaints.
- Constant rework.

Transformation Process

- Lean maintenance training for staff.
- Definition of KPIs for the service department.
- Installation of Andon boards to facilitate. communication and job assignment.
- 5-minute meetings for the mechanics and spare parts team.
- Kaizen for maintenance kits assembly (spare parts and materials).
- Kaizen for continuous flow — including vehicle reception, registration, online data entry, maintenance, car wash, and customer service.
- Implementation of Gemba walks and Leader standard work.

Results

- Delivery time = 2 hours.
- 45% increase in capacity (using the same resources).
- 28% reduction in service cost.
- Became #1 car repair center for the dealership in only 6 months.

LSSI
LEAN SIX SIGMA INSTITUTE

Lean Logistics

What is it?

- A work philosophy that eliminates waste in supply chains.
- Lean Logistics integrates all required processes in order to prevent interruptions in the service and production processes

Benefits:

- Ensured minimum inventory levels across supply chains.
- Reduction of variation in real demand data across supply chains.
- Improved customer delivery and service response time.
- Reduction of logistics costs: transportation, warehouse, deliveries, etc.
- Reduction of overbearing tasks and unnecessary movement.
- Reduction of environmental impact and pollution caused by excessive or unnecessary transportation.

Limitations to Productivity	Lean Logistics
Overburden	Long or unusual shifts Unsafe work areas
Variability	Inconsistent job scheduling Discrepancy between order and delivery (time, characteristics, etc.)
Overproduction	Planning before analyzing forecasts/trends Continuous rescheduling
Excess inventory/ Resources	Excess purchasing (e.g., to take advantage of volume discounts) Excess inventory due to continuous program changes
Waiting & Searching	Searching for people, documents, orders, etc. Inefficient receipt and order management
Defects/Errors	Planning, scheduling, and forecasting errors Incorrect purchase orders
Unnecessary Transportation & Movement	Redundant planning and scheduling
Overprocessing	Improving all processes except the main constraint/bottleneck
Non-utilized talent	Employees limited to specific tasks Not elaborating strategic purchase plans

Lean Logistics
Procurement & Purchasing

Procurement & Purchasing: Negotiate with suppliers to define the MSL (Minimum Stock Level) for the raw materials inventory (using Kanban for calculations and replenishment management), ensuring purchases for the supplier and supply availability for the manufacturer.

Shipping: Reduce the OTD (Order-To-Delivery) cycle time using multi-disciplinary teams to coordinate every step of the order management process.

Lean Inventory: Implement a perpetual inventory system with real-time data entry (using bar codes) and daily reconciliation reviews to improve precision, reduce inventory levels, and reduce storage costs.

LSSI
LEAN SIX SIGMA INSTITUTE

Traditional supply chain

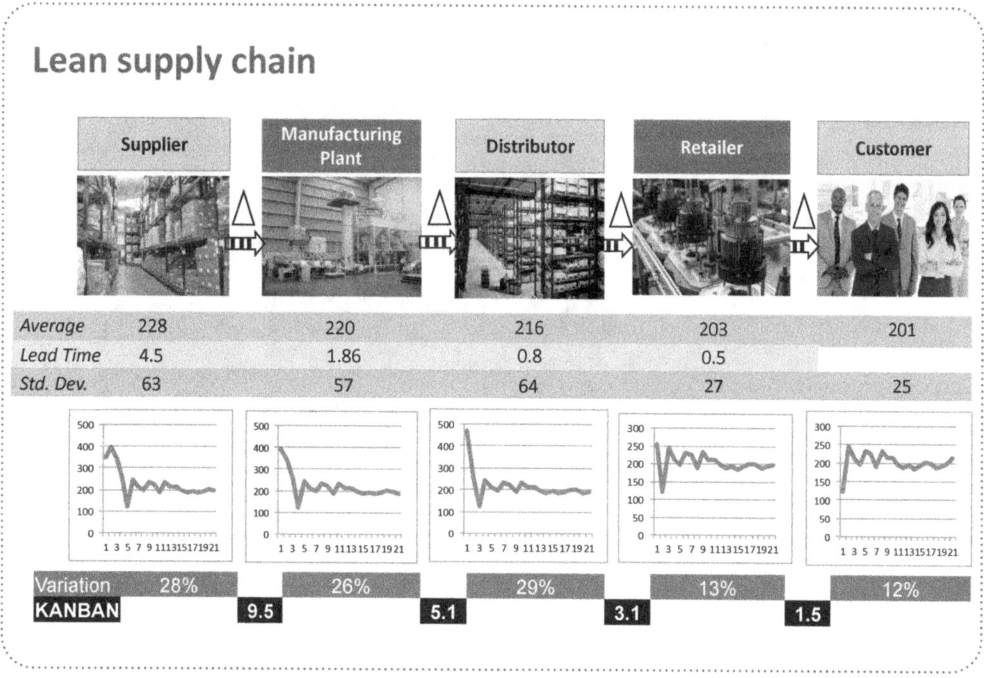

	Supplier	Manufacturing Plant	Distributor	Retailer	Customer
Average	1353	668	477	395	201
Lead Time	25.7	5.00	9.25	3.3	-
Std. Dev	1091	397	158	69	25

	Supplier		Manufacturing Plant		Distributor		Retailer		Customer
Variation	81%	129234	59%	14567	33%	11092	17%	4874	12%
Days		94.0		10.3		14.9		7.6	

Excess inventory found throughout the supply chain.
All parties have different information since they use different forecasts.

Lean supply chain

	Supplier	Manufacturing Plant	Distributor	Retailer	Customer
Average	228	220	216	203	201
Lead Time	4.5	1.86	0.8	0.5	
Std. Dev.	63	57	64	27	25

	Supplier		Manufacturing Plant		Distributor		Retailer		Customer
Variation	28%		26%		29%		13%		12%
KANBAN		9.5		5.1		3.1		1.5	

Lean Manufacturing

What is it?

It is a collaborative work system in which value streams deliver high quality products at a target cost range and manufacturing operations are optimized by managing the system's constraints – constantly analyzing results and making decisions to improve, adjust, and control processes.

Benefits:

- Significant improvement of product quality
- Reduced delivery time
- Reduced production costs
- Improved communication
- Reduction of WIP and FG inventory levels
- Increased adaptability to changes in demand
- Reduction in non-value adding activities
- Ability to increase product mix

Limitations to Productivity	Lean Manufacturing
Overburden	Dangerous tasks Heavy goods loading and unloading Poor cleanliness
Variability	Inconsistent costs and quality Variability in production times
Overproduction	Producing more than is being sold Producing before products are required
Excess inventory/ Resources	Holding excess "just in case" inventory
Waiting & Searching	Approvals: quality, production, etc., before next steps in process Searching for people, material, documents, orders, etc.
Defects/Errors	Material selection errors Production errors Rework for products not fulfilling their functions
Unnecessary Transportation & Movement	Unnecessary transportation of tools and equipment Inefficient logistical processes Inefficient placement of material
Overprocessing	Packing and unpacking between processes Continuous reprogramming and rescheduling
Non-utilized talent	Employees limited to specific tasks Process imbalances Little cross-training and multi-skilled labor

LSSI
LEAN SIX SIGMA INSTITUTE

Lean manufacturing – Small business turbine mfgr.

Before

- Capacity = 20 – 30 turbines per day.
- Backorder = $80,000 USD.
- Inventory = More than $2 million USD.
- Delivery time = 3 – 4 weeks.
- High per-unit production cost.
- Constant Rework.

Transformation Process

- Lean Six Sigma training.
- Implementation of 5S Housekeeping to improve order and cleanliness.
- Implementation of Hoshin Kanri and box score.
- Use of Gemba walks.
- Installation of Andon boards in work areas.
- Implementation of a talent development program combining cross training with different compensation models.
- Redesign of the company's layout with manufacturing cells instead of traditional departments.
- Design and implementation of Kanban "pull" system.

Results

- Capacity = 50 – 70 turbines per day.
- Backorder = $ 0 USD.
- Inventory = $650,000 USD.
- Delivery time = 2 days (max.).
- Reduction of per-unit production cost of 23%.
- Increase in quality = 95%.

Lean Accounting

What is it?

- Lean Accounting aims to eliminate waste, prevent overburden, and minimize variation in accounting and administrative processes to develop a work system that benefits the value stream.

- The function of the accounting and finance teams is to ensure that internal and external creditors have the right resources and information to ensure continuity of the business and further value creation for customers.

Benefits

- Elimination of waste in administrative and accounting processes.
- Understanding of the real costs of products and services.
- Development of improved design, sales, and production strategies.
- Improved decision-making in terms of value created for customers and the company.
- Elimination of bureaucracy that prevents better communication and – therefore – better results.
- Accurate measurement of the financial impact of Lean Company implementation.

Limitations to Productivity	Lean Accounting
Overburden	Long shifts required to complete work Constant work-related stress
Variability	Inconsistency in accounting and financial analysis that results in discrepancies and rework
Overproduction	Time-consuming and low-value-added processes, activities, and paperwork
Excess inventory/Resources	Inefficient allocation of resources to fulfill functions
Waiting & Searching	Long waits for approval and information Searching for documents, customer orders, people, etc.
Defects/Errors	Errors in accounting, invoicing, payments, and financial analysis Repetitive financial analysis and rework
Unnecessary Transportation & Movement	Inefficient logistics of people to get work done (e.g. meetings, customer and supplier visits, etc.) Inefficient internal and external document sharing
Overprocessing	Unnecessary reports and analysis Redundant processes to comply with workplace politics
Non-utilized talent	Not asking for feedback Not assigning talented employees to more challenging tasks

Lean Accounting
Accounting improvements

Real-time costing: Eliminate monthly reports and generate real-time reports for each manufacturing and service cell to understand the real daily and weekly costs.

Invoicing: Optimize invoice design and structure with only the most important information – and implement 5S Housekeeping and Andon – to expedite the invoice process, avoid rework due to incomplete information, and improve collection of payments.

Accounts payable: Reduce amount of credit notes issued and past due backlog by centralizing the accounts payable system, optimizing approval procedures, reducing and simplifying supplier appointing, and reviewing single monthly invoice reports.

Lean IT

What is it?

- Lean IT ensures the safety and availability of information the organization requires to operate and supports all key processes in identifying, installing, and maintaining the optimal hardware and software that contributes to speed, quality, and data security across all value streams.

- Lean IT aims to eliminate overburden, variability, and waste in all systems in regard to the use of information and technology to supports key company processes.

Benefits

- Simplification and standardization of systems used to gather, store, and analyze information.
- Improvement of speed and quality of the information used in decision-making processes.
- Optimal selection of reliable technology to fulfill key functions at the lowest cost and highest quality.
- Elimination and mitigation of risks via the elaboration, communication, and implementation of business continuity plans.
- Robust software, hardware, and technology to ensure speed and quality.

Limitations to Productivity	Lean IT
Overburden	High amount of open, pending, or unresolved tickets
Variability	Use of independent/incompatible systems in different areas of the organization
Overproduction	High amount of open, high-cost, low-impact projects
Excess inventory/ Resources	Too many unprocessed, irrelevant, or outdated files and documents that take up storage space
Waiting & Searching	Gathering information, preparing reports, integrating databases, etc...
Defects/Errors	Data entry errors
Unnecessary Transportation & Movement	Constant need for IT staff to be present in order to solve computer or software issues
Overprocessing	Unnecessary emails and communication to follow-up on open tickets
Non-utilized talent	Not integrating information from all areas into a single system

LSSI
LEAN SIX SIGMA INSTITUTE

Before

- Too many software development projects in process.
- Too much time required to process and analyze data.
- Low use of technology for transactional processes.
- Work-related stress.

Kaizen – IT Systems

- Cloud software implementation.
- Integration of systems to avoid duplicate data and reports.
- Use of robots to automate repetitive transactional processes.
- Use of artificial intelligence to process large amounts of data.
- Digital box score to process data from all value streams.

Results

- Significant reduction of data entry errors.
- More time can now be allocated to decision-making.
- Improvement in the speed and quality of decision-making processes.

Lean Quality Management

What is it?

- Lean Quality Management is a customer-focused system that aims to improve speed and quality across an organization's key processes in order to deliver high-value products and services to customers.
- It is a set of interconnected processes that will help companies fulfill customer demand, increase the value created, and achieve continuous improvement.

Benefits

- Simplification and standardization of quality management activities.
- Stress reduction for employees as a result of effectively managing complex quality systems.
- Increased awareness of the importance of quality systems as tools and not as additional workload.
- Ensures best practices, processes, and documents have a real positive impact on quality as perceived by customers.

Limitations to Productivity	Lean Quality Management
Overburden	Lack of knowledge to maintain a quality management system (e.g., audits, documents, etc.)
Variability	Lack of uniformity or standardization in handling documentation, conducting audits, and overall communication
Overproduction	Work done on generating documents or improving processes that do not add value
Excess inventory/ Resources	Excess amount of irrelevant files and documents
Waiting & Searching	Unorganized files, documents, and scheduling
Defects/Errors	Auditing errors
Unnecessary Transportation & Movement	Inefficient document or information sharing (e.g., physically moving across rooms, buildings, etc.)
Overprocessing	Unnecessary emails to share irrelevant documents or to keep records on file
Non-utilized talent	Best practices are not documented, and lessons learned are not communicated across teams

LSSI LEAN SIX SIGMA INSTITUTE

Lean Quality Management: Improvements

Quality system: Simplify and standardize processes, document best practices, and leverage technology to communicate instructions in order to significantly reduce setup times, nonconformities, and audits.

Reduction in receipt inspections: Define the verification criteria and control plans together with suppliers and require them to provide quality assurance certificates, in order to minimize receipt inspections and ultimately reduce the time spent receiving, inspecting, and handling material.

Becoming a Lean Company takes time...

"Patience, persistence, and perspiration make an unbeatable combination for success."

Napoleon Hill (1883-1970)

Lean Industry 4.0

The Fourth Industrial Revolution

Learning objectives

1. Understand what is Industry 4.0.
2. Understand the key elements and implications of the Fourth Industrial Revolution in improving productivity.
3. Understand the key elements of Industry Review examples regarding the changes that will unfold as technology revolutionizes today's world.

Content

> Background
> What is Industry 4.0?
> Industry 4.0 elements
> Implementation examples
> Conclusions

Lean Industry 4.0

Chronology

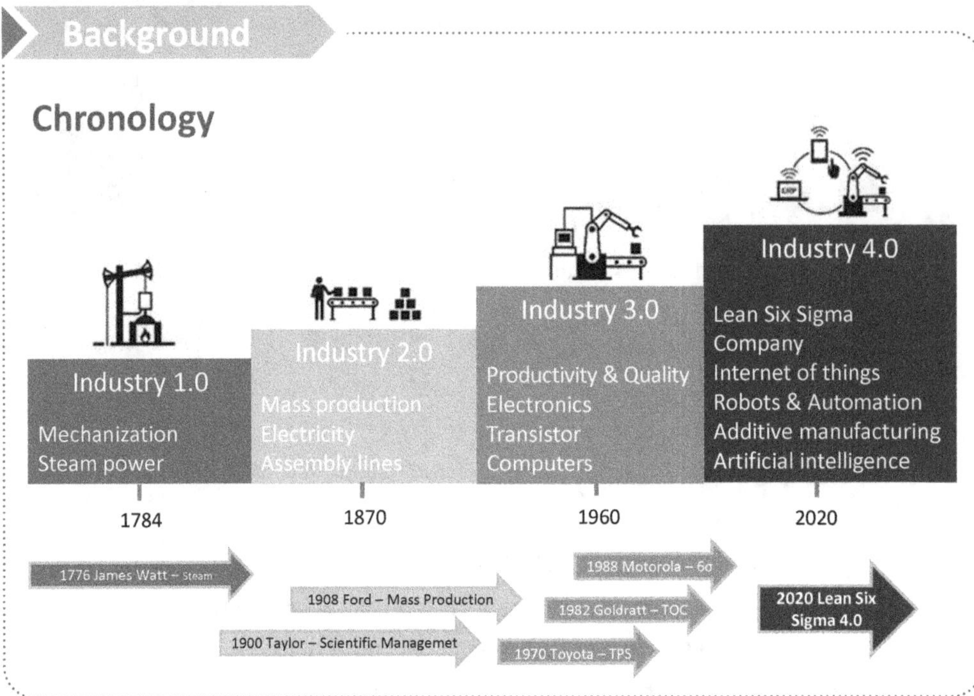

Technological Revolution

It significantly and positively impacts lives around the world through the discovery and use of new technologies.

Socially

How we relate to each other

Economically

How wealth is distributed

Ideologically

How we think

Organizationally

How we think

LSSI
LEAN SIX SIGMA INSTITUTE

Digitalization of everything

Digitalization does not mean operating in a faster and automated manner. That occurred during the previous revolution. Digitalization means doing things more intelligently – measuring and using information to make decisions.

The term Industry 4.0 was first used in **2011 at Hannover Messe,** one of the world's largest trade fairs.

It describes the information-driven transformation of processes in a connected cyber-physical environment of data, people, systems, production and service assets.

The context of the term's usage was on how organizations can **integrate cyber-physical** tools and systems into their processes to interact with the physical world.

What is Industry 4.0?

Abundance of information

Nowadays, machines and systems provide structured data which we can use to better perceive and understand the world around us.

Interconnectivity

The ubiquity of the information represented by mobile and cloud technologies allows us to connect in a global network that improves collaboration with one another.

New business models

Enable new ways of doing business that we had not considered a few years ago.

Interconnection – P2P, M2M, M2P

Systems of interconnected networks sharing information and access to data.

Trends

- The auto industry will be transformed.
- Companies using cloud software will gain competitive advantages.

Uber owns no vehicles.

Airbnb owns no property.

LSSI
LEAN SIX SIGMA INSTITUTE

Industry 4.0 Opportunities

The five senses and their equivalent technology

Sight – video cameras and presence detectors

Hearing – audio Frequency detectors

Touch – humidity and temperature sensors

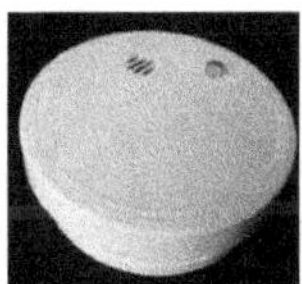

Smell – particulate matter sensors

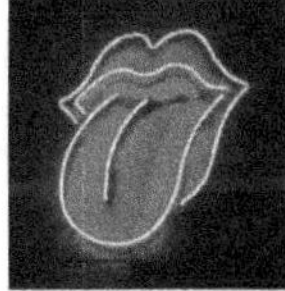

Taste – ph meters and contaminant sensors

Isn't industry 4.0 just an extension of the previous revolution?

No. The digital revolution broke down the barriers between the physical and digital worlds.

We are now using wireless technology, renewable energy, and data-driven thinking.

Industry 4.0 Elements

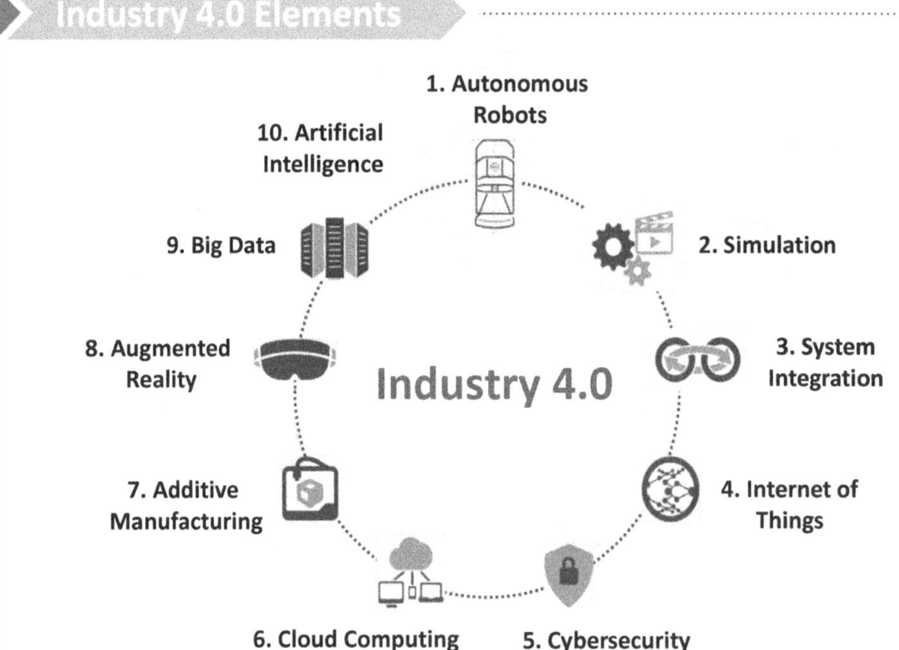

LSSI
LEAN SIX SIGMA INSTITUTE

1. Autonomous Robots

- A new set of low-cost robots has been developed to detect, collect, and sort items.

- These robots can perform many common tasks and be involved in various functions such as warehousing, grocery, accounting, sales.

- They become less expensive to produce and easier to use by the year.

Examples

- **Warehouse Robots**
  - Self-guided vehicles.
  - Zero accidents.
  - High productivity

- **Repetitive tasks: Megatech**
  - Financial services: automated invoicing for late payments, portfolio improvement (+341%).

2. Simulation

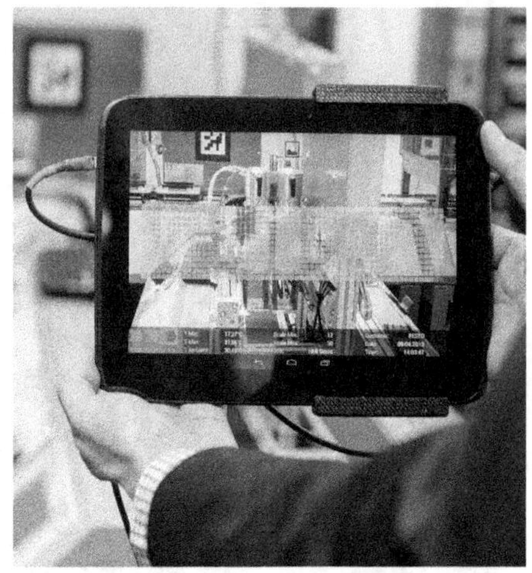

A simulation is a real-time, approximate imitation of the operations of a process or system.[1]

- It allows for advanced optimization and control, as well as early detection of problems.

- It enables an advanced comparison of actual vs. expected performance based on the experience of thousands of similar teams.

- It helps identify improvement opportunities and reduce warranty expenses.

[1] J. Banks; J. Carson; B. Nelson; D. Nicol (2001). *Discrete-Event System Simulation*. Prentice Hall. p. 3.

Examples

- **Company:** Skarnes Inc.

- **Objective:** Improve the performance of automated storage and retrieval systems.

- **Initial performance:** 70 pallets per hour.

- **Result:** 100 pallets per hour (43% improvement).

LSSI
LEAN SIX SIGMA INSTITUTE

3. System Integration

- Provides a centralized platform that imitates a standardized process to collect, analyze and store data for improved decision-making.

- Access to internal and third-party data analytics.
  - SAP, Oracle, Microsoft, Apps.

- Adds value though new functionalities by linking various IT systems, services and/or software together and interconnecting their functions.

4. Internet of Things

- Global network devices that capture, process, and share data to provide high-value information for decision-making.

- It is no longer just computers that are connected, but also many other devices – including clocks, refrigerators, sensors, smartphones, and work equipment.

- It is one of the drivers of the new revolution.

- It is the interconnection of everyday objects with the Internet.

Examples

- **Healthcare**: Telemedicine, pacemaker, sleep monitor

- **Home**: Thermostat, lighting, watering

- **Security**: Cameras, motion sensors, alarms

- **Agriculture**: Sowing, irrigation, sourcing weather data

- **Daily Activities**: Fitness, car, keys, coffee, reservations

- **Business**: Transactions, production, dashboards, etc.

LSSI — LEAN SIX SIGMA INSTITUTE

5. Cybersecurity

The protection of computing infrastructure:

- Software
- Databases
- Files
- Hardware
- Networks

The exponential increase in digitalization also increases the risk and exposure of the data itself.

Secure business-to-business connections that enable visibility and optimization of the entire supply chain.

Risk is not only in personal data

Our Conversations

Blockchain

A blockchain is a decentralized, distributed ledger that is shared across a network of computers and is used to record transactions across them. It is a **decentralized database** that stores digital pieces of information – or records – as immutable blocks.

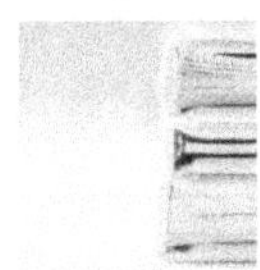

Distributed ledger

- Each member of a blockchain network (called nodes) owns a copy of the ledger
- All transactions are encrypted

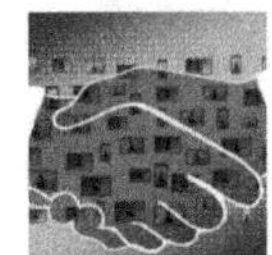

Consensus algorithm

- There is no central authority responsible for validating the integrity of the information
- Each record is validated by each node of the network

Smart contracts

- Transactions are validated and released if certain rules and conditions are met

Digital currency

- Enables secure exchange of currency as each transaction is a unique piece of information.

Blockchain technology can be applied to practically any industry.

Its basic advantages include decentralization, immutability, security, and transparency.[2]

Implementation

- **Government**: Transparency, fraud reduction (smart contracts)

- **Healthcare**: Medical records, insurance, clinical trial results

- **Notary Public**: Private key access to files, transfer of document ownership

- **Supply Chain**: Reduce delays for paperwork, transparent transactions

According to the Brooking's Institution, 97% of Fortune 500 companies have been hacked. The question is not if it will happen, but when my data might be breached.

[2] A. Patel (2014). *The Top Advantages of Blockchain for Businesses.* SmartDataCollective.

6. Cloud Computing

- Cloud computing is the scalable availability of computer system resources that do not require direct active management by users.

- These resources enable users to access services such as data storage and have computing power in flexible ways.

- At may times, users can access these services for free, or only pay for the resources they consume.

Examples

Siemens
Constant monitoring of teams around the world that charge only for services consumed, not for technical equipment.

Tesla
- Model update.
- Bug fixes.
- Vital indicator monitoring.

7. Additive Manufacturing

3D Printer in NASA.

- Creation of lighter, stronger, high-precision parts that are added (usually in layers).

- Increased flexibility and elimination of unnecessary components.

- One-piece runs and smaller production batches.

- Lower time and cost requirements as compared to traditional manufacturing.

Examples

Additive Construction

3D wall printing.

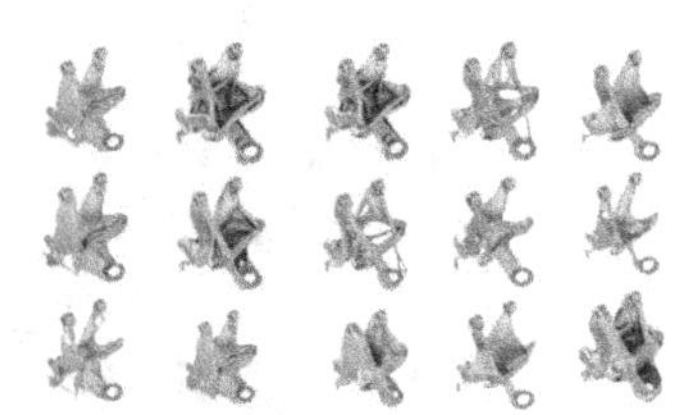

Components

Prototype and
Fabrication
(General Motors
Consolidation of
8 parts into one).

Healthcare

3D printed
prostheses
and organs.

LSSI
LEAN SIX SIGMA INSTITUTE

8. Augmented Reality

- Real-time, accurate visual information.

- Onboarding and training.

- Error reduction and improvement opportunities.

- Future state process simulations:
    - Layout.
    - Design.
    - Team configuration.

Examples

Remote Support

An expert explains how to solve an issue by demonstrating a real-time fixing procedure.

Design

Online 3D rooms that enable visualization of room design and accommodation of true-to-scale furniture.

Training

Step-by-step coaching of personnel.

9. Big Data

- Allows significant data-capturing and processing capability in order to provide valuable information that improves decision-making.

- The amount of data generated by devices such as sensors, engines, and systems in general are growing at an exponential rate.

- Big data technology can help us capture, analyze, process, and extract these large amounts of data from extremely complex data sets.

- It is useless to have data capturing-technology if we cannot store and organize it appropriately.

LSSI
LEAN SIX SIGMA INSTITUTE

10. Artificial Intelligence

- AI is the discipline that seeks to teach machines how to perform tasks, solve problems, and make decision that normally require human intelligence.

- This is done by learning patterns and classifying information.

- Composed of different technologies:

    - Computer vision.
    - Machine learning.
    - Deep learning.
    - Big Data.
    - Robotics.

Examples

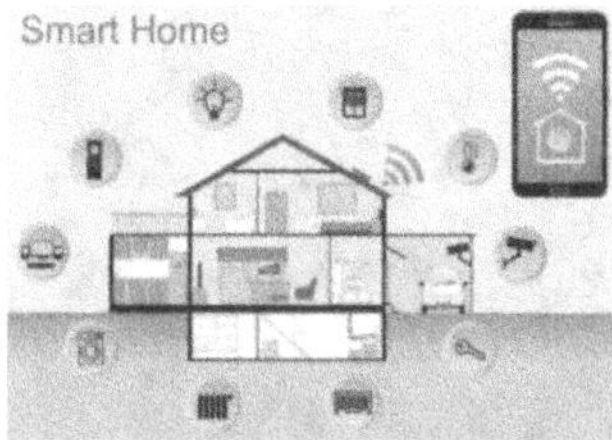

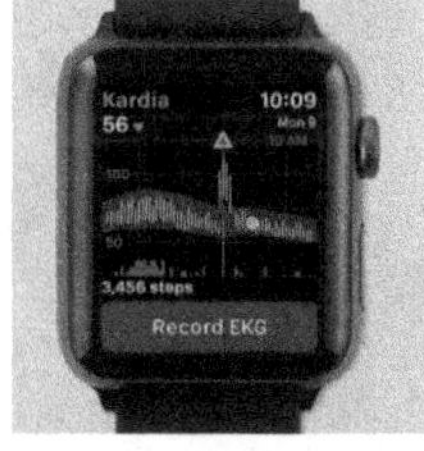

Autonomous vehicles

Capable of interacting with satellites and other vehicles to minimize human-driving errors and prevent accidents.

Smart Homes

Connected home applications and sensors that switch devices on and off according to certain criteria (e.g., AC, security system, lighting).

Health & Fitness

Monitoring vital signs and analyzing information to prevent heart problems.

Implementation Examples

Connected homes

Manufacturing

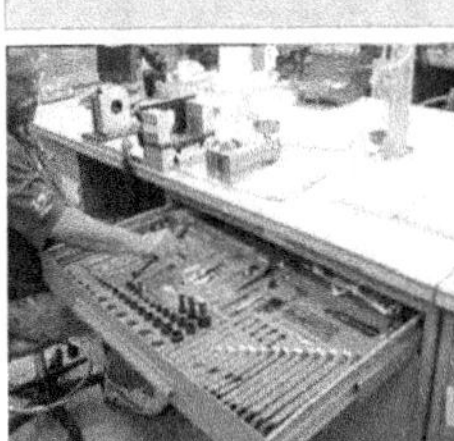

LSSI
LEAN SIX SIGMA INSTITUTE

Healthcare

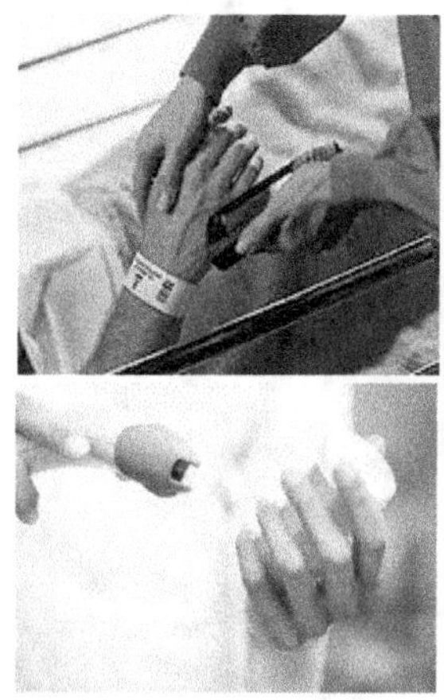
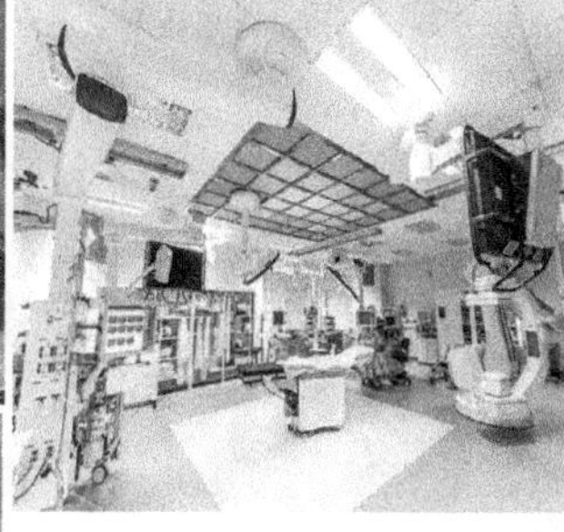
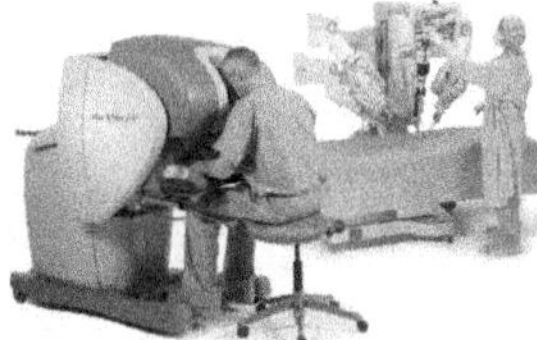

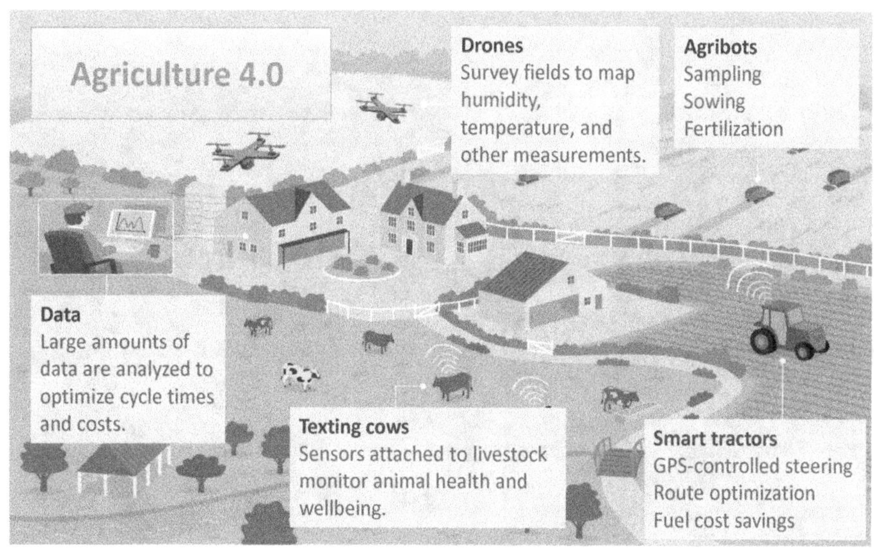

Agriculture 4.0
Drones
Survey fields to map humidity, temperature, and other measurements.
Agribots
Sampling
Sowing
Fertilization
Data
Large amounts of data are analyzed to optimize cycle times and costs.
Texting cows
Sensors attached to livestock monitor animal health and wellbeing.
Smart tractors
GPS-controlled steering
Route optimization
Fuel cost savings

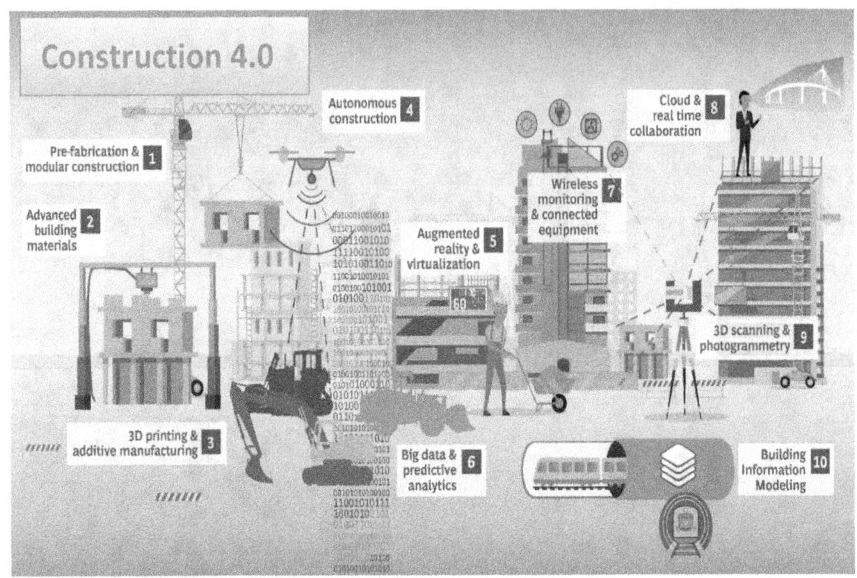

LSSI
LEAN SIX SIGMA INSTITUTE

Energy Lean 4.0

10-20 % of total energy cost.

Thermography:
Leaks and insulation

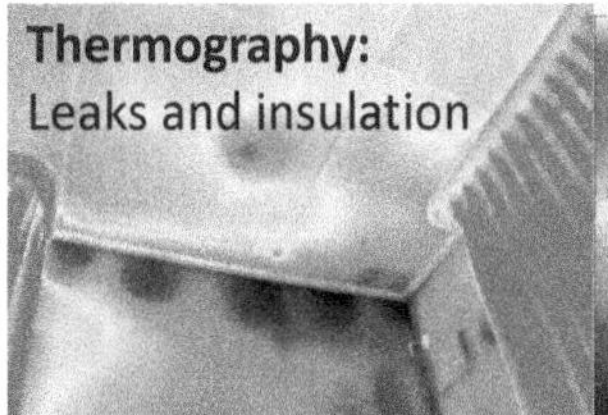

Monitor IoT:
Electricity / Production

Ultrasound:
Gas leaks and electricity

Technology:
AA-Efficient
Artificial Intelligence

60 %

Is it possible that as many as two thirds of workers will see their functions automated?

Machines have
the ability to
learn faster
than humans.

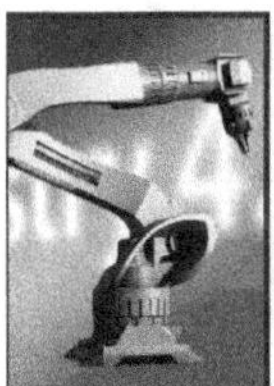

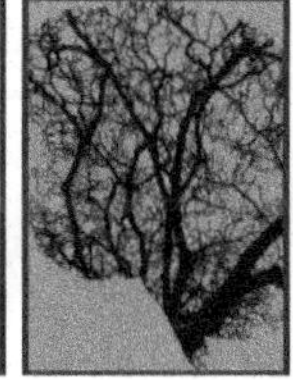

Impact

Technology will continue to improve our quality of life.

The democratization of technology tends to reduce production costs.

Growing another Billion by 2030

In 2050, 55 countries will have 30% of their **population** be 60 years of age or older.

Upcoming global Pension crisis

Declining birth rate

LSSI
LEAN SIX SIGMA INSTITUTE

Emerging economies

In less than a generation, **developing economies** went from low cost production sites to becoming the destination of value-added products, services, and investments.

The U.S. and Europe will steadily lose ground to China and India.

Share of world GDP (PPPs) from 2016 to 2050 (est.).

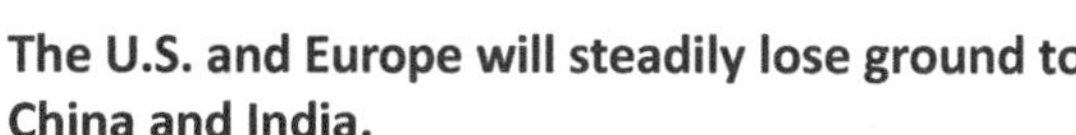

Sources: IMF for 2016 estimates, PwC analysis for projections to 2050.

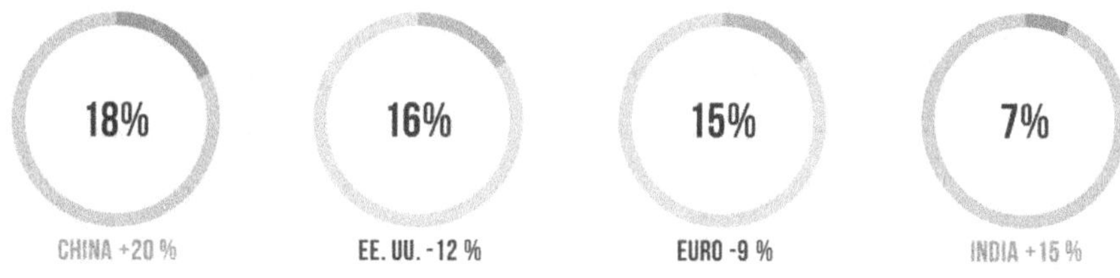

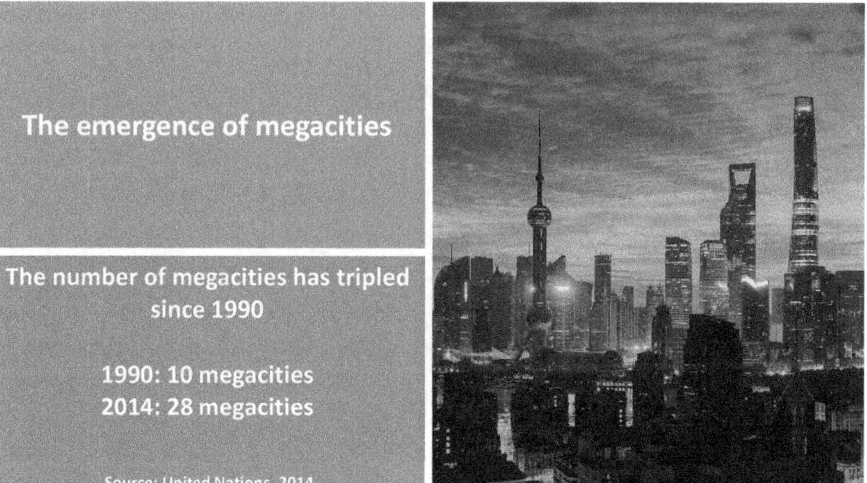

Speed

What's the difference?

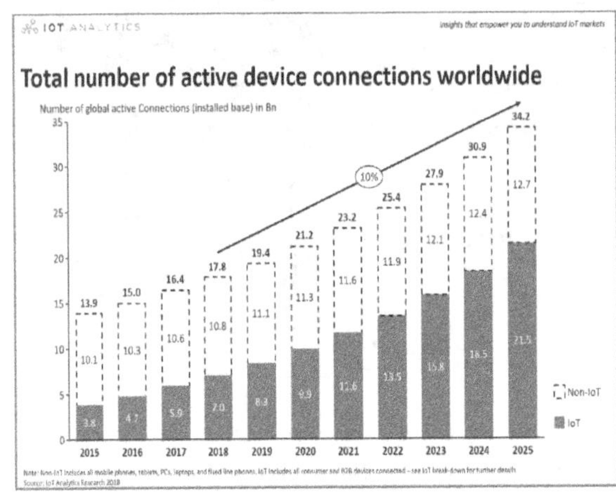

Exponential growth

Over 57% of the world's population has Internet access (Internet World Stats, 2019).

As of 2018, the global number of connected devices exceeds 17 billion (IoT Analytics Research, 2018). This number is expected to nearly double by the end of 2025.

Scope

What's the difference?

Growth does not know borders

Although some countries benefit more than others, there is growing evidence indicating that regions that have not been able to ride the initial wave of technology adoption and accelerate their development process are starting to do so with Industry 4.0.

LSSI
LEAN SIX SIGMA INSTITUTE

Who will be the first affected?

1. **Work as we know it**

2. **The education system**

3. **Traditional structures**

4. **Governments**

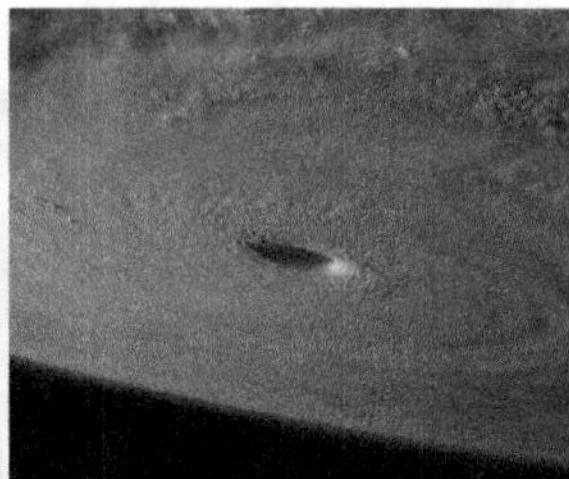

Skills Inventory

2015	2024
1. Solve Complex Problems.	1. Solve Complex Problems.
2. Teamwork.	2. Critical Thinking.
3. Personal Management.	3. Creativity.
4. Critical Thinking.	4. Personal Management.
5. Negotiation.	5. Teamwork.
6. Quality Control.	6. Emotional Intelligence.
7. Service-Oriented.	7. Decision-Making.
8. Decision Making.	8. Service-Oriented.
9. Attention to Detail.	9. Negotiation.
10. Creativity.	10. Cognitive Flexibility.

Sources: *Future Jobs Employment,* World Economic Forum.

LSSI — LEAN SIX SIGMA INSTITUTE

Who benefits?

The economy

Communities

Those who prepare

Simulation with FlexSim

Learning objectives

1. Understand what simulation is as well as its benefits.
2. Understand how to use the main functions of FlexSim.
3. Develop a simple model to practice the knowledge taught.
4. Interact with an advanced model in order to understand the benefits of running simulations.

Content

> Background
> What is Simulation?
> Benefits
> Simulation with FlexSim
> Using FlexSim
> Exercises
> Conclusions

Background

Production systems:

- Are complex.

- May be dependent on other processes.

- Can represent thousands of possible combinations and outcomes.

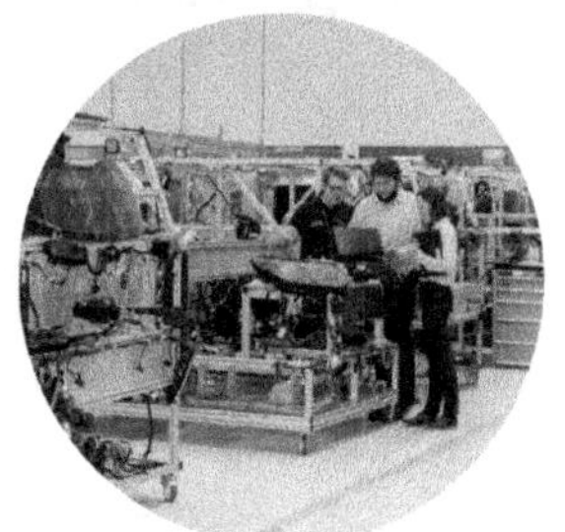

How can we improve the system, without interrupting production, while simultaneously minimizing risk?

This problem could be solved by using spreadsheets, diagrams, or even programming codes. But still, are these tools...

Pointing us to the right decisions?

...in the shortest possible time?

...with a low margin of error?

- **Simulation** is the only tool that allows us to quickly examine complex systems.

- It finds the optimal **solution** by considering all **factors** influencing the system.

LSSI
LEAN SIX SIGMA INSTITUTE

What is Simulation?

Definition

A **simulation** is an experimentation with a simple computer imitation of an operating system as it would progress through time, for the purpose of better **understanding** and/or **improving** that system.

S. Robinson, *Simulation: The Practice of Model Development and Use,* 2004, p. 4.

Simulation models are generally used to **represent** business models, systems, and processes.

Key concepts

Unlike other tools, simulations allows us to represent:

- **Interdependence**
  - The behavior of one element affecting other elements in the system.
- **Randomness**
  - Variation in events represented by statistical distributions.
- **Reliability**
  - Events and/or situations such as failures, scrap and stoppages.

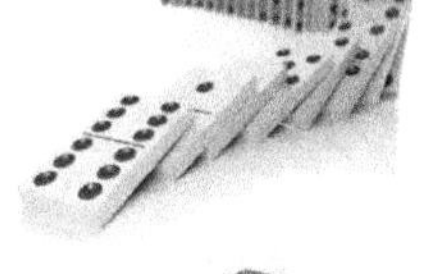

These aspects can be elaborated on without having to create complex mathematical representations.

What questions can simulation answer?

- Can the current operation be improved?
- How many people are required to operate the system?
- How is capacity determined?
- How many trucks and forklifts will be needed?
- Are optimal delivery routes being used?
- Are we using optimal layout distribution and storage systems?
- Is it convenient to open a new warehouse or distribution center?
- Is it necessary to implement a higher level of automation?
- When will the investment be recovered?

The cost of making changes increases with time

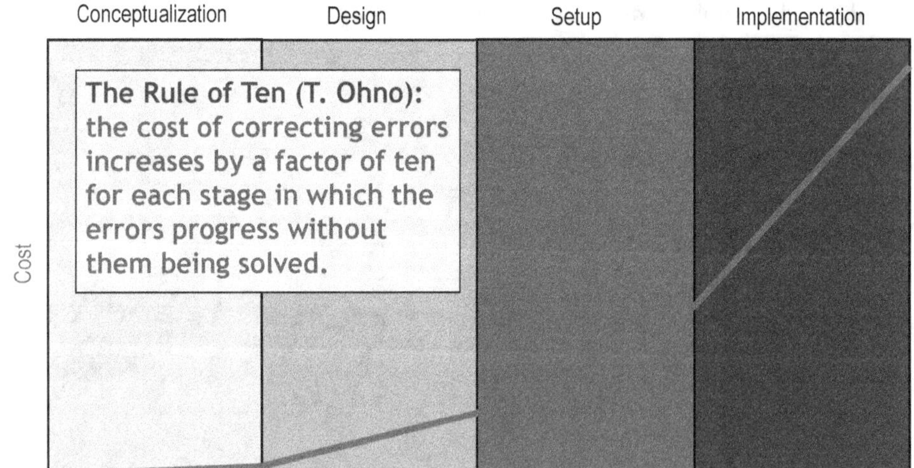

LSSI
LEAN SIX SIGMA INSTITUTE

Advantages of simulation

- Allows you to **evaluate** improvement strategies without disrupting real operations, therefore mitigating risk.

- Makes it possible to **identify** bottlenecks indicating the current state and degree of utilization for different resources.

- The simulations can be performed **at a fast speed,** allowing you to see several months or years worth of operations in a matter of minutes.

"The simulation is the best place to make mistakes."

Benefits

- **Improves decision making**
  - Carry out feasibility evaluations to prevent issues and identify the best course of action.
  - Generate statistics and other useful metrics to visualize and analyze information.

- **Reduces costs and optimizes processes**
  - Assess the functionality of resources without the need to invest.
  - Discover improvement opportunities by identifying and eliminating waste.

- **Further communication**
  - Present new proposals using a 3D model with precise process flows and accurate dimensions.
  - Explain the behavior of processes to both the work team and people external to the operation.

Simulation using FlexSim

- FlexSim is a 3D simulation software that models, simulates, predicts, and visualizes industrial and commercial systems for several industries. It is both powerful and easy to use.

- It uses discrete-event simulation and object-oriented programming, providing **flexibility** and **connectivity**.

Application across several industries

FlexSim is designed to simulate systems and processes for any type of industry. For example:

- Manufacturing.

- Material handling.

- Logistics and supply chain.

- Healthcare and more....

LSSI
LEAN SIX SIGMA INSTITUTE

Distinctive features

 ### Virtual 3D environment

- Realistic graphics with a high degree of detail and precise distribution.

Model layout

- Intuitive logic that allows you to program flows without using programming code.

Distribution-fitting

- ExpertFit module that adjusts inputs to one of 40 statistical distributions.
- ExpertFit is a leading distribution software

 ### Model analysis

- Dynamic dashboards that allow for real-time visualization of KPIs and generation of customized reports.

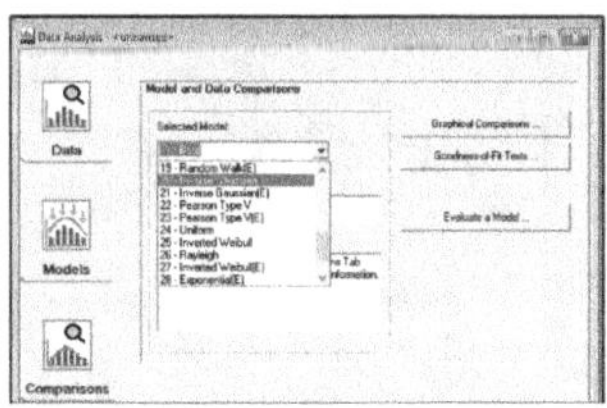

Optimization

- Experimentation module that uses algorithms to simulate hundreds of different scenarios to find the optimal solution.

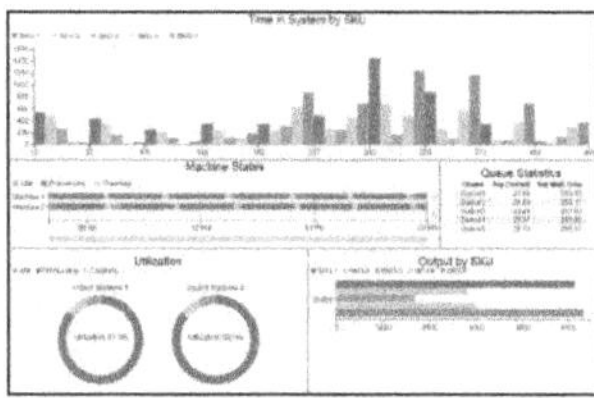

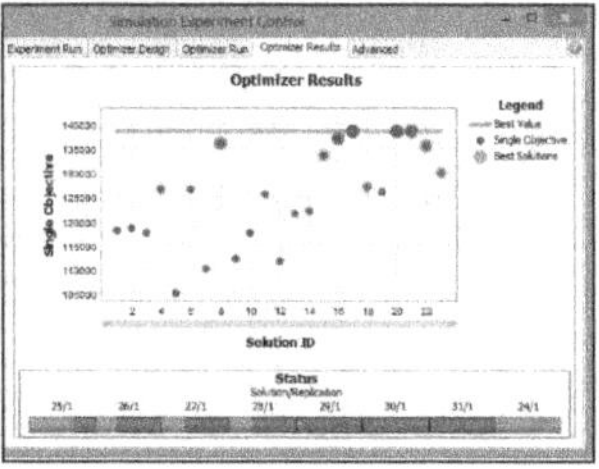

More than just simulation

How does FlexSim fit in with the Pillars of Industry 4.0:

- Digital Twin: virtual system integration.

- PLC* Emulation (Autonomous Systems).

- Cloud Computing.

- Extended Reality (VR and AR).

- Big Data + Data Analytics.

*Programmable Logic Controller.

Using FlexSim

Overview

Elements of the user interface

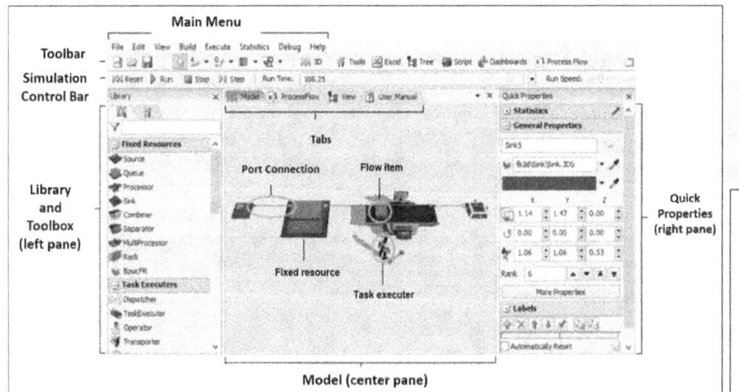

Navigating the model

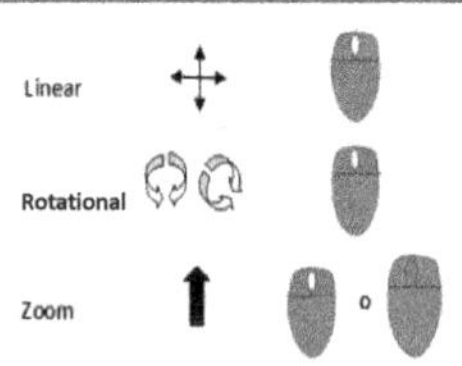

LSSI
LEAN SIX SIGMA INSTITUTE

Types of objects

There are 3 main types of objects with different functions within the simulation model:

- **Flow Items:** Objects that move or "flow" through the simulation model usually from one station (typically a fixed resource) to another. Flow items can represent products, customers, documents, parts, or any other item moving to and from various stations in the system.

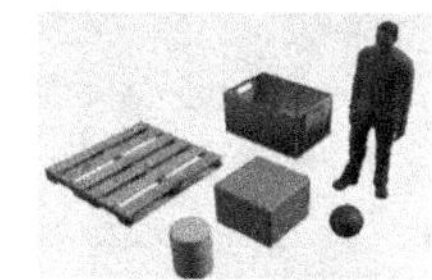

- **Fixed Resources:** Objects that remain stationary within the 3D model. Each fixed resource performs a specific function, such as creating, storing, or processing flow items. Fixed resources can represent workstations, machinery, inputs, outputs, etc.

- **Task Executers:** Objects that move around in the 3D model and perform tasks such as transporting flow items, operating machines, etc. They can represent operators, forklifts, robots, cranes, AGVs, and any means of transportation.

Object properties

Objects can be edited in the Properties window.

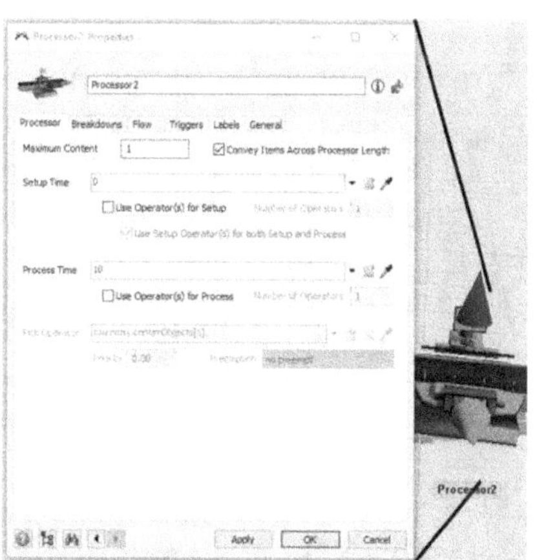

- An object's Properties window is opened by double-clicking on it.

- This window allows you to **edit variables** such as time intervals, content, flows, rules, visual aspects, and more.

- Each class of objects has its own unique properties.

Ports and Port Connections

Objects in the simulation need to be connected in some way in order to interact during a simulation model. One of the ways in which objects can be connected is through ports.

There are two types of ports in FlexSim:

- **Input & Output ports**
  Determine input and output **flows** for flow items as they pass from one fixed resource to another.
  - To connect: Drag using the 🖱 + the "A" key on the keyboard.
  - To disconnect: Drag using the 🖱 + the "Q" key on the keyboard.
- **Central ports.** Connect **fixed resources** to task executers by creating a reference point between objects.
  - To connect: Drag using the 🖱 + the "S" key on the keyboard.
  - To disconnect": Drag using the 🖱 + the "W" key on the keyboard.

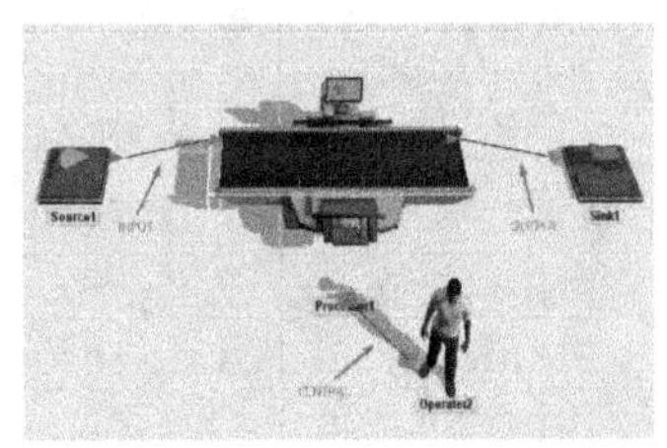

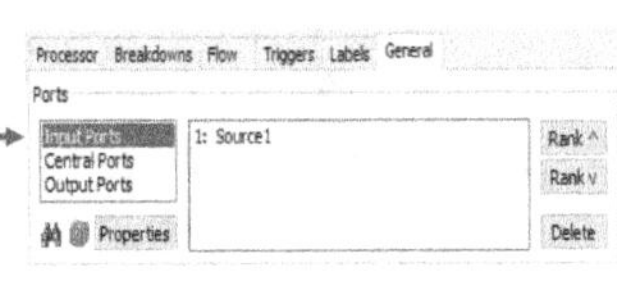

Connections can also be modified in the Properties window.

Before the simulation...

Before modeling, it is recommended to carry out the following activities:

- **Define** the purpose of the simulation and the problems to be solved.

- Determine clear **objectives** and **scope** to manage expectations.

- **Map** the process on a flowchart or value stream map (VSM).

- Establish the system **inputs** and gather data if necessary.

LSSI LEAN SIX SIGMA INSTITUTE

Exercise 1

It is time to build the first simulation model using FlexSim.

Procedure:

1. Open a new file/process flow.

2. Add objects as shown in the image.

3. Connect objects according to their port and activate transportation.

4. Configure variables in the Properties window.

   - Time between arrivals for Source 1 = 30 seconds.

   - Processor 1 cycle time = 20 seconds.

   - Queue 1 maximum capacity = 30 parts.

5. Run the simulation.

6. Discuss results.

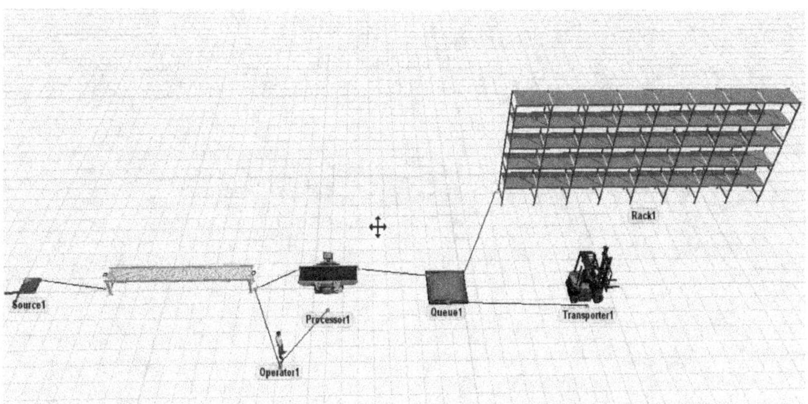

What types of waste can be identified in the simulation?

Exercise 2

Decision-making: Evaluate the incorporation of a new processor.

Procedure:

1. Use the same file from exercise 1.

2. Modify the Time between arrivals for Source 1 to 15 seconds.

3. Copy and paste the line to create a new scenario.

4. In the second line, add a second workstation.

5. Add dashboards to show utilization for the processors and the throughput of the rack.

6. Run the simulation for one hour (3,600 seconds).

7. Analyze and discuss results.

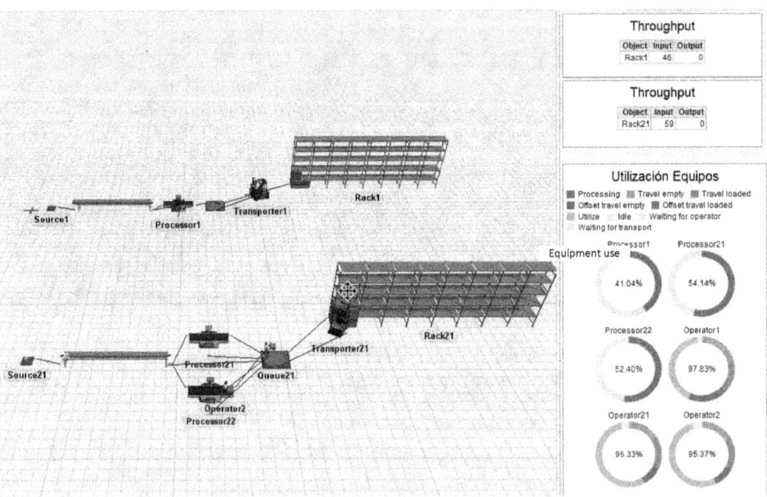

Should we incorporate a second processor?

LSSI
LEAN SIX SIGMA INSTITUTE

Exercise 3: Lean Shop Case/Current State VSM

For the third model, we will simulate the **Lean Shop** case reviewed during the Yellow Belt course.*

Procedure:

- Review the case.
- Follow the instructor's or coach's instructions.
- Discuss results.

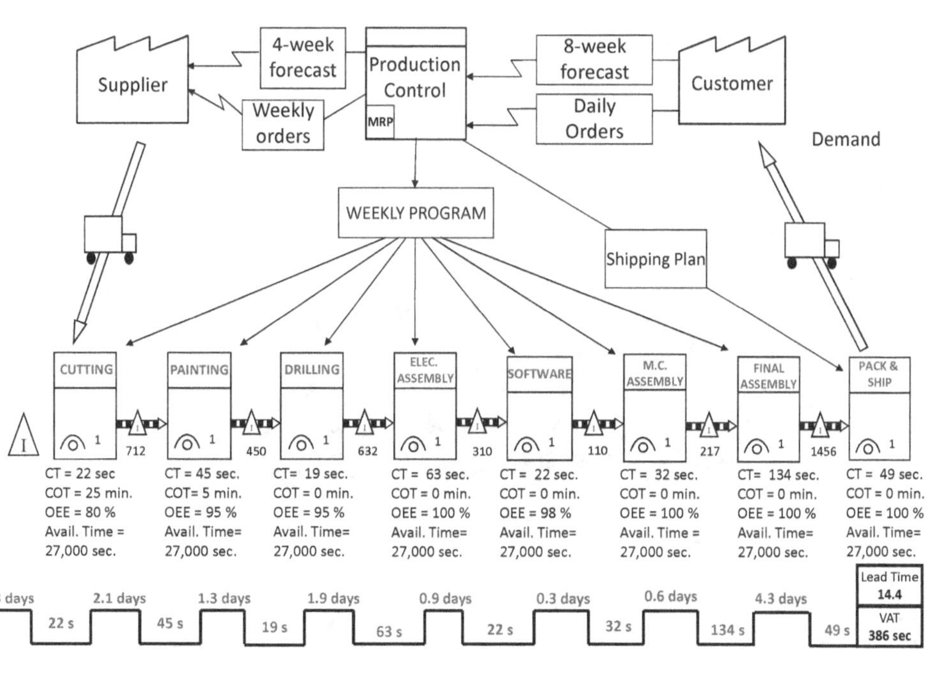

Create a Spaghetti Diagram

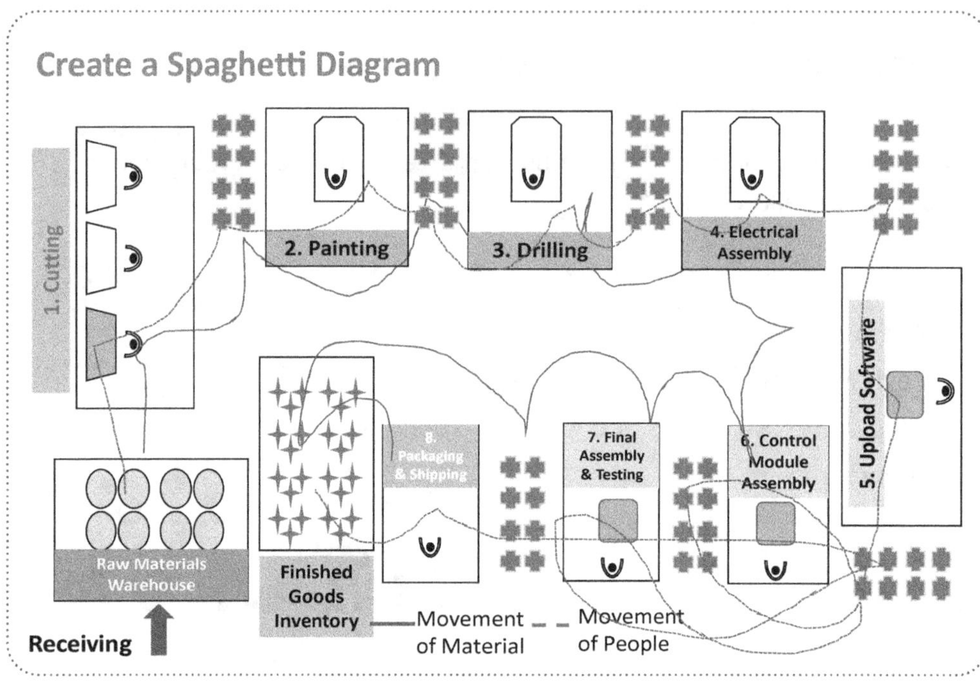

Current State VSM Model Simulation

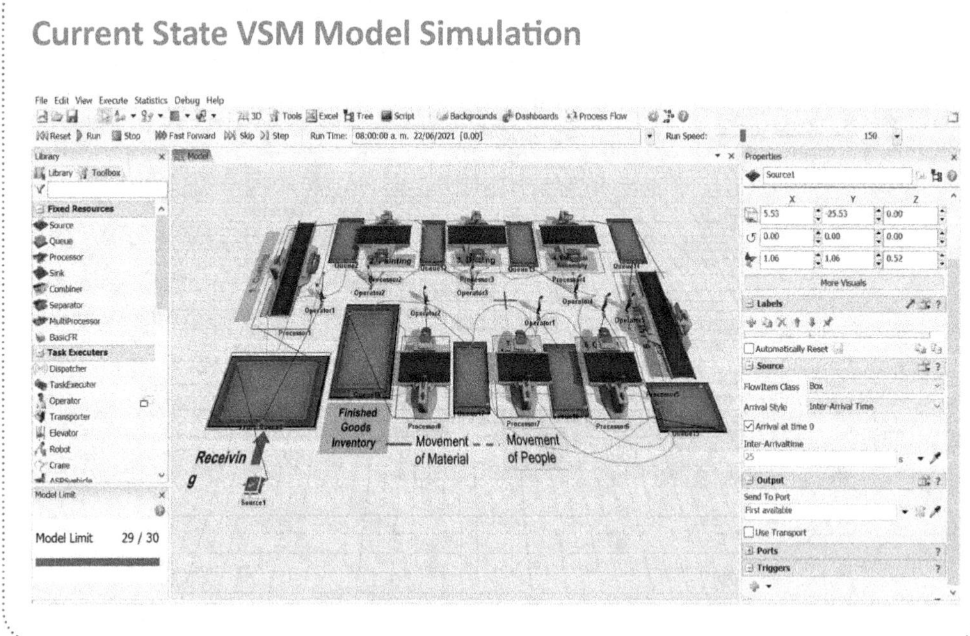

LSSI LEAN SIX SIGMA INSTITUTE

Exercise 4: Lean Shop Case/Future State VSM

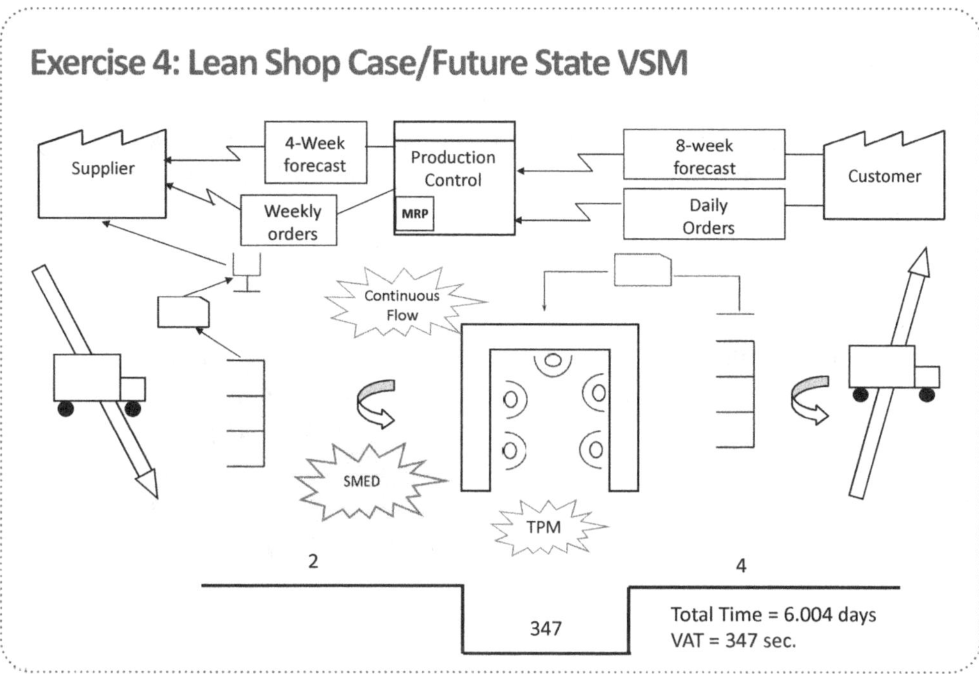

Simulation of the future VSM

Develop the Future State VSM Simulation Model for the Lean Shop exercise.

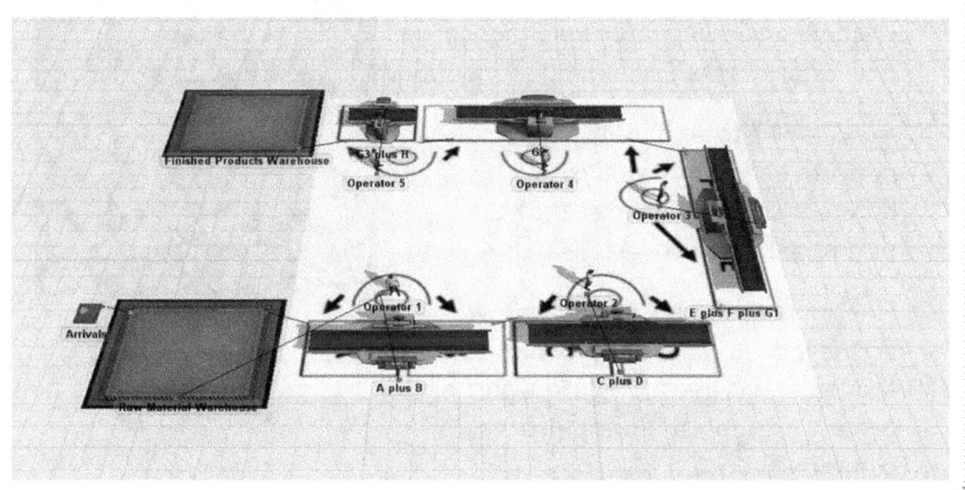

Exercise 5: Simulation with an advanced model

The objective of this exercise is to interact with an advanced model of the Lean Shop case in order to understand the benefits of running simulations.

Instructions:

- Explore the model.
- Modify variables.
- Analyze results.

> **Conclusion**

- Simulation allows us to represent **complex** systems by taking into account all factors influencing the system – including interdependence and randomness.

- FlexSim is a tool that helps us perform a **dynamic** analysis for different scenarios and reduce the risk of making mistakes.

- FlexSim is becoming rapidly known across industries and is growing at a fast pace. It is becoming a key part of **project** presentations and **process** communication.

LSSI
LEAN SIX SIGMA INSTITUTE

Leader Standard Work

A guide to clearly define the work of Leaders in a company

Learning objectives

1. Understand the key elements of a Lean Management System.
2. Learn how to integrate Leader Standard Work into a Lean Company System.
3. Understand the elements that ensure the proper functioning of Leader Standard Work.

Content

> Background
> What is Leader Standard Work?
> Benefits
> Key elements
> Who participates?
> How is LSW implemented?
> Examples
> Visual Management – Andon
> Daily Accountability
> Disciplined Leadership

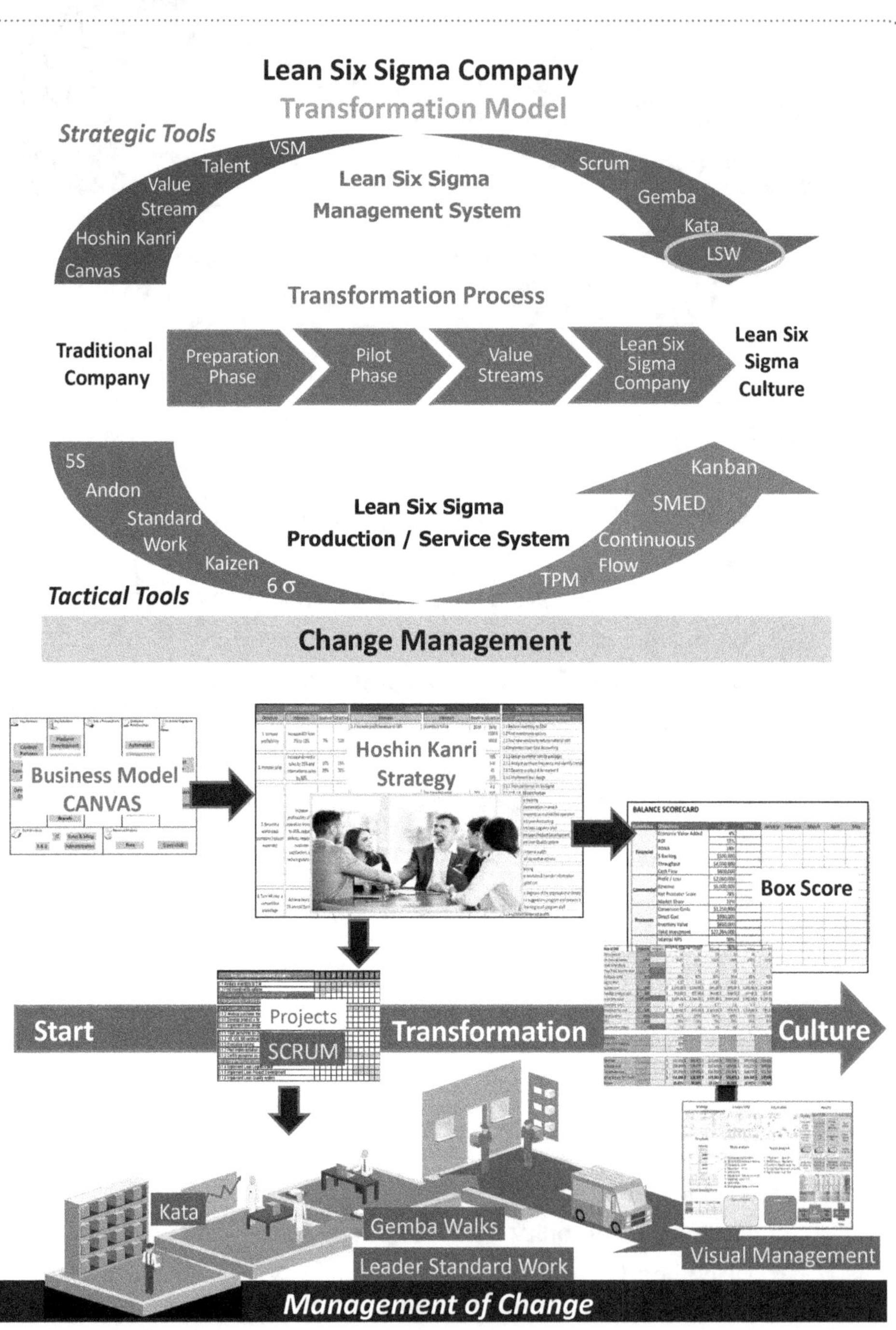

Lean Six Sigma Company
Transformation Model
Strategic Tools
VSM
Talent
Scrum
Value
Stream
Gemba
Kata
Hoshin Kanri
LSW
Canvas
Lean Six Sigma
Management System
Transformation Process
Traditional Company
Preparation Phase
Pilot Phase
Value Streams
Lean Six Sigma Company
Lean Six Sigma Culture
5S
Andon
Kanban
Standard Work
SMED
Kaizen
6 σ
Continuous Flow
TPM
Lean Six Sigma
Production / Service System
Tactical Tools
Change Management
Business Model CANVAS
Hoshin Kanri Strategy
BALANCE SCORECARD
Box Score
Start
Projects
SCRUM
Transformation
Culture
Kata
Gemba Walks
Leader Standard Work
Visual Management
Management of Change

Background

Scientific management

Frederick Taylor was an Industrial Engineer who analyzed workflows and developed *Scientific Management,* which later became the foundation for Standardized Work.

His work contributed to the development of:

- Time-and-motion studies in the steel industry.
- Tooling standardization.
- Sales planning departments.
- Management by Exception (MBE).
- Instruction cards for workers.
- Calculation rules for the cutting of steel and metal.
- Cost calculation methods.
- Employee selection based on tasks.
- Compensation methods.

Frederick Taylor

Good employees vs. Good supervisors

- When highly-skilled employees are promoted to supervisors or team leaders, they often don't have the knowledge or qualifications they need to be successful.

- As a result, they may stop performing activities for which they are experts and turn into bureaucratic supervisors.

- Usually, their roles are not clearly defined nor supervised, and therefore they end up working in a reactive manner.

- Their talent and experience are not fully utilized since they spend more time supervising than leading.

- They don't always teach what they know due to a lack of time or because they don't think it is one of their responsibilities.

Standard work for operations

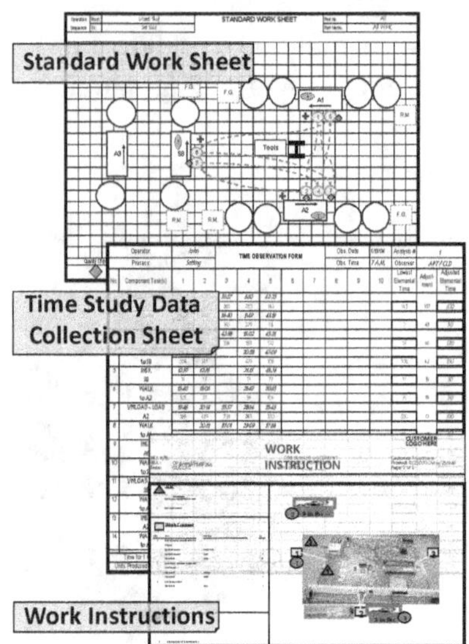

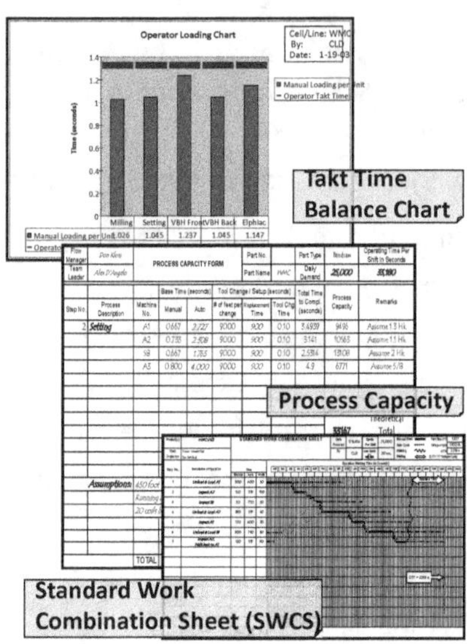

The missing link: The Lean Management System

- When most organizations implement Lean, they often miss a key ingredient:

    - *A methodology to ensure its continuity.*

- Yet, the only way to sustain Lean practices is to have a
Lean Management System.

- A Lean culture grows throughout a company and is strengthened by *strong management systems*.

LSSI
LEAN SIX SIGMA INSTITUTE

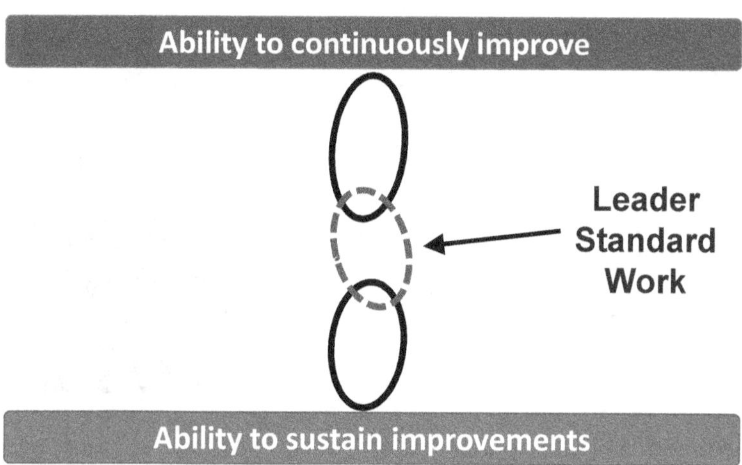

A Lean culture is the result of its management system.

Lean Management System

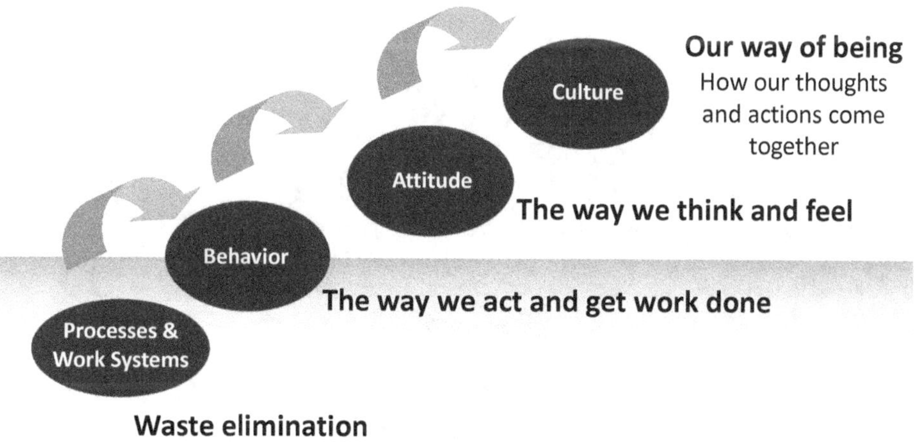

A healthy

Lean Management System

=

A healthy

Value Stream System

Development of a Lean Management System

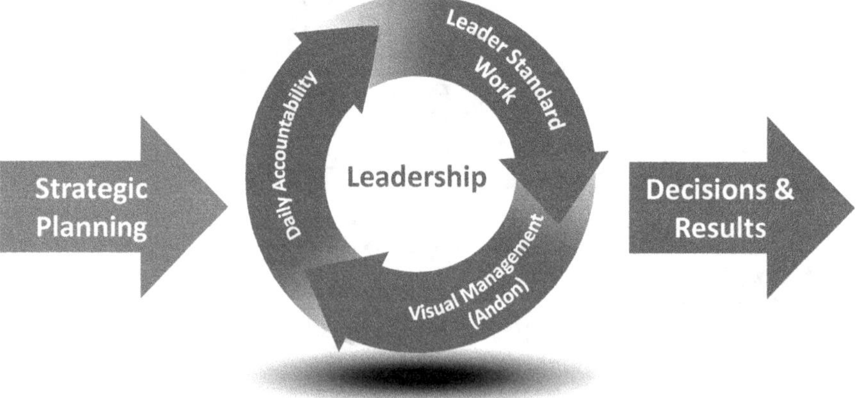

LSSI
LEAN SIX SIGMA INSTITUTE

What is Leader Standard Work?

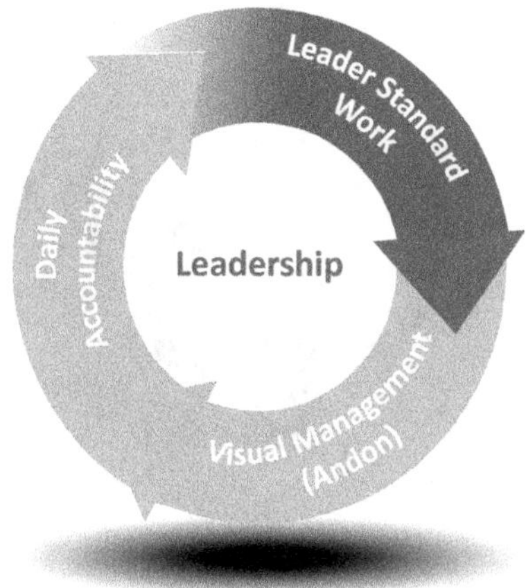

Strategy Execution

- It is the engine of the Lean Management System and the most influential tool for a Lean culture transformation.

- It is a methodology for reviewing the workplace.

- It relies on the process, not people.

- It is a systematic approach for detecting opportunities.

- It is a list of activities that must be carried out to sustain the work system:

  - Audits, meetings, project reviews, etc.

Visual Management for Daily Performance

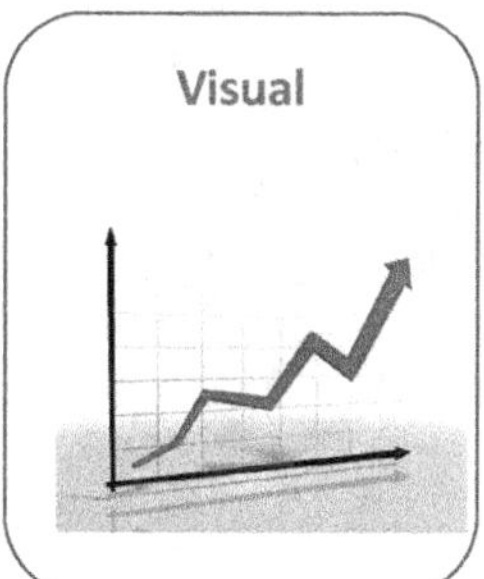

Visual

Timely

Promotes Action & Learning

Leader Standard Work

- Help leaders shift from a *focus* on *results* to a *focus* on both *processes and results.*

- Help new supervisors and managers become *high-performance leaders.*

- Provide a *structured and documented system* that can be easily understood and taught.

- Eliminate *on-the-job improvisation.*

- Challenge leaders to become *teachers and problem-solving facilitators.*

Leader Standard Work sustains and furthers improvements

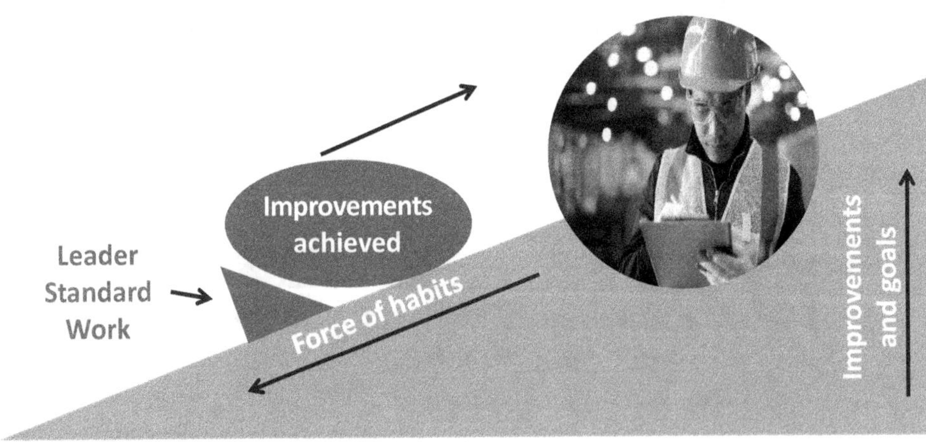

Key elements

Elements that should work together → "System"

When improving the stability of a process, it is important to apply the elements of Lean Management = A road that is paved and free of potholes.

Lean roles

	Who?	Lean Role	Tools/System
Strategic	Leaders	Guide and sustain Lean initiatives	Lean Management System
Tactical	Value Stream managers, supervisors, and team leaders	Implement and control Lean operations	Lean Company tools and methods

Leader Standard Work System

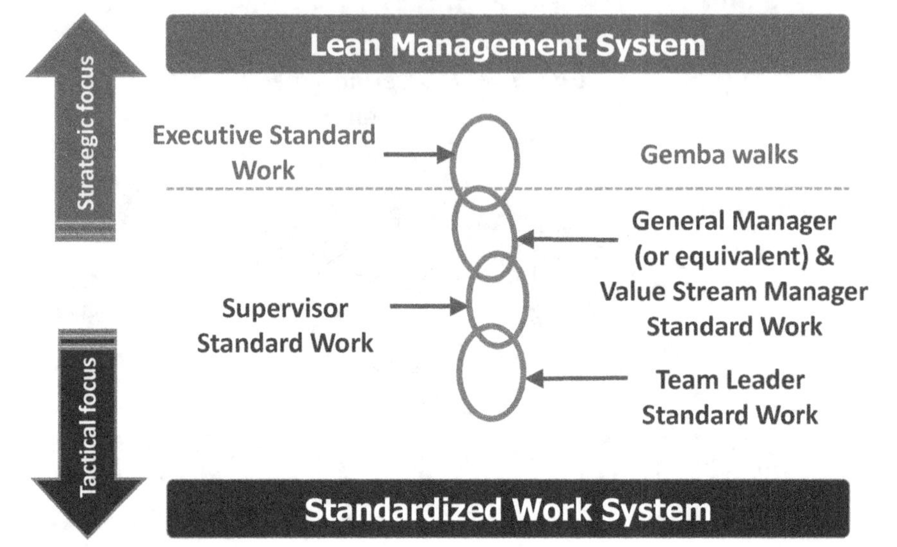

Anyone responsible for leading one or more individuals.

All leaders are teachers, since they:

- Informally train others at the workplace.

- Solve problems by removing barriers and help develop improvement ideas.

- Understand the details of the business.

LSSI
LEAN SIX SIGMA INSTITUTE

How is LSW implemented?

- By developing routine tasks that allow for the management of key activities required to meet customer demand.

- By ensuring that standard work is implemented at the value-adding processes.

Structure and results

Day by-the-hour boards

Value Stream boards

Team Leader

Daily

- Pre-shift meeting.
- Review and adjust work plans/schedules.
- Monitor production kickoffs.
- Submit verification sheets.
- Meeting at the department-results board or Value Stream board.
- Define work plan/schedule for the next day.

Multiple times per day

- Work on open Kaizen activities.
- Update the day-by-the-hour production board.
- Train operators as needed.
- Monitor machine and process setups.

Team Leader Standard Work represents about 80% of their workday.

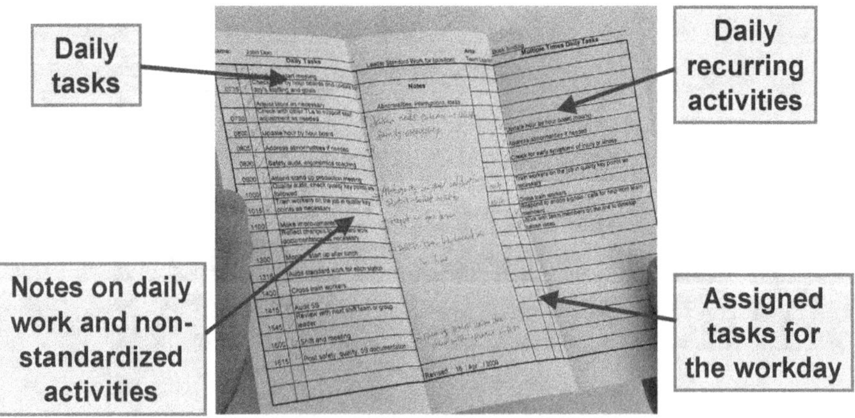

LSSI
LEAN SIX SIGMA INSTITUTE

Supervisor

Daily

- Change-of-shift meeting.
- Monitor production kickoffs.
- Submit KPI monitoring sheets.
- Lead department/area meeting.
- Attend Value Stream KPI Review meeting.
- Audit standard work at work cells or pods.
- Conduct Gemba walk along with team leader.
- Establish plans for the next day.

Multiple times per day

- Follow the workflow of their areas / departments.
- Review performance boards and take necessary actions.
- Assist team leaders in any way necessary.
- Monitor start and end times for production runs.

Supervisor standard work represents about 50% of their workday.

Visual Management – Andon

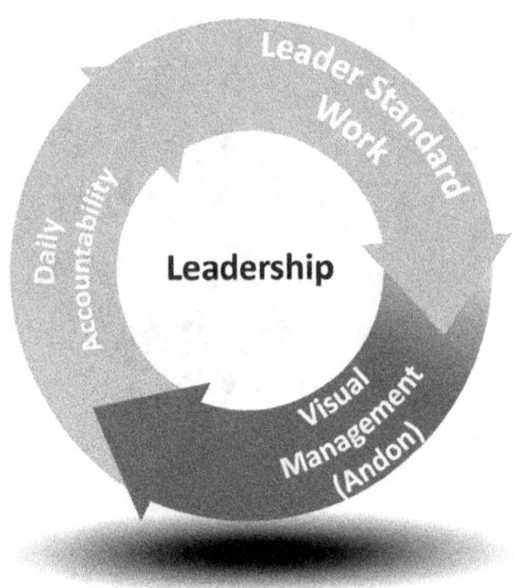

Visual Management is a *planning, control,* and *continuous improvement system* that integrates:

- Simple Visual tools that allow you to understand unusual conditions at a glance.

- Standard Work Management, which ensures adherence to continuous improvement processes.

*Visual Management is **NOT** Desk Work!*

Visual Management and its benefits

- "Understanding at a glance."

- Reinforces the use of graphs and charts instead of numbers and words.

- Clear, actionable information at the place of communication.

- Aimed and maintained by those performing the work, who are the first to detect anomalies.

- Linked to business metrics and overall business goals.

LSSI
LEAN SIX SIGMA INSTITUTE

Value Stream performance board

- It is a tool that helps us "see" the business (as if looking at it through a window).

- It presents relevant supporting data and information such as:
  - The organization's goals.
  - Continuous improvement initiatives.
  - Key Performance Indicators (KPIs).

- Information is written in an easy-to-understand manner (visuals, graphs, etc.).

- Represents a progressive management style.

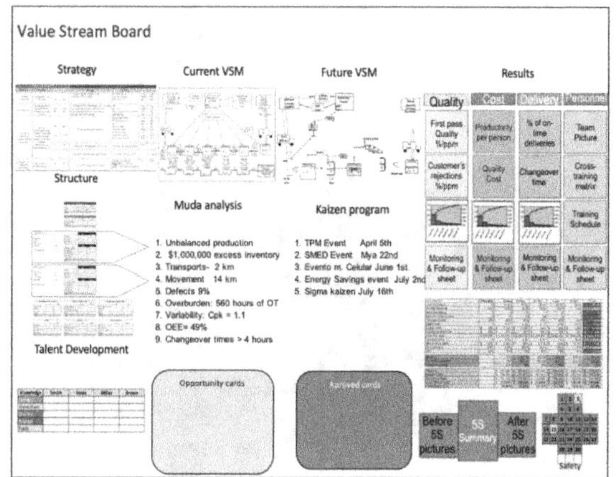

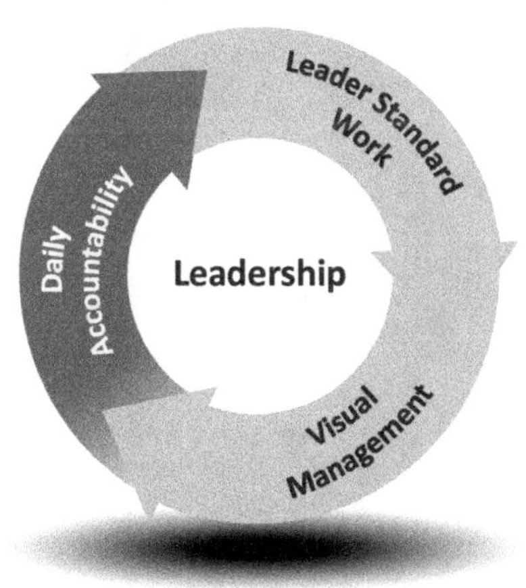

- A series of meetings by level within an organization
  - Levels: Work streams, Supervisors, Value Streams

- Decision-making and resolution development to close the gap between objectives and current state.

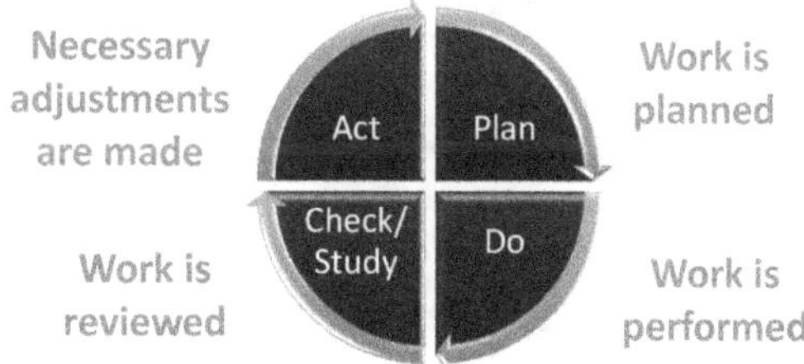

Daily Accountability ("pre-shift meetings")

Daily performance review meetings

There are three levels:

- Level 1: The work team meets at the start of the day
  - The team leader meets briefly with his/her team.

- Level 2: Supervisor meetings
  - The supervisor meets with team leaders and support area representatives.

- Level 3: Value Stream meetings
  - The Value Stream manager meets with supervisors and supporting department coordinators.

LSSI
LEAN SIX SIGMA INSTITUTE

Daily meeting characteristics (all levels)

- Brief – typically less than 15 minutes.

- Everyone remains standing at the work area.

- Activity progress is measured based on the objectives set forth on the performance boards.

- Used to ensure communication between leaders at all levels.

- Follow-up on improvements, customer issues, problem-solving, and employee issues.

Daily meeting expectations (all levels)

- Participants present issues that need to be addressed.

- Supporting staff participate in each meeting and at every level (as needed).

- Leaders at each level assign tasks, keep their staff organized and on track, and request assistance from the next level up (whenever necessary).

Example

The review includes tasks that were scheduled to-be-completed the day before the meeting as well as those to-be-completed on the day of the meeting.

- Completed = Green label

- Not completed = Red Label

  - A new due date is scheduled and added along with the reason why the task was not completed on time.

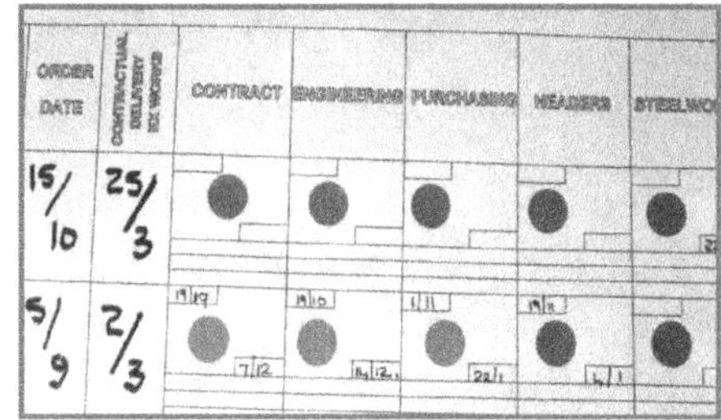

Daily actions

- Checklist (focused on exceptions only):

  - Hour by hour boards.
  - Situation boards.
  - Standard work of operators.
  - Standard work of leaders.

- Situation boards are evaluated to take immediate actions.

- The boards are updated daily.

LSSI
LEAN SIX SIGMA INSTITUTE

Disciplined Leadership

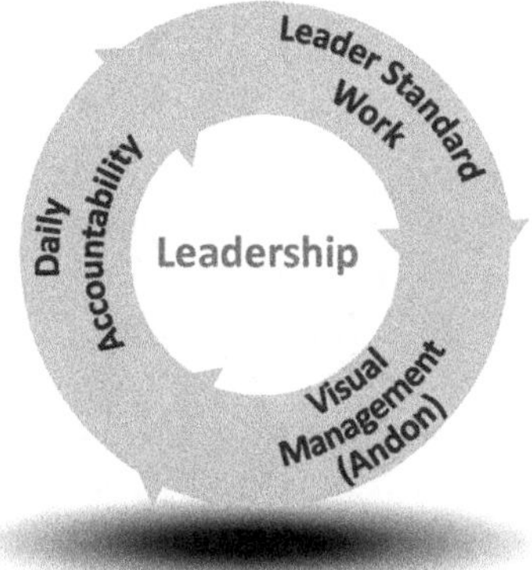

Strategy Execution

- Disciplined leaders always keep **purpose** in mind and use management systems to guide teams towards the future state.

- Disciplined leaders feel comfortable taking **risks** and are eager to bear the burdens of leading in a humble way.

- Disciplined leaders are constantly **learning**, training teams, and finding ways to improve the current state.

- Disciplined leaders **harmonize** the Lean Management System and Lean operations to achieve maximum effectiveness.

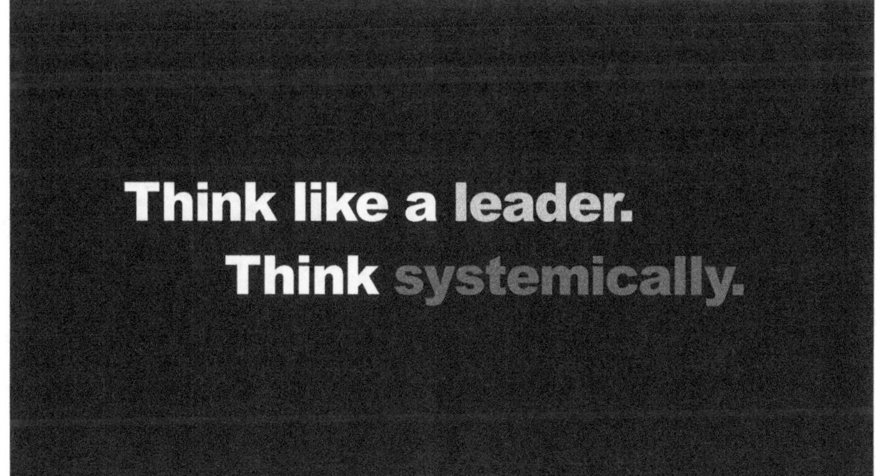

The Gemba Walk

*Culture is achieved by practicing every day
where the work happens*

Learning objectives

1. Understand how to use Gemba Walks as a strategic tool and how to implement them.
2. Understand the importance of good management habits that advance high-impact initiatives.
3. Know how to implement Gemba Walks to develop a long-term culture of continuous improvement.

Content

> Background
> What is a Gemba Walk?
> What is it used for?
> Who participates?
> When is it used?
> Procedure

"When you are out observing on the Gemba, do something to help them!

If you do, people will come to expect that you can help them and will look forward to seeing you again on the Gemba."

Taiichi Ohno

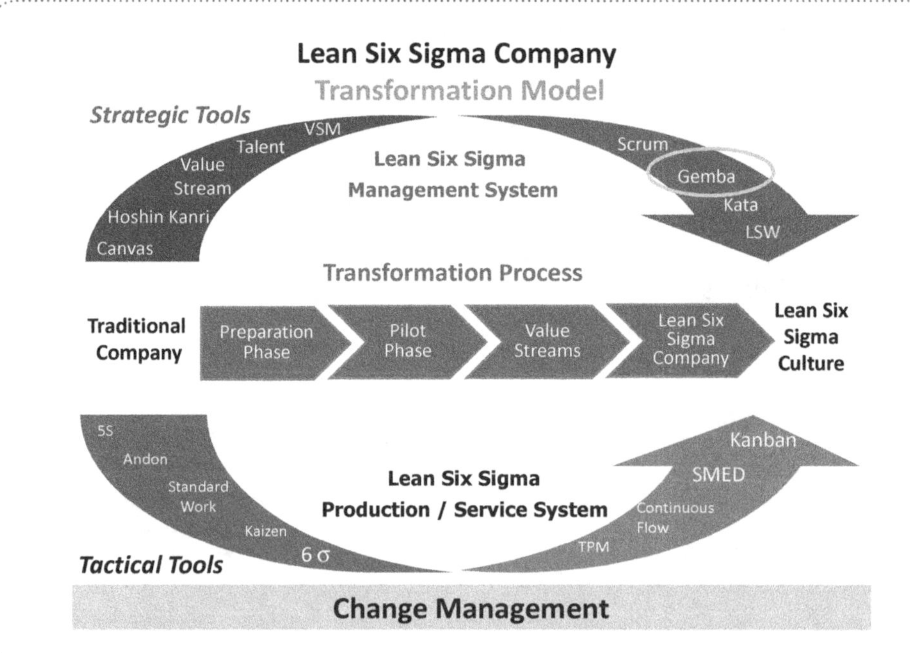

LSSI
LEAN SIX SIGMA INSTITUTE

- **Gemba walk** is a concept that was developed by *Taiichi Ohno*, who is known as the father of the Toyota Production System (TPS).

- The development of the TPS is also attributed to *Shigeo Shingo* and *Eiji Toyoda*. Today, TPS is generically known as *Lean*.

Gemba Walk

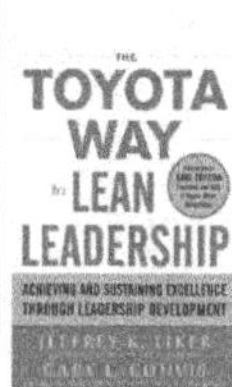

Shigeo Shingo   *Taiichi Ohno*   *Eiji Toyoda*

- Lean Six Sigma has developed into a **worldwide movement**.

- Lean tools – including but not limited to VSM, Kanban, SMED, 5S and Hoshin Kanri – have helped organizations in every industry achieve *remarkable results*.

However:

- Results are usually sustained for a short period (typically 1 – 2 years).

- People typically do not acquire long-term habits.

- Continuous improvement programs often end due to a lack of leadership and momentum.

Traditional companies

- Executives of world-class companies spend at least 80% of their time planning and executing high-level strategies.

- But how do they spend the rest of their time?

- If only 20% of their time is **spent where the work happens (the Gemba),** then they need to adjust their priorities.

Source: *Harvard Business Review.*

Gemba Walk		
Activity	**Time**	**%**
Management		
Participate in meetings		
Read and answer emails		
General paperwork		
Interact with staff		
Write and read reports		
Track expenses		
Other		
Contact with Customers		
In person		
By phone		
By email		
Other		
Work in Process		
Learn and coach		
Problem solving		
Improvements (Kaizen events)		
Learn about and understand issues		
Eliminate barriers		
Walk through the process		
Other		

Evolution: with and without a Lean management system

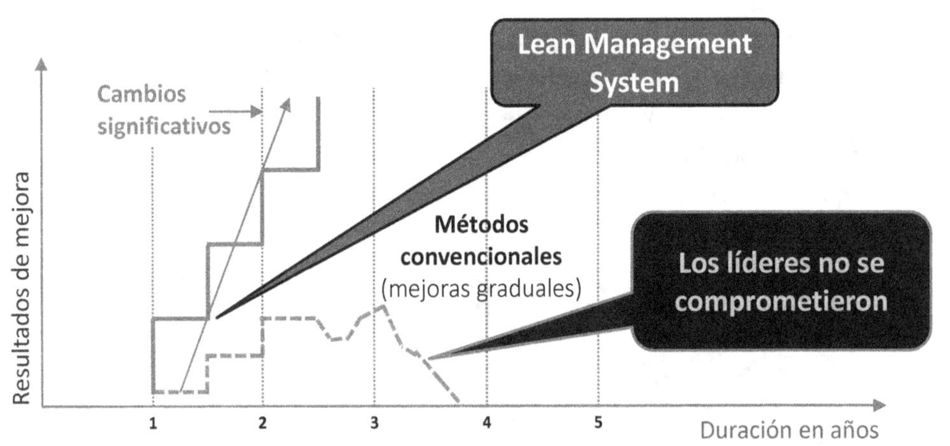

LSSI
LEAN SIX SIGMA INSTITUTE

What is a Gemba Walk?

The literal translation of Gemba is **"The real place"**.
Meaning: **The place** *where value is created*.

The idea is simple:

- Visit *the place* (Gemba).

- Observe and understand the process(es).

- Talk with the people, ask questions!

Leader Standard Work

LSSI

NAME: JEFF SALES

TIME	TASK
8:00 AM	Meeting (on the floor)
8:15 AM	Gemba Walk
8:30 AM	Review Alicia and Jorge's LSW
8:45 AM	Emails/ Voice Mail
9:00 AM	Prepare for a meeting
9:15 AM	Meeting
9:30 AM	Meeting
9:40 AM	Production Board / Open items
10:00 AM	Review first production run performance
10:15 AM	
10:30 AM	Task follow-up
10:45 AM	
11:00 AM	Project time
11:15 AM	Project time
11:30 AM	Project time
11:45 AM	Project time
12:30 PM	Review 2nd production run performance
12:45 PM	
1:00 PM	Results presentation meeting and task follow-up
1:15 PM	Time for pending tasks
1:30 PM	Time for pending tasks
1:45 PM	
2:00 PM	
2:15 PM	
2:30 PM	Review 3rd production run performance
2:45 PM	
3:00 PM	
3:15 PM	Costing simulations
3:30 PM	
3:45 PM	
4:00 PM	
4:15 PM	Review on-time delivery performance

Notes / Changes

DAY	TIME	TASK
Mon	9:00 AM	Production plan and shipping schedule
Tue	11:00 AM	
2nd Tue.	9:00 AM	Project review
3rd Tue.	9:00 AM	Cross-training review

What a Gemba walk is NOT

- Walking around without a purpose.

- An opportunity to identify other people's mistakes.

- A time used to solve problems and implement changes.

- Observing the work area from one's desk [e.g., video].

What is it used for?

Focus on the process:

The purpose of the Gemba walk is to *observe* processes, not to evaluate people's individual skills.

Observe, learn and understand:

- It is helpful to adopt the mindset of a student during a Gemba walk.

- Keep an open mind and ask open-ended questions.

- The leader is here to learn – not to judge or give advice.

Why use Gemba Walks?

Companies tend to be **vertical** and complex; managers report to higher levels of management (e.g., CEO) for directions.

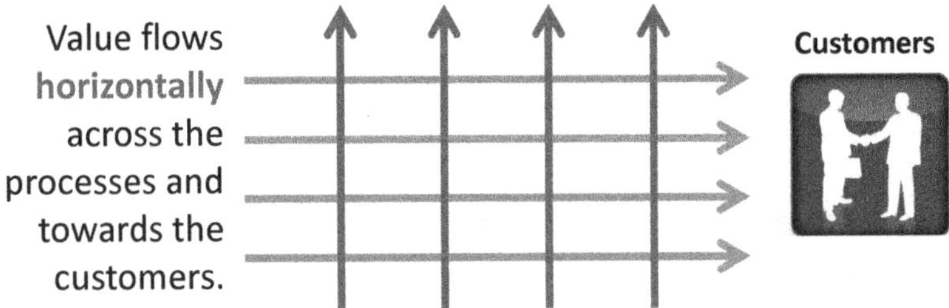

Gemba walks help managers observe and reconcile the vertical and horizontal elements of a company.

Why go to the Gemba?

- To fully understand how value is created in the organization.

- To build trust and working relationships between company leaders and employees.

- To demonstrate management's commitment to Lean initiatives.

- To increase accountability and ownership within the organization.

Addressing constraints

- **Logistical**
  - Layout, physical environment, walls, divisions, distances, etc.

- **Behavioral**
  - Orders or services are started but not finished, habits, cultural differences, etc.

- **Management**
  - Strategies, politics, norms, rules, metrics, infrastructure, etc.

Eli Goldratt

The Gemba Walk

Gemba walks are effective if the entire company structure thinks lean.

- Senior management and vice presidents.

- Functional managers.

- Value stream managers.

- Area leaders.

- Team leaders.

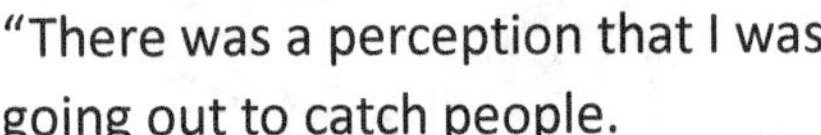

**Bob Nardelli, CEO
The Home Depot**

"There was a perception that I was going out to catch people.

Over time they understood that I just wanted to see [the process] like a customer. I can do my job better if I have first-hand exposure to 'the good, the bad, and the ugly.'"

When is it used?

- Senior management and vice presidents → Once a month.

- Functional managers → Once a week.

- Value stream managers → 2 - 3 times per week.

- Area leaders → 3 - 5 times per week.

- Team liders → Everyday.

LSSI
LEAN SIX SIGMA INSTITUTE

Toyota Motor Corporation Philosophy

Fujio Cho
Former CEO (1999-2005)

- **Go see.**
  - "Senior management must spend time on the front lines."
- **Ask why.**
  - "Use the 'Why?' technique daily."
- **Show respect.**
  - "Respect your people."

Where do Gemba walks take place?

At the location of:
- the value streams and support processes
- the areas or functions that involve customers and suppliers.

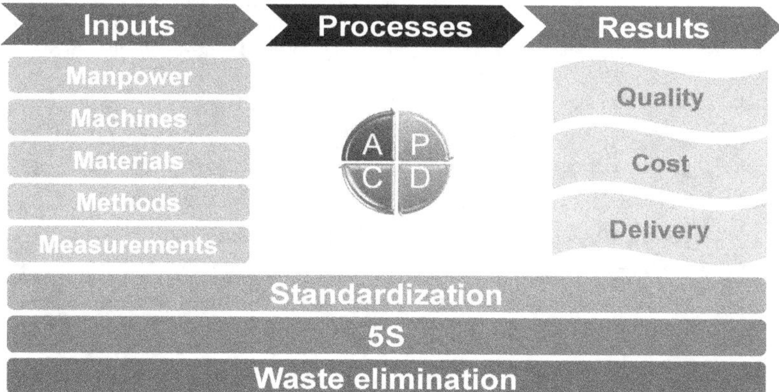

Where do Gemba walks take place?
The 3 Flows

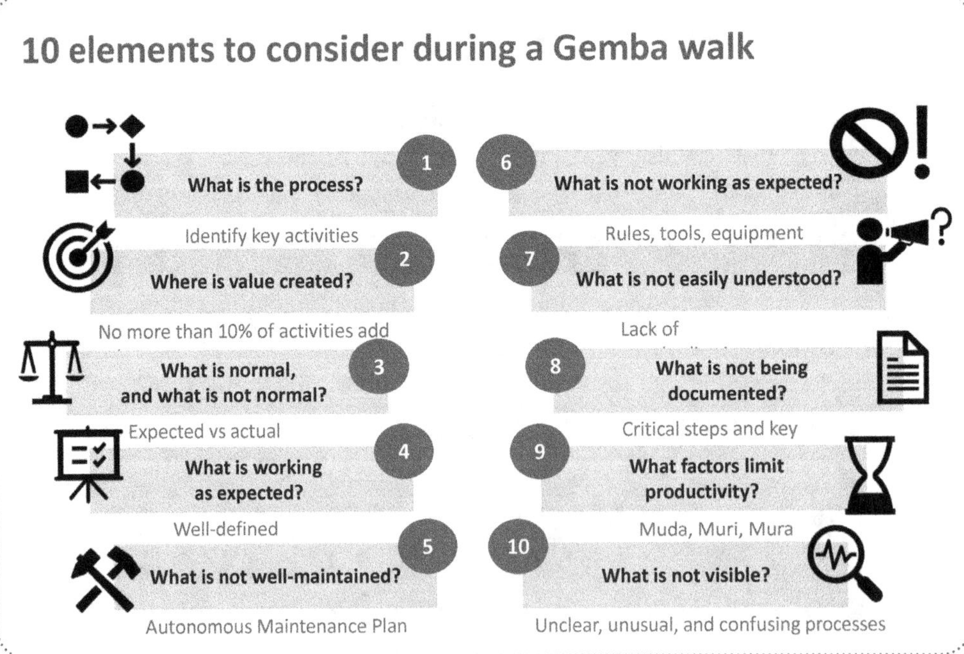

10 elements to consider during a Gemba walk

LSSI
LEAN SIX SIGMA INSTITUTE

Be mindful of the 3 enemies of productivity

Non-value added activities

Variability

Over-bearing tasks

Main muda

Overproduction

Waits

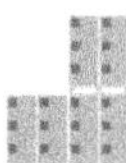

Transportation

Unnecessary processes

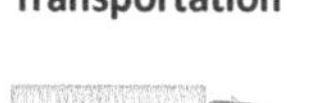

The big wastes

Movements

Errors and rework

Excess inventory

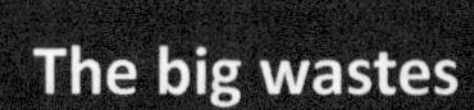

Talent without action

Preparing for the Gemba walk

Structuring your approach:

- The *observer* must have a ***profound interest*** in understanding the company's processes.

- Leave all ***assumptions*** and ***opinions*** behind.

- The objective is to fully understand the behaviors in the Gemba and how they relate to the current activities and overall functions.

Prepare your questions

Who?	What?	When?
1. Who should perform the activity? 2. Who is performing the activity? 3. Who else can perform the activity? 4. Who else should perform the activity? 5. Who is involved with the 3 MUs?	1. What should the activity accomplish? 2. What does the activity accomplish? 3. What else does the activity accomplish? 4. What else should the activity accomplish? 5. What are the 3 MUs creating?	1. When is the activity performed? 2. When should the activity be performed? 3. At what time is the activity performed? 4. At what other time can the activity be performed? 5. When are the 3 MUs present?

Where?	Why?	How?
1. Where is the activity performed? 2. Where should the activity be performed? 3. Where else can the activity be performed? 4. Where else should the activity be performed? 5. Where are the 3 MUs present?	1. Why is the activity being performed? 2. Why are we performing the activity there? 3. Why are we performing the activity that way? 4. Why do the 3 MUs occur?	1. How should this activity be done? 2. How is this activity being done? 3. How is this activity done in other places? 4. Is there another way to do this activity? 5. How are the 3 MUs developed?

3 Mu's = Muda, Mura, Muri

LSSI
LEAN SIX SIGMA INSTITUTE

Focus is key

- Show respect.
  - Avoid scolding people and interrupting processes.
- Engage in direct interaction with employees.
  - Ask open-ended questions.
- Ensure people feel listened to.
  - Make sure their feedback and comments are considered.

A Gemba walk is a great opportunity to strengthen Lean culture!

Procedure

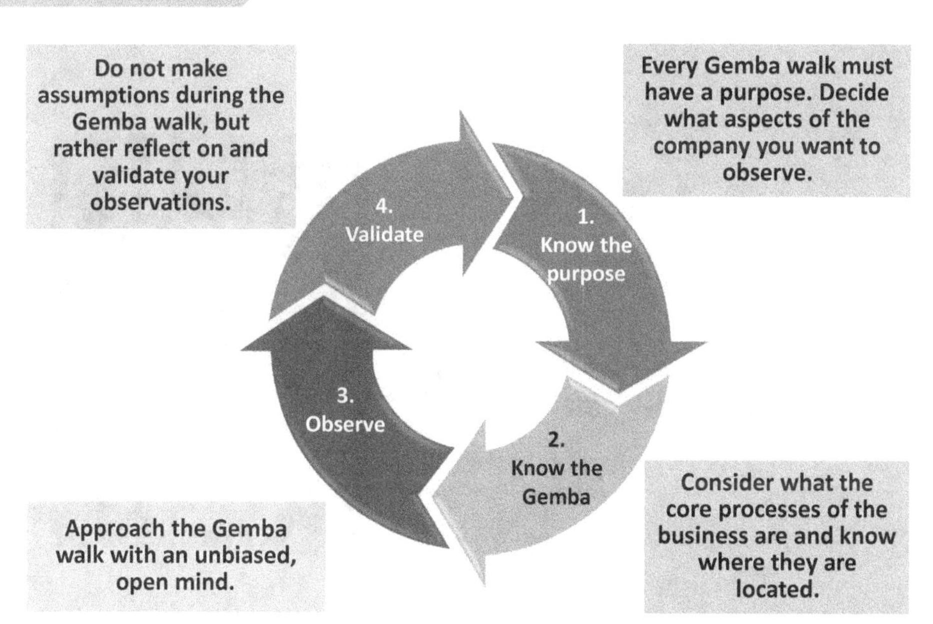

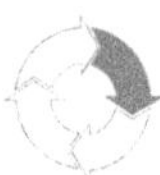

1. Know the purpose

- If you do not know why you are performing the Gemba walk, then there is no reason to do it at all.

- Walking around without a purpose is inefficient and counterproductive.

- Answer the following questions prior to the walk:

  - What will I be observing and why?
  - What am I trying to understand?

Always answer these questions before a Gemba walk!

Define a theme for the Gemba walk

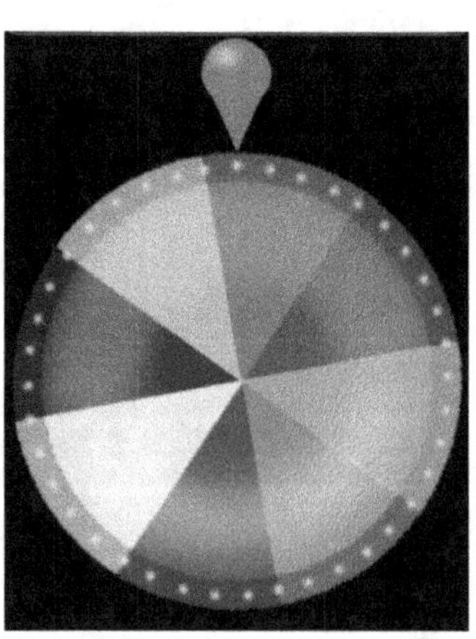

- Safety.
- Customer service.
- Productivity.
- Quality.
- Cost.
- Innovation, creativity, and learning (new ways to solve problems).
- Specific issues.
- Maintenance.
- New product development.
- Identifying customer requirements.

LSSI
LEAN SIX SIGMA INSTITUTE

2. Know the Gemba

- Targeting only the main area of operations for your **Gemba Walk** limits the company's improvement opportunities.

- **Gemba** is the place *where value is created for the customer*:

  - Office space.
  - Customer visits.
  - Sales.
  - Etc.

- The **Gemba** is the place where the activity that you are trying to understand and improve is being performed.

Example

Define the path to walk for different themes.

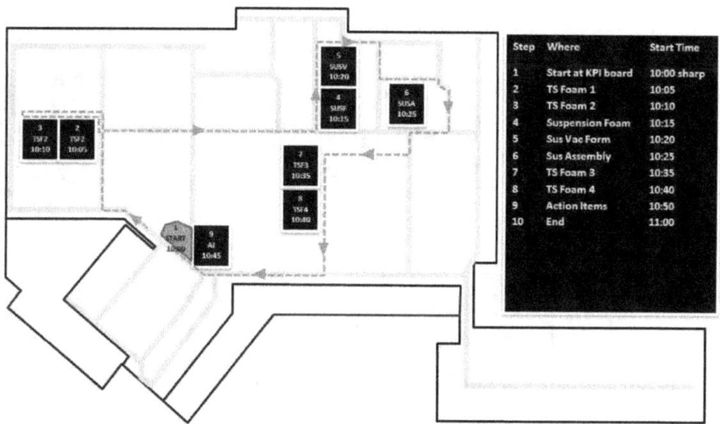

Step	Where	Start Time
1	Start at KPI board	10:00 sharp
2	TS Foam 1	10:05
3	TS Foam 2	10:10
4	Suspension Foam	10:15
5	Sus Vac Form	10:20
6	Sus Assembly	10:25
7	TS Foam 3	10:35
8	TS Foam 4	10:40
9	Action Items	10:50
10	End	11:00

3. Observe

Anyone can watch his or her surroundings, but observation requires skill and focus.

- *What* is being observed and *how* it's being observed are both important.

- Observe beyond the process:

  - People.
  - Equipment.
  - Materials.
  - Methods.

- Keep in mind the different activities, connections, and flows.

- Have both a big picture and a detail-oriented approach.

Example

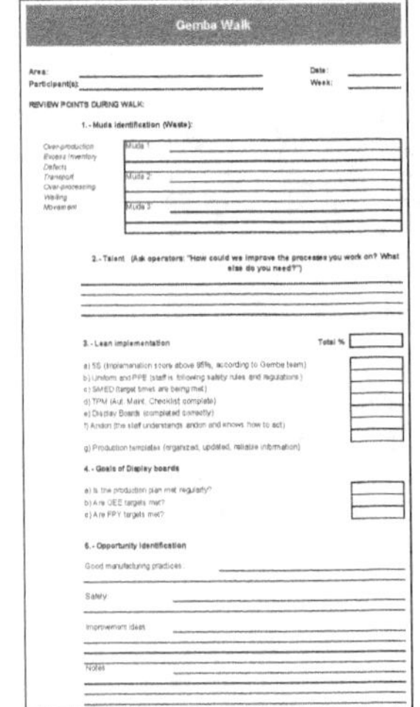

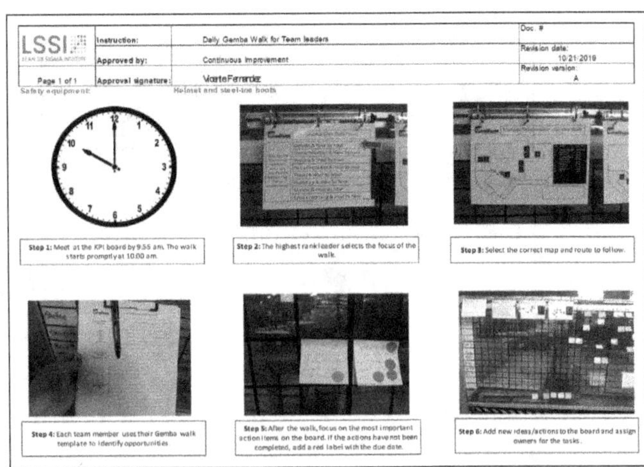

LSSI
LEAN SIX SIGMA INSTITUTE

Sample questions to ask

Observation – Do's

Best practices

- Observe all elements in a process (SIPOC diagram):
  - **S**uppliers.
  - **I**nputs, material, and tools.
  - **P**rocesses and the quality expected.
  - **O**utput.
  - **C**ustomer expectations.

- Try observing from different places and angles.
- Ask open-ended questions.
- Record observations and answers to your questions.
- Take your time; do not rush.

Observation – Don'ts

- Don't go on the walk already having decided on a change or improvement.

- Don't conduct the Gemba walk just to check it off your to-do list.

- Don't judge or correct people's work.

- Don't interrupt others.

- Don't make assumptions.

4. Validate (and define actions for improvement)

- Don't assume that what you see is all there is

- There are some things the human eye cannot see (e.g. problem-solving process).

- If you are unfamiliar with the standard work, then it is very challenging to deal with process anomalies.

- When an observation is complete, validate your conclusions with the gathered information.

- Generate ideas and convert them into an action plan for improvement.

LSSI
LEAN SIX SIGMA INSTITUTE

Example

Generate ideas and place them in an action plan board.

If the ideas/actions have not been completed, then deadlines are assigned using red labels.

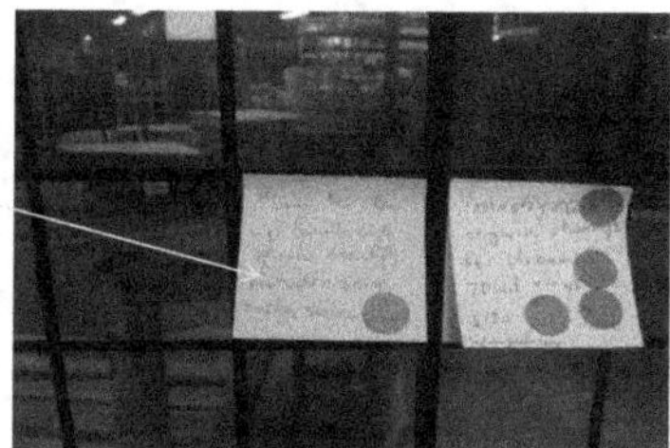

Conclusion

The Gemba Walk

- A Gemba Walk is the best way to fully understand a process that creates value and how we can improve it.

- Walking the Gemba is a habit that needs to be developed to sustain a Lean culture.

**Lean Six Sigma.
Management System
for Leaders**

Luis Socconini, Carlo Reato

**Lean Six Sigma White Belt.
Certification Manual**

Luis Socconini

**Lean Six Sigma
Management.
Certification Manual**

Luis Socconini

**Lean Service.
Certification Manual**

Luis Socconini

**Lean Six Sigma Yellow Belt.
Certification Manual**

Luis Socconini

**Lean Six Sigma Green Belt.
Certification Manual**

Luis Socconini

**Lean Six Sigma Black Belt.
Certification Manual**

Luis Socconini

**Lean Company. Más allá
de la manufactura**

Luis Socconini

**Lean Six Sigma Green Belt,
paso a paso**

Luis Socconini, Eduardo Escobedo

5S Practical guide to improve quality and productivity

Luis Socconini, Marco Barrantes

Lean Energy 4.0. Guía de Implementación

Luis Socconini, Juan Pablo Martín

Lean Manufacturing. Step by step

Luis Socconini

Inteligencia directiva. Manual para liderar equipos

Jaume Llopis Casellas

Cómo gestionar la cadena de suministo

Ed Weenk

Economía circular. Un enfoque práctico para transformar los modelos empresariales

Rozanne Henzen, Ed Weenk

Sincronización y sinergia empresarial

Matías Birrell Rodríguez

Tecnologías para liderar el futuro

Marc Busom

Productos y servicios inteligentes y sostenibles

Llorenç Guilera, Antoni Garrell

Brutau, 160 – 08203 Sabadell (Barcelona) – Tel. +34-931 429 486 – marge@margebooks.com – www.margebooks.com

www.ingramcontent.com/pod-product-compliance
Lightning Source LLC
LaVergne TN
LVHW080422200726
843507LV00004B/691